AMY FISHER

◆

My Story

AMY FISHER

◆

My Story

by AMY FISHER
with SHEILA WELLER

POCKET BOOKS
New York London Sydney Tokyo Singapore

POCKET BOOKS, a division of Simon & Schuster Inc.
1230 Avenue of the Americas, New York, NY 10020

ISBN: 0-671-86558-7

First Pocket Books hardcover printing April 1993

10 9 8 7 6 5 4 3 2 1

POCKET and colophon are registered trademarks of
Simon & Schuster Inc.

Printed in the U.S.A.

NOTE

◆

This is Amy Fisher's story. I have had numerous conversations and interviews with her, and the story that results is told largely through her memory and her perspective. Joseph Buttafuoco has a different version of events. It is not included in this book.

In various media, Mr. Buttafuoco and his wife, Mary Jo, alone or through their attorneys, have called Amy Fisher "a liar." In addition, Mr. Buttafuoco has denied that he:

- ever had an affair with Amy Fisher;
- has ever been to the Freeport Motor Inn & Boatel;
- ever talked to Amy Fisher about killing his wife;
- taught Amy Fisher how to use a gun;
- introduced Amy Fisher to prostitution;
- knew Amy Fisher was a prostitute;
- was ever a pimp;
- was ever a drug dealer;
- ever had a sexually transmitted disease.

I tried to reach Mr. Buttafuoco for an interview to address some of the assertions in this book. Through his attorney, Marvyn Kornberg, he refused to be interviewed.

Some portions of this book are written in the first person, in Amy's voice; others are in the narrative third person. The change is indicated by a row of ◆ ◆ ◆.

NOTE

The names of most of Amy's peers have been changed in this book, as have certain identifying characteristics. The names of individuals in the escort service industry have been changed as well.

Reasonable literary license was taken in reconstructing two scenes, reported in the third person, featuring Maria Murabito, in which dialogue and small setting details were simulated, hewing very closely to the substance of events, concerns, and conversations reported by Ms. Murabito and by Amy.

My interviews with the various investigators, private and police, occurred in December 1992 and January 1993, one and two months after the Nassau County district attorney announced that he was not going to prosecute Joseph Buttafuoco.

—Sheila Weller
March 1993

CONTENTS

♦

CONTENTS

PART 3

PART 4

AMY FISHER

◆

My Story

Prologue
"Lyin' Eyes"

♦

The Eagles are my favorite group of all time. Even though I was just a baby when they were popular, I got into them from their *Hotel California* CD, which Joey always played in his car. He kept it in his glove compartment, along with his Ray-Ban shades and his other CD's, all neatly lined up. His favorite CD was *A Decade of Steely Dan*.

Joey changed cars like other people change underwear. (Joey himself wore no underwear.) I'm not kidding. In the year that he was my boyfriend, he had a black Caddy with smoked windows and pinstriping, then a green Toronado, then an old truck. Then he thought he'd be cute and drive a copmobile: a Grand Marquis with black-smoked windows. Then he got an old racing car—a Delta '88, with a souped-up engine and black limo tint. Finally he settled on his white Lincoln Continental. Looking at a newspaper from my Nassau County Jail cell last summer, I saw a picture of him taking Mary Jo to her doctor appointments in that car. A chauffeur drove.

If Joey was picking me up at my house, he'd drive Mary Jo's car—a Jeep with a pink script *M J* on the driver-side door—so my dad wouldn't recognize his honk. Joey did that during the first month and a half of our relationship, because when you're still sixteen, like I was then, you have a junior driver's license and you're not allowed to drive a car at night. He'd probably tell Mary Jo he was going to the shop to help his friend Dave paint. Dave had a Formica-cabinetry business on the side, and he did the spray-painting at night at the shop, Complete Auto Body & Fender Inc., that Joey's father owned. Joey was a repairman at Complete. Sometimes Joey would help Dave with those cabinets. Mostly, though, between June 1991 and May 1992, he would *tell* Mary Jo he was helping Dave. Dave would lay out the mica doors and start spray-painting them mauve. Joey'd go upstairs and make love with me. I guess if Mary Jo called the shop Dave would say Joey was busy mixing paint.

I had alibis, too. I'd run out the door, saying, "Mom, Dad, I'm going with Michelle and Julie (during the first month of our relationship), or Maria and Lori (if it was after August 1991). They thought I was going out with my girlfriends: at best, getting pizza and renting Nintendo games; at worst, cruising Francis Lewis Boulevard, where kids drive up and down and hang out in a parking-lot-turned-flea-market in their decked Camaros and Trans-Ams with their doors open and their sound systems high.

But I was going with my lover, Joey Buttafuoco, a married man more than twice my age. I am five years older than Joey's older child with Mary Jo.

By the time I came running out, Joey'd have made the U-turn—my street, Berkley Lane in Merrick, Long Island, dead-ends on an inlet of Baldwin Creek—so I could hop right up and in. Joey would be leaning back behind the wheel, the diamond stud in his left ear twinkling through the sideview mirror like a star. "Hi, babe," he'd say, nuzzling me with his grinning, tough-looking, smashed-nose face. "I love you." (He said "I love you" to me from day one!) We'd kiss. The first day we ever made love, we made out in a car as my father walked by. I had to duck quick.

He'd have changed from the baggy pants and tight T-shirt he wore at work (sleeves rolled up, like a guido James Dean) into a pressed dress shirt and sport jacket. He'd have on his Big John jeans and lizard-skin cowboy boots. I would be wearing cowboy boots and tight Levi's just like him. I loved us dressing alike.

As he shot out Berkley and made the right onto Hewlett—a curvy, tree-lined street of big family houses like mine—he put his right hand on my left leg. He could practically circle my whole lower thigh between his pinkie and his thumb. He is six-foot-one and 240 pounds. I am five-foot-four, and, because Joey liked me skinny, I dieted with Acu-Trim, down from one hundred to eighty pounds. My waist was twenty inches back then.

As our relationship progressed—and I got my real driver's license—I would drive out and meet Joey, usually at Complete Auto Body. If it was Monday or Tuesday, I'd come to him a few hours after a date with a client I prostituted for. (I never did tricks at night—just after school. Or I'd cut school to meet a client, if a lucrative call came in.)

When Joey cut off money he'd been giving me to pay back a debt I'd incurred and strongly suggested I become an "escort," he said I didn't have to have sex with the men. When I found out I did, it was too late to back out. I just got used to it.

I'd park my black Chrysler LeBaron in the Complete lot and go upstairs to the apartment Joey kept over the shop. At my earlier client's request, I'd be wearing my black-matte spandex miniskirt, with only a G-string underneath, and a black crop-top with long sleeves and a satin-trimmed collar and cuffs over one of the Frederick's of Hollywood push-up bras Joey bought for me. When I first met Joey, I wore baggy jeans and sweatshirts. I was embarrassed by my body. I was sixteen, but I thought I looked fourteen. Joey made me feel like a woman. Still, clients from the escort service told me that I was "childlike" and that they liked that. One man who was about forty, when I told him I was seventeen, said, "You're not the youngest I've had."

It turned Joey on to hear me talk about what I did with those gross, pathetic dentists and lawyers and businessmen. At the time I liked to think that *I* was ripping them off and that *they* were suckers because I was making $150 off them for fifty minutes (a prostitute's hour is like a psychiatrist's). Being tough is a very important part of who I think I am. But with the help of the psychiatrist I had at Huntington Hospital (after my suicide attempt in September 1992), I am beginning to see now that *I* was the sucker, that *I* was the one being used and degraded.

At the time, though, I didn't think so. I exaggerated—I lied—to make my prostitute life sound sexy for Joey.

"Did he do it *hard?*" Joey would whisper as we started to make love in his bed in the makeshift bedroom he fixed up next to his home gym, two floors up from Complete.

"Yeah, Joey," I'd whisper back.

"This hard, babe?" He'd show me what he meant.

"Yeah, Joey."

"Am I better, baby?" He expected a moaned yes. (It wasn't an accident that the only decoration in the room was a Superman sticker stuck in the center of the headboard of the bed.)

"Yeah, Joey. Oh, yeah, Joey."

Of course he was better. He was a *god* next to the man I spent 4 to 4:50 P.M. with. That man weighed about 400 pounds and stank. I had to sit on that motel bed with that horrible man, rubbing his flabby back with Jergens lotion, whispering about how nice and thick his hair was, checking my watch every two minutes and holding my breath.

I would come home from my tricks and go upstairs to my bedroom, with my James Dean poster on the wall and my collection of Teddy bears propped on the dresser and bed. I'd go into the bathroom and brush my teeth for five minutes. And then I would always throw up.

After Joey and I made love, we would drive out to a restaurant for dinner. Joey would slip the *Hotel California* disc into his disc player. He always fast-forwarded to "Lyin' Eyes." He loved that song, but for a reason I couldn't put my finger on, it made me uncomfortable. I thought it was very sad. It's about a girl who dresses up for a rich old man. It's about a prostitute.

Joey said the girl in the song reminded him of me. Sometimes Joey'd sing along, his raspy voice over Don Henley's raspier one. We'd turn on to the Southern State Parkway. When the song's chorus came on—"You can't hide your lyin' eyes/And your smile is a thin disguise . . ."—Joey stamped his left boot against the car floor to the *"hide"* and the *"eyes"* and the *"smile."* When the part of the song came on where it tells that the girl is a prostitute—the part where it talks about her lying to her boyfriend about going out to see a friend, while she's really going to the "cheating" part of town—Joey would turn the volume up.

In the song, the boyfriend she comes running back to has "fiery" eyes. He makes her feel the way none of the men who pay her feel. He's better than any of them. After her night of prostitution, she comes running into his arms.

Joey liked that song because he was that "fiery"-eyed boy who the

4

prostitute couldn't wait to run back to at the end of her night. It was true. The more I was with them, the more I wanted to run back to Joey. Joey knew that very well.

As we drove into Elmont, I would hold Joey's hand and touch his smooth fingernails, which I'd just polished a couple of days before. He liked me to give him manicures: hold his big fingers in my little ones, file his nails, paint the clear polish on with the tiny brush. (What is it with big men and dainty fingernails? Same as big men and little dogs. Joey had this shih tzu that he loved more than anything in the world. He told me he was *furious* when Mary Jo gave it away one day when he was at work because it was a bother to care for.)

When I polished Joey's nails, I felt in control. I liked that. Control. Toughness. Strength. I have this motto: No matter what people do to hurt or scare or humiliate me, I will not cry. I developed that motto growing up. My aunts and my grandmother—and, later, my three best girlfriends: Maria, Lori, and especially Jane—showed me how to protect myself by accentuating that toughness. Maybe I listened to them a little too literally. I know that I listened to *Joey* much too literally.

"You are a very literal person," my lawyer, Eric Naiburg, has told me.

"You make pacts like a marine does: '*Semper fi,*' " said our private investigator Richie Haeg.

Someone else put it this way: "Amy, you have all the subtlety of a Mack truck."

Yeah: a Mack truck loaded with lit dynamite, with broken brakes, going 120 miles an hour toward a brick wall.

Joey would park in the lot of King Umberto's and we'd walk past the row of limousines: his arm around me, my head up to just under his shoulder. We'd be wearing our matching cowboy boots, our matching jeans. We'd enter the big, modern Italian restaurant with its smoked-glass windows and the framed pictures of politicians and other bigshots on the walls. As the hostess led us to a table, people's eyes would lift up for a second and then they'd go back to their eating or talking. I hoped they thought Joey and I were engaged. Joey would hail the waitress and order two shrimp marinara entrées. He loved seafood and he never asked me what I wanted; he just ordered me what he ordered himself. "The man should do the ordering," he always said. I felt taken care of. I loved those magic nights.

In the last part of "Lyin' Eyes," the girl is hanging her head in the middle of a very different kind of night—a long, bad night. She is crying. She is looking at the stars and the sky and wondering how her life got "so far gone" and "crazy."

At 10 P.M., when I'm locked back in, I know the night will be "another long one," like they say in the song. But unlike the girl in the song, I can't see the stars, or the sky. (What I can see, looking through the steel grates on this small window, are three rows of barbed-wire fencing and, beyond that, tops of trucks moving up an interstate to Canada.) The guards wake us up at 5:15 A.M., so I have had plenty of time to wonder how things got "so crazy" and "so far gone" that at 11:30 A.M. on May 19, 1992, I walked up the two stairs to the front porch of Joey's house at 1 Adam Road West in Massapequa, and, after his wife, Mary Jo, came out and we started talking, I took out a gun that I'd bought.

I remember how excited Joey was when he realized I was really going to buy the gun. "The thing—the piece—did you get it?" he asked me on the phone, at 8:30 in the morning, four days before. He woke me up to ask me that.

Joey was at work when the shooting occurred. School had not yet let out for the summer, so his children were not in the house. I was in disguise—my hair was tucked under a cap. Joey's having an alibi by being at work, the kids not being home, my disguise—these were not accidents.

Except, when I got to the front porch, I knew I couldn't do it, even though shooting Joey's wife had been my idea. I pulled my cap off. I wanted to talk to Mary Jo instead.

We did talk. She was dismissive toward me. She said, "Get the fuck off my property," then turned around to go back into her house. I got angry and I hit her with the gun and it went off. For this—for buying the gun and planning the shooting; for causing the injury that almost killed her—I will be remorseful every day of my life.

I know what I really wanted from Mary Jo, what would have made everything different that day and all the days after that. You won't believe me if I tell you, now, what it was. But I think you'll understand once you know a little bit more about my life. So I'll save it for later in this book.

Joey turned me in. He denied everything—not just his role in encouraging the shooting, but his role in my becoming a prostitute. As everyone knows now, he denies that we ever made love. He says he fixed my car a lot and that he had pizza with me once.

Do you know what it feels like to have your existence in a person's life denied like that? It makes you feel invisible. Erased. Like you're worse than a piece of shit. That's why I didn't want Bill Clinton to be elected President. I could never forgive him for how he treated Gennifer Flowers. (I was a Perot supporter.) He made her into a ridiculed nonentity who had to beg for a scrap of credibility, while he was dismissing her as a liar and the media was calling her a slut.

As another very famous media-designated "slut" and "liar" half her age, I felt for her—a lot.

During the course of my prosecution and in the media circus that followed, other men and boys—Steve Sleeman, Chris Drellos, Peter Guagenti, Paul Makely—denied or lied about other things. Three of them were wooed by offers of big money; one by the offer of a reduced-count criminal charge. No betrayal was worse than Paul Makely's. Last September, when I was at my lowest ebb, Paul lured me to Future Physique, the gym he co-owns, which had been wired with secret cameras by the TV show "Hard Copy." Paul got a lot of money from "Hard Copy" for baiting me into saying things he acted like he wanted to hear while the hidden cameras rolled. For that spectacle, broadcast all over television for days, I lost my chance to testify against Joey before a grand jury. I was labeled by the district attorney, Fred Klein, as a "revolting" and worthless potential witness with "no credibility," and all investigations of Joey were dropped. That's how it happened that, three months later, on December 1, Joey Buttafuoco was holding hands with his wife at a press conference in a local hotel, making jokes about how the newspaper photographers were fighting with the TV cameramen to get their picture. He had just announced: "Amy Fisher is a liar and has zero credibility. The district attorney knows she's a liar and has no credibility. The *court* now knows she's a liar and has zero credibility." While he was doing that, I was handcuffed in a van, on my way to prison.

The night after that fateful "Hard Copy" aired, Joey's brother,

Bobby, had walked into the gym and told Paul Makely, "Thanks for helping my brother out."

In one of the last lines of "Lyin' Eyes" the girl is chided, sarcastically, for screwing her life up.

Am I ever the girl in that song.

Now I know why that song always made me uncomfortable when I'd hear it with Joey. I was listening to my awful destructive choices, stupidly dressed up as glamour. I was hearing my fate in advance.

My name is Amy Fisher, and I am eighteen years old, and I am in prison serving a five- to fifteen-year plea-bargained sentence for allegedly shooting Mary Jo Buttafuoco in the head. Before I entered Albion Correctional Facility, near Rochester, New York, last December, I spent a total of two and three-quarters months in Nassau County Jail—one month while I was still seventeen. My bail was $2 million—the highest bail ever set in the county for a non-homicide. A kid from my area who killed both his parents got bail half as high. A few months after my case, in the next county over, an arrested child molester who kidnapped a ten-year-old girl and chained her by the neck for sixteen days in a closet-sized dungeon as fortified as Saddam Hussein's bunker got held on bail only *one-quarter* of mine. (Later it was raised to slightly over half my bail.) If I serve my minimum sentence with no early release, I will, at twenty-three, have spent more than a fifth of my life incarcerated. I'm in a white-columned, red-brick, medium-security prison, but it feels like I'm in a zoo cage.

The first thing I am going to do when I get out is change my name. Wouldn't you, if you were me?

It was real handy for people to have made me into a demon and a freak the way they did. That way, no one had to ask questions. Questions like: Why, in a country where people make so much money glamorizing sex and violence and getting away with things, is it such a shock when a young person acts on those messages that have been shoved down all of our throats? Questions like: How come even the adults who piously condemned me supported my exploitation by reading about me in the tabloids and watching me portrayed (largely inaccurately) in two TV movies? Questions like: Why, in our system of justice, are big, tough men exonerated, protected, called credible *even when no one believes them,* while screwed-up young girls end up serving those men, feeding their egos, fueling their fantasies, polishing their nails? Going to prison alone.

For six months after the shooting, I thought if I somehow ran into Joey and no one was watching or listening to us, he would ask, "How'd you fuck it up?"

And I would whisper back, "I don't know. I just know that I need to find out."

But Joey would be referring to the shooting. I would be referring to my life.

That's what I'm trying to do in this book—figure out the "why" while I go back and relive it all. The book is written mostly in my words, but also with a professional writer, Sheila Weller, telling the parts of the story that are beyond my point of view.

I am a blunt person, and you'll get that bluntness here. I have to warn you: The truth about the week of the shooting is hard even for *me* to read now. I am still trying to figure out how I became the person who could plan, and do, and want to get away with that. But I will tell you this: I did not act alone. There are two people walking around now—one making money as the husband of the victim; the other, a female, working at a shopping center—who should be where I am. *They* weren't stupid. *I* was.

On December 1, 1992, I stood before Judge Marvin Goodman and said, "I realize what I did was terribly wrong. I put Mrs. Buttafuoco and her children in so much pain, and for this I am deeply sorry. If I could take the pain away, if I could change everything, I would. Your Honor, the truth is, I did something so awful and I wish that I could take it back." Then I said, "It is also the truth that I had an affair with a married man, and it is also the truth that when Joey Buttafuoco learned of my intentions toward his wife, he encouraged me. These things, Your Honor, they are all true. They are facts."

This book takes off from those words. I want to push the truth through these window grates and these three rows of barbed wire—right up to the liars' lying eyes.

You probably think, "Amy Fisher could never be *my* daughter." You're probably right. Still, please; listen to me for a second. It wasn't so long ago that I was going on ski trips, wanting to help the Native Americans, dreaming of being a fashion designer, thinking it would be a big deal for me, a fifteen-year-old, to date an eighteen-year-old college freshman. Two and a half years ago, if you were to come across me with my friends Debbi and Jennifer and Heather at the Taco Bell in the mall, I swear, you would have looked at me and never have imagined my fate.

Here's what I know: It doesn't take long for a girl to destroy her own life.

Other girls my age—working on having good hair and good jeans and staying thin for their boyfriends, driving around in their Trans-Ams, LeBarons, and Firebirds, looking for love with their doors wide open and their sound systems up, those girls have asked themselves questions like I am now asking. "What am I so scared of that I can't feel anything?" "How come men keep using me? And how come I never feel used?" "Where's my sense of limits and consequences? Where's my self-respect?" (And, I will add for myself alone the biggest question: "How did I lose my respect for human life?") Though the pain those other girls feel is just a fraction of the pain I've inflicted on others, and though their reasons for asking the questions are not nearly as extreme as mine are, maybe if I work on answering the questions for me, those other girls can use them, too.

Am I really a demon, a freak? Or could I be your friend or your sister or daughter?

Here is my story. Read it, and try to understand me. Then decide the answer to that question for yourself.

♦ ♦ ♦

PART

i

1

Long Island Baby, 1974

◆

Amy Elizabeth Fisher was born at 9:26 P.M. on August 21, 1974, at South Nassau Community Hospital. She was, and would remain, the only child of Roseann and Elliot Fisher, twenty-one and thirty-eight, respectively, of Wantagh, Long Island. The couple had met two years before when Roseann Vise, a Long Island native, the eldest daughter among five siblings, came to work part-time at the fabric store Stitch 'n Sew, which Elliot owned. Soon the reserved young Queens College fashion design major and the older entrepreneur, a twice-divorced man of less than serene temperament, were in love. They were married in the backyard of her parents' Wantagh home.

It was from that modest house that Roseann had, as a girl, biked off several mornings a week on her *Newsday* paper route. Roseann was a Long Island girl, and among the other factors that lay, like hidden markers, on the path of her tiny daughter's fate were the sociological characteristics of Long Island.

Despite being just a bridge away from Manhattan for most of the first half of the century, much of Long Island, cut off from train service and threaded by local roads, lay sleepily agricultural and stubbornly undeveloped. Then, after World War II, whole neighborhoods of struggling blue-collar workers, seeking the good life, migrated to a cluster of South Shore towns. The transformation of Long Island from rural to suburban was sudden, thorough, wholesale. Especially affected was the more western of its two counties, Nassau. There population increased 65 percent in the 1940s and 93 percent in the 1950s. Towns filled with inner-city apartment and row-house dwellers bloomed en masse on former duck ranges and potato fields. The nation's most famous postwar "instant" community, Levittown, planted 17,447 houses on this soil. (The choicer, hillier North Shore held the older towns and the faded mansions of the jazz age's gold coast, immortalized in F. Scott Fitzgerald's stories.) Making use of the 118-mile Atlantic coast front and the highways that Robert Moses battled native reluctance to build, the new homeowners bought cars and boats, flaunting them showily, less like the privacy-priding farmers and frontiersmen who peopled more western U.S. suburbs than like the sidewalk-seasoned boulevardiers they had only recently been.

These new residents brought a culture of their own. For while the suburbs of nearby Westchester County were built upon foundations laid by earlier WASP residents, the South Shore Long Island suburbs offered a blank canvas on which to paint urban ethnicity. Though the island had a recent history of disparate extremism (from the violent Prohibition-era shootouts on Rum Row to an unsettling native surge of support for the Ku Klux Klan in the 1920s), the new bloc of residents—primarily Catholic, secondarily Jewish—came with their own ethos. The tone of many of their communities would remain ethnic working class, less "Ozzie and Harriet" than arriviste "Honeymooners," with milkmen's, firemen's, butchers', and steve-dores' sons proudly tending hard-won lairs with finished base-ments, barbecue pits, and wall-to-wall carpet. Sociologist and Long Island resident Donna Gaines calls these blue-collar bedroom towns "turnpike suburbia." Other local sociologists wonder if the rich communality of those immigrant cultures was lost in the rush to privatization.

By far the largest single ethnic group to settle there were the Italians, some of whose compatriots had arrived, decades earlier, from their native country to landscape the grand Old Westbury estates and stayed on to form enclaves. (The Irish were the second most populous settlers; Middle European Jews and Germans third and fourth, respectively). Today, Nassau and

Suffolk are the two most densely Italian-American contin
counties in the country; Long Island, the most Italian-American
mega-suburb in the United States. Today, one out of every four Long
Islanders is part or wholly Italian in origin. In many areas of the
island, that ratio is one out of two. The flavor of Long Island's
culture derives strongly from its largest ethnic population, and
because Italian-Americans marry out of their group at rates lower
than other groups and tend to stay in close proximity to their
parents, that flavor has not been greatly diluted as the first suburban generation gave way to a second, and the second yielded a
fledgling third.

According to Dr. Joseph Scelsa, sociologist, ethnotherapist, and
director of the John D. Calandra Italian-American Institute at the
City University of New York, the hallmarks of the Italian-American
ethos were imported by Sicilian immigrants in the 1880s and have
survived in urban East Coast culture to this day, despite the fact
that their principal reason for being was the social reality of
end-of-the-nineteenth-century Italy, not end-of-the-twentieth
America. They include the valuing of a kind of primal macho,
"Robin Hood" justice—self-administered since institutions are
deemed untrustworthy, the notion that children's accomplishments
should not exceed their parents' (so future generations will not
stray far from home, thus remaining available to care for their
elders later on); pride in artistic expression and self-ornamentation;
and the idea that women, once married, must relinquish many of
the freedoms they previously enjoyed*—in exchange for undis-
puted psychological dominance in the deeply valued family. This
last quid pro quo, Dr. Scelsa says, may offer a certain traditional
power for women, but, in our distinctly modern—indeed, feminist
—times, it also causes frustration. And, because, Scelsa says,
heterosexual socializing for married women is more frowned on
among Italian-Americans than among many other ethnic groups
("the tradition of chaperonism is strong"), it also makes for male
jealousy.

---

*It must be remembered, however, that the only woman who ran for the
highest elective office in U.S. history ever offered to a woman (Vice-
President) was Geraldine Ferraro, an outer-borough New York Italian-
American woman married to an Italian-American man.

Taken together, all of these elements suggest an expressive, high-energy culture—one might even say a *charged* culture—struggling to balance the tension between a revered past and a compelling present. Played out over the island's resortlike geography and filtered through its mesh of other suburbanized ethnic groups, these values are distilled into something that might be seen—at cursory glance, at least—as a Long Island subculture. Its adherents are more physical and practical than academic or professional; at once restless and traditional. They dress in leisurewear (the men's upper-body clothes tighter than the women's), live close to their parents, enjoy a low divorce rate, are concentrated in building-trade careers, and move, in American cars, through a world of marinas, turnpikes, fast-food restaurants, automotive garages, bowling alleys, hair salons, arm-wrestling tournaments, family weekend barbecues, discos, beach clubs, bodybuilding gyms, church fairs, and shopping malls.

There's an aggressive rather than a bucolic feeling about western Long Island, residents note. In the same way that Seattle has its rain-induced depression and Los Angeles its Santa Ana syndrome, local folklore attributes flashes of temper to something called "mid-island fever," caused, it is said, by the Long Island Lighting Company's (LILCO) practice of stringing, not burying, utility wires. Health activists wonder if this same practice, among others, is what has made for the fact that Nassau County has a rate of breast cancer conspicuously higher than that of the rest of the nation. "There's an aggressiveness that reaches even to the driving," says writer and social critic Barbara Ehrenreich, a twenty-year resident. "People drive more hostilely here than anywhere I've ever lived."

All suburban subcultures are affected by the forces that shape their wedge of time in America. Being born on Long Island—or anywhere in the United States—in 1974 meant coming to maturity at a time in which more families had two parents working than not; in which materialism and acquisition were prized and encouraged by the social and political elites; in which drug use fanned out from the counterculture to the working class; in which the advent of music videos linked the imaging of violence and sexuality and made it more explicit,

attractive, and pervasive than had been true for prior generations of popular-music fans.

Being born in 1974 meant coming to maturity at a time in
which better nutrition had plummeted the mean age of menses
(from fifteen in the early decades of the century to the current
twelve and a half), leaving American girls physically mature at a
vulnerable age. It meant being fourteen when a fourteen-year-
old won the country's most coveted modeling contract, when
sixteen was the national average age for first intercourse, and
when the number of fifteen-year-old girls who were having sex
had risen from one out of seven to one out of four over a
fifteen-year period. It meant being exposed to afternoon soap
operas whose sex content went up over 100 percent from 1980 to
1990, and to a brand-new genre of 4-to-6 P.M. "issue" shows that
focused almost entirely on violence and sexuality. It meant
becoming a teenager when, according to the first national
prevalence-of-sex-abuse study, 27 percent of American women
defined themselves as having been victims of sex abuse in their
youth. It was a time when the number of hours of homework
that high-school students actually did had halved; when the
only group in the U.S. not to experience a decline in mortality
were adolescents, plagued by an epidemic of homicide and
suicide; when private psychiatric hospitals' intake of teens had
risen, in less than twenty years, from 6,000 to 200,000; when
weapon use in high schools increased 33 percent in a single year
(1991–1992), with metal detectors newly installed in fully
one-fourth of America's largest school districts; and when, in
one ten-state area, 41 percent of teenaged boys and 21 percent
of teen girls believed that they could freely purchase handguns.

If Long Island spawned a somewhat restless, macho culture,
the last two decades of American life had created conditions
that made exploitation, confusion, recklessness, and violence
more endemic and acceptable to younger and younger people.
Such confluences of factors create traps not for the many but for
the few—in affluent neighborhoods, the *very* few.

Amy Elizabeth Fisher appears to have been one.

◆ ◆ ◆

2
Tracy's Closet

♦

Did you ever feel you could be surrounded by a hundred people, with everyone patting you on the back and telling you how great you are—and still feel all alone? Did you ever know that you had the kind of life where someone looking at you from the outside would say, "Wow, that person's got it all together"—and yet if someone could watch you from the *inside,* he could tell that you wanted to cry?

That was me, as a real little girl.

I've gotten the feeling I'm not supposed to say that. I'm not supposed to "complain." People think because my parents bought me things—nice clothes and, later on, cars—it's the sign of a terrible spoiled brat to say you felt terribly sad and alone as a child. When I was on "Inside Edition," talking about how I felt as a child, the interviewer, Nancy Glass, gave me a sort of quizzical, judgmental look when I started to talk that way. "But how can you *say* that when your parents did so much for you?" she asked.

"Why?" I challenged her. "Because they bought me *things?*"

Everyone knows you can feel sad and alone even if you've been materially well cared for, even indulged. And anyone who lives in America today knows that kids cannot *not* be aware of material goods. Television and advertising constantly bombard us with how important it is to know, and have, the right things. Why do adults put on this phony-shocked, moralizing act when they confront a well-off kid who went wrong like I did? They should know better. They live in this country. They were kids themselves.

Another myth about me is that I didn't like being an only child and wanted to be part of a big, bustling, old-fashioned, around-the-dinner-table family—that I wanted to get married and have that kind of family myself. That was the view portrayed in the ABC-TV movie. That's ridiculous. I didn't care about the size of my family, and I sure didn't want to rush out and get married. Most of the girls I know don't want to do that, either.

Isn't it funny how adults feel they have to start pulling out "The Waltons" when they deal with someone like me? Is a certain kind of behavior from a girl only understandable if we can say, "Oh, but you see, she was *really* just *dying* to be this sweet, innocent, humble old-fashioned girl instead of who she was"?

So let's get this straight: I don't think I wanted, or received, any more or less than other kids in a lot of other suburbs want and get. And I don't have any problem with being a racy, independent girl. I *like* being that.

The only thing is, I wasn't that independent girl. Terrified, defensive girls are not independent. Exploitable and self-destructive is what they are. I am only now learning that fact.

It's 1980 and I'm six years old, waking up in my bed in our house in Wantagh, filled with my usual sadness and dread. How come I feel that way? The school I go to, Mandalay Elementary, is so close you can see it from the roof of my house. I walk the two blocks to school alone, which suits me just fine. (I've been secretly crossing boulevards for a whole year.) So it's not the prospect of walking to school by myself that fills me with dread the minute I open my eyes. But dread is what I feel upon awakening. *Something* about going to school is making me feel very wary and sad. I can't figure out what. I'm not even trying to figure it out (I'm just six!), but that sadness has me inside of it. It's like a big tub of water I'll never get out of. It's not fair to wake up, six years old, and feel like that.

It sure isn't my room. My room is great. It's by far the brightest room in the whole house. I've got a white carpet and brown rug and light wallpaper. It's a real "girlie" room. I've got dolls and stuffed animals all around and my mother puts fresh flowers in the room, so it will smell nice all the time. It's trouble to keep changing the flowers and the water. Other girls' moms don't do that. But my mother does it without thinking twice.

I can tell I am the light of my mother's life. I can just *feel* it, from the way she is with me. Anybody who's ever had a parent like that knows what I mean. That parent can never punish you. That parent always tells you she loves you. But, the sad thing is, that parent still cannot protect you in that secret way you need and crave and can't—or don't—explain.

I get up and get dressed and my mother comes into the bathroom and brushes and gels my hair. Sitting behind me, with my hair in her hands, my mother seems so old. (A little girl always wants her mom to be old.) But she is really just twenty-one years older than me—twenty-seven. Today, twenty-seven is shockingly young for the mother of a six-year-old. (I have friends who are twenty-one and twenty-two.)

Maybe she seems old because my mother is an "old" twenty-seven. She already has a very responsible and complicated life. She has me, and she has my father, who is forty-four now (*that's* really old), and has just had a heart attack. Because of his heart attack, he has to stay home. The two fabric stores my parents own together (my dad owned one first—he met my mom when she worked for him there—and then they opened a second) are now all hers to manage and take care of. While my father stays home, doing the books and working on his investment portfolio—as he has been doing since I was four—my mother is out at Stitch 'n Sew in Levittown (there is also one in Freeport), opening the shop at 9, waiting on customers, overseeing part-time workers, and closing the store at 5. She has even turned the stores from selling straight fabrics to the more unusual fabrics and crafts. Then she comes home and she's the wife of an ill man. And the mother of a six-year-old.

I have no idea how hard all of this is on my mother. I just know that I love her so much and I want her so much to be there when I come home from school. But she *isn't* there; she's at work. That's probably why I wake up so sad about school—going there means coming home. And home after school is not a happy place. It is a lonely and sometimes scary place. Coming home means not being protected, not being protected by my wonderful mother, who is now brushing my hair but will soon go to work and disappear.

At school, I look like I fit in. Everybody thinks I fit in. I don't fit in at all.

Today—it's a cold, snowy day—I hatch a plot as I walk the two blocks to school. To my six-year-old logic, it's brilliant, foolproof: I am going to run away. I have two best friends, Tracy and Nicole. We're like *this:* The Three Musketeers. Nicole's father owns a pizzeria. (Throughout this story, you will get a lot of pizzerias!) Tracy's father is a lawyer and her mother works, like mine does. Tracy has older brothers who are always torturing her, so today, in first grade, Tracy and I talk. We decide we can solve all our problems by me running away and living with her. I'll be her ally against her torturing brothers, and she'll give me a place to stay so that I never have to go home after school.

That place is Tracy's bedroom closet.

Today I ask myself, What must a child be feeling that she dreams of escaping her life to live in a closet? And I answer, Very, very bad about herself. Back then, though, Tracy's closet was like a beacon of hope.

Two days later is the perfect day! It's snowing again. Because it is one of those rare days that my father is out of the house, my mother has hired an after-school baby-sitter for me, a high-school girl. We sit and watch TV. Then: The phone rings. "Your dad will be home soon," the baby-sitter says, putting on her big fat, down coat. She goes into the backyard for a moment. I resolve to myself; If my father is coming home, then I am going to Tracy's closet!

I put on my galoshes and walk very fast to Tracy's house. When I get there I tell her, "I never want to go home again!"

Tracy's closet is huge. She's even put a pillow in there for me. I'm excited. I'm at peace. I'm happy with my new life. Tracy will hide me in her room, bring me food, and everything will be good.

Three hours later, my mother has figured it out. She isn't stupid; she knows I'm *somewhere.* She's called Tracy's mother and Tracy's mother has come into her bedroom and—well, there I am.

Tracy's parents drive me home.

That was the only time—ever—that my mother hit me. As soon as I got home, she looked at me with a face lined by hours of worry on top of two years of daily stress, turned me over her knee, and slapped my butt till it was red.

"Why did you do that?! You had me worried out of my mind!"

yelled this woman who never raised her voice at me. All the frustration of the difficult juggling act that was her life at twenty-six came out in that spanking, that plea.

Then, because we both were exhausted from her outburst and my shock at it, we got our coats and we went out for pizza, and as we sat there chomping into the doughy crust, we both calmed down.

First she was going to punish me: "You can't watch 'Buck Rogers' tonight."

But by the time we got home, she relented, or forgot. The night proceeded as usual: my dad being waited on; my mom doing the waiting-on; me, watching TV.

I never did answer her question, "Why did you do that?!"

So here's that answer now.

I was afraid of being alone with my father.

My father, Elliot Fisher, terrified me.

Sure, I have a couple of good memories of him. I remember going to the park with him and him teaching me how to throw a baseball. And when I see pictures now of me sitting on his lap and smiling, I realize, Gee, I must have done that; I must have felt good enough to smile. But I can't *really* remember sitting on his lap. And when I think of him teaching me to play ball, mostly I remember how, if I wasn't throwing the ball right, he would come over and show me for fifteen minutes how to do it. But somehow his emphasis was always on what I was doing wrong.

I was always doing something wrong. I could never please my father.

My father used to always tell me he wished I was a boy. "Why didn't you come out right?" he said. Now there was no one to carry on his name. My father always called me "beautiful" in front of other people, but when we were alone, he put me down. I think he really wanted me to be the best, but it ended up that he made me feel like I was stupid. Once I came home from school and told him about a picture game we'd played in art. We were all supposed to draw pictures of what we wanted to be when we grew up. I drew a picture and labeled it LAWYER. My father said, "You're not smart enough."*

---

*Today, an authoritative source on Amy's potential says: "Amy Fisher is a very bright girl. If two or three things had been different in her life, she

But just disappointing him was like a luxury. Angering him was what I really feared. Most of the time, when we were home alone together, I walked around, trying to avoid him. I never wanted to disturb him, never wanted to make a sound. We would be home alone together in the house from the time I was four till I was six—and then after I was eight and a half. (Between the ages of six and eight and a half, I was with my grandmother almost every day after school.) Starting from when I was five, I was always doing something for him: making him a sandwich, emptying the dishwasher, even running the vacuum. (Only when my mother came home, he always told her *he* did those things.) He would lie down on the couch and say, "Amy, get me a soda." "Amy, get me a glass of water." "Amy"—if he thought I disappointed him—"look what you did to me, you're trying to kill me."

My father was a formal man. When I close my eyes I picture him sitting in front of the television, watching the Financial News Network, with his glasses way down on his nose, lifting his cup of coffee to his lips with one hand and holding the saucer with the other, lecturing me about the Dow Jones Industrial Averages. I would be sitting on the floor in front of him, secretly intimidated, worried about his temper, trying not to say anything stupid—and ending up not saying anything at all. That's why, when I got older, I always went for the totally opposite kind of man—the easy, outgoing " 'ey, yo!" guido who I never had to bite my tongue and feel stupid around.

My father was a big man—over six feet tall. He constantly slapped me. I would tell my mother sometimes, but I could never quite communicate how terrifying it felt when his hand hit my cheek. It doesn't sound so bad, a child whining in a small voice: "Mommy, Daddy slapped me." It sounds like an exaggeration. Also, if you love somebody—and I know my mother loved my father—it's hard to believe a father's touch is a slap and not a pat. But it *was* slapping. Other times he'd push me, hit me, throw me in my room, leave, come back again.

One time, when I was home alone with him after kindergarten, I was drinking hot chocolate on the coffee table in the den. Then I went up to my room. Suddenly he was on top of me, grabbing me by

---

could be on her way to becoming a doctor now."

the hair, screaming at me to clean up the mess I'd made, pulling me into the den and pushing my face into the table. It was just a little spill and I was only five years old, but I thought I'd committed a major sin.

I was so small next to his big, angry body!

The minute I went to get a rag to clean it up, he was screaming again: "What are you doing? Where are you going?"

After I finished, I went to my room. I sat there in my little-girlie room, with the sweet-smelling flowers my mother cut and all the dolls and stuffed animals. It seemed so sad that even in that room, I wasn't safe. Any time he wanted he could come in and demand, "Look at me when I talk to you!" He would say whatever he had to say, then leave. Sometimes he'd be in and out of my room for what felt like hours. I couldn't do anything else but sit on my bed, frozen and scrunched up, praying he wouldn't come back. *If I am very quiet,* I would think, *maybe I will disappear. Maybe all the pain of this will go away.*

Once, I was sitting at dinner with my father. A box of Kodak film was on the table, I can't remember why. "Spell 'develop,' " my father challenged.

I got scared. I got confused. "D-E-V-O . . .?" "D-E-V-V?" "D-E-V-E-L-U-." I kept screwing up. I have no idea how long I sat there struggling to spell that dumb three-syllable word for my sternly disappointed father, but it felt like it was an hour. My father wouldn't let me leave the table until I spelled it. Not only did I have to spell it, but I had to say it and spell it again, and again, and again. "Develop. D-E-V-E-L-O-P. Develop. D-E-V-E-L-O-P. Develop. D-E-V-E-L-O-P." I don't think I will ever forget how to spell that one word, even if I get severe Alzheimer's disease.

Just recently I've started to think about the stress my father must have been under then. To not be able to work because you're sick. To be furious that your body's betrayed you. To be anxious that any minute you might have a heart attack and die. Maybe, having suddenly lost so much control, he had to regain it by controlling me. I understand it, and I know there were a lot of good intentions in his wanting me to be perfect. Still, at the time, I was very small and very powerless. And very, very scared.

My father grew up in Brooklyn, but his relatives were scattered about and we didn't see them often. Aside from a few Passover seders at those relatives' houses, I didn't get much of a sense of his family. Maybe that's what happens when your father is thirty-eight when you are born; he's already had a life before he married your mother. In my father's case, he had two lives, I guess. He was married twice before.

I never learned anything about my father's first wife, but his second one had a baby girl from a previous marriage, whom he adopted. As the family story goes, when they divorced, not long before he and my mother got married, that second wife made a deal with him. He didn't have to pay any more child support, she offered, as long as he had no more contact with the daughter. I've been told that I played with my eleven-years-older step-half-sister when I was very little, but I can't remember.

Once, when I was about ten or eleven, I asked, "Daddy, were you ever married before?" He said yes, but that it was none of my business. I never asked him that question again.

When I would wonder aloud to Joey about our future together, he would always reassure me, in his animated way: "See, your *father* was as much older than your *mother* as I am to you, and *he* was married before, and *he* had a child from a previous marriage—and *they're* still together, *right? See?* There's a future for us."

Although mostly my parents' relationship was like two ships passing in the night, sometimes my dad and mom fought. I didn't mind it when they fought, for two reasons: one, in focusing on my mother, my father was leaving *me* alone; two, if the fighting got bad enough, I hoped that maybe they would get divorced. Once my dad threw a garbage pail at my mom; another time he ripped pictures off the wall (I remember they were pictures of *me*). Other times, he would mentally torture her. (I defined it that way, anyway.) I would listen to them fighting and she would call out to me, "Get on your clothes, Amy. We're going to Grandma's!"

And I'd say to myself, "Yes! This time, we're going! We're leaving!" And I'd get all excited, but then she'd give in and we wouldn't go.

But I did spend lots of time with Grandma. My mother's parents didn't like my father very much. They thought he was too old for my mother (my father was just six years younger than my grandmother) and they didn't especially like it that he was a different religion. He is Jewish; they are Catholic. (I was raised with no religion, which is okay by me. I'm too opinionated for religion.) But I think they could have overcome both of those objections if my father had treated me better than he did.

I loved my grandmother. I felt so safe with her. From the time I was six till I was eight and a half (when she died of cancer), she would come every day after school and take me to her house. I was so close to her, sometimes I slipped and called her "Mommy" by mistake. She didn't really seem like a grandmother. She was only forty-four when I was born. (She had my mom when she was seventeen.) But what a character she was! I get my toughness (the *good* toughness, that is) from Grandma Angela Venza Vise.

Grandma was a big, heavy Sicilian woman. Five-foot-eight. Dark skin. Dark eyes. She grew up in Bensonhurst, the Italian section of Brooklyn, just like the grandparents and even the parents of the girls who would become my teenaged best friends. My grandpa, her husband, was different, though. He came from the South. He wasn't Italian; he was a mixture of a lot of different things, including English and even a tiny bit of American Indian. (Maybe that's why I have such an affinity for Native Americans; why I like visiting the local reservations on Long Island, decorating my room with their crafts; why I wanted to do volunteer work with them.) He had light skin, black hair, and blue eyes. He was supposed to have been quite a looker, and quite a wild one, when he was young. And I heard he was a drinker.

As the family story goes, Grandpa, while in his late teens, was running moonshine. When he was on the verge of being arrested, he escaped up north, staying with his sister and brother-in-law in Brooklyn. That's where he met my grandmother. She got pregnant; they had a shotgun wedding. My mother was born, and then, soon after, my uncle Tommy. When they were little, they were disciplined in that spare-the-rod-and-spoil-the-child way that was popular then. Sometimes they were beaten with belts.

But all that was long over by the time I really needed my grandmother, when I was six. Because, after that day in Tracy's closet, it was agreed that Grandma would take care of me after school. Her house in Wantagh became my haven and she became my protector.

Here'd come big, bustling Grandma, picking me up after school. After having been an old-fashioned mother most of her life, she now had a job managing an office of mail-order-photo workers. She got out of her job early on account of me—we'd get to her house and she'd throw something in the oven for dinner and turn on her Italian station and sing to it.

Grandma doted on me and hugged and kissed me, but she never let me complain. She taught me to be plucky and selfsufficient.

"Grandma," I'd call out, "I lost my doll."

"Look where you left it!" she'd holler back.

"Grandma, I still can't find it."

"It's up Aunt Tillie's ass."

When I got out of line, she'd smack me. Lightly. With a smile. I felt her love, like sunshine. I kept coming back for more.

She was as tough and sensible as an old boot and she had all the culture of a bullfrog. And you didn't want to get near Grandma's table when she tried to get fancy with food. Her tomato sauce was great, but have you ever tasted beef teriyaki or pheasant, cooked by a Italian grandmother from Bensonhurst? I wouldn't recommend it, on a dare.

Grandma Vise had five kids in all, and my three youngest aunts—Alana, Harriet, and Mary Lynn—were like big sisters to me. Especially Mary Lynn. She was fourteen when I was born. We had a special relationship that continues to this day.

Aunt Mary Lynn was, pure and simple, my idol. My role model. She was pretty and sexy and funny and loving and tough. She looked like Cher: long jet-black hair, which she wore in a feathered style, like Charlie's Angels. Long body. Long nails. Long legs. Tight jeans. Smart mouth. *No one* pushed Mary Lynn around. *No one* told *her* what to do. I want to be tough like Mary Lynn, I'd think. I want to be that cool.

Mary Lynn lived up to my hopes as my loving corrupter. She would take me shopping and buy me jeans so tight I'd have to lie down to zip them up. She would sneak me into movies I wasn't supposed to go to—movies where the characters said dirty words. (My mother would turn into an angry Mary Poppins when she found out.) Mary Lynn and her boyfriend Jimmy took care of me a lot. They liked playing Mommy and Daddy, with me as their kid. Jimmy was this lanky guy who worked in a pet store. He didn't have much money but he had a lot of heart. He had long, long hair and a great tattoo, and he had a boa constrictor as a pet, which he sometimes wore draped around his neck. I wanted a fun, sexy, tattooed boyfriend like Jimmy.

AMY FISHER

Mary Lynn was like my fairy godmother. When I'd go to sleep at Grandma's on weekends, Mary Lynn would tuck me in in her bed. When I opened my eyes, she'd be next to me on the bed, asking, "How'd ya sleep, Amy? D'ya sleep good?" It was only years later that I realized that she purposely waited for me to fall asleep before she went out on her date. Even if Jimmy was impatient, even if a movie was starting, even if a party was under way, Mary Lynn would wait—until 10, 11 P.M.—until my breathing was nice and steady before she got up from the side of my bed. Sometimes she waited until midnight. And in the morning, the first thing I'd see when I opened my eyes was Mary Lynn standing over me, with her cool, cagey, you-and-me-are-buddies smile. Mary Lynn wanted me to think she hadn't left my side through the night. She knew about my morning dread.

"Come on, Auntie Mary, time to play," I'd say.

She'd make breakfast while I put on "The Smurfs." She was the best.

I definitely became my grandma's and my aunt's kid. A tough little scrapper, street-smart rather than book-smart. I notice mothers running after their five-year-old kids now and I think, Phew! Am I glad Mary Lynn just let me do my own thing—and Grandma was too busy to notice.

When I was five and my cousin Tommy (the son of my mom's brother) was three, we'd wait for Grandma to start cleaning the house: then, when she wasn't looking, we'd steal change out of her jewelry box and take ourselves out to Burger King for lunch. To get there, we had to cross Jerusalem Avenue, a busy thoroughfare. God knows what the people in the cars thought, pulling to a stop for these two toddlers, one of them still in diapers! But we made it to Burger King and back before Grandma even knew we were gone.

I was cagey: I figured out how to *not* get in trouble, how to make sure the adults were doing something else before I signaled Tommy that we should go on our way. My talent increased, the older I got. By the time I was eight and Tommy was six, we were taking twenty-minute jaunts down to Wantagh Avenue, going into a bowling alley and playing video games. Eleven-year-olds who thought it was great that *they* came alone looked at us and went, "What? *These* little kids?"

Today, although my cousin Tommy lives 5,000 miles away from me—in Hawaii—his personality's stayed so much like mine.

"Please!" I write him from prison, "please don't turn out like me! Don't do the things I did!"

I was a tomboy. Tommy and I would wear cowboy boots (a habit I never gave up) and play with our little spaceships and watch "BJ and the Bear" and "Buck Rogers" on TV. Mary Lynn and Jimmy would let us see action movies: *Any Which Way You Can, Any Which Way But Loose, Canonball Run.* My favorite movie was *The Champ,* with Ricky Schroder and Jon Voight. I felt for that plucky kid who loved that broken-down but wise old dad of his, who believed in the guy, despite it all, who would do anything for him. I never cried at movies, but I left *that* movie drenched in tears.

Now, I see that being the scrappy kid sidekick to the glamorously knocked-around guy was a role that grabbed me a little too much. My tears for Ricky Schroder and Jon Voight foreshadowed the future between Joey and me.

I'm going to tell you another thing that happened to me. This involves something a man close to the family used to put me through when I was such a tiny girl I didn't even have the words to tell anyone else about it. It started when I was about three and ended when I was about six.

This man would stick his fingers inside me and touch me there. It would really, *really* hurt.

I'd say, "Stop!"

This person would say, "Shh! Be quiet."

It was *terrifying* and yet, his voice was soothing—soft.

Sometimes when I was in my bed, he would come in. He would take my hands and say, "They're cold." And then he'd take my hands and put them on his penis and rub them up and down. He'd rub my feet and then he would put them there, too. I can still picture my little feet, sticking out of that blue blanket. And I remember lying in bed naked and him holding me. I was a really little, little girl.

And I remember this: These were the only times that this man was ever nice to me. The only, only times.

♦ ♦ ♦

"These were the only times that this family member was ever nice to me."

This idea that Amy learned—that sexual compliance buys

29

kindness from a man—is a lesson driven home to many incest victims.* Harvard University psychiatrist Dr. Judith Herman has written, in her landmark 1981 book *Father-Daughter Incest:*

> The relationship between father and daughter, adult male and female child, is one of the most unequal relationships imaginable. It is no accident that incest occurs most often precisely in the relationship where the female is most powerless. The actual sexual encounter may be brutal or tender, painful or pleasurable; but it is always, inevitably, destructive to the child. *The [man close to the family or] father, in effect, forces the daughter to pay with her body for affection and care which should be freely given. In doing so, he destroys the protective bond between parent and child and initiates his daughter into prostitution.* [Emphasis added.]

If the words that Amy closed her earliest childhood memories with are archetypal, so are the words that she opened with: "Did you ever feel you could be surrounded by a hundred people . . . and still feel alone?" In her long-term study of incest survivors, Dr. Herman found that "the most common complaint was a feeling of being set apart from other people. Many women described themselves as 'different' or stated that they knew they could never be 'normal,' even though they might appear so to others."

Later in this book, Amy speaks of feeling different from her friends—"off on her own track," feeling the alienation of "a female James Dean."

If one looked, with a psychologist's tools, into six-year-old Amy Fisher's future, prostitution might be dimly visible. An

---

*"Incest" is clinically defined as sex between a female child and an older, close relative. So incest literature, such as Dr. Herman's, takes the father-perpetrator as the norm, the violator is just as likely to be the child's stepfather, uncle, grandfather, or a nonrelated male in a position of trust within the family—a neighbor, therapist, clergyman, or servant. It is this broadened definition of "incest" that is operative in explaining Amy's childhood abuse.

exploitative older lover would also be in that picture. For, according to experts in the fields of both incest and prostitution —interviewed for purposes of this book—the future for girls who suffer perceived verbal and emotional abuse from a father, and sexual abuse by a man close to the family, is often marked by a series of desperate adaptations that are necessary simply to get through early life without incapacitating fear, but that often escalate into severe victimization at the hands of a potent male agent. This sad, and not always visible, course starts with survival.

"A child is extremely powerless; a child wants to please her parents very badly; children crave love as much as they crave food," says Dr. Diane Glazer, Ph.D., a Los Angeles psychotherapist. Glazer is one of the few therapists listed by the American Psychological Association as a specialist in treating middle-class prostitutes. Glazer's patients, none of whom has ever been as young as Amy Fisher, come mostly from two very different— indeed, almost opposite—types of families. In one type, "the group" is so paramount, boundaries are so blurred, and relationships with the outside world are so discouraged, the girl feels she has no separate self. The girl is *locked into* into this family. In the other type of family, authority is always shifting from one parent to the other and a kind of every-man-for-himself ethos prevails. The daughter is *pushed out* out of this family.

According to a recent major study, at least 75 percent of all prostitutes were sexually abused as children. Most of that abuse was performed by a close, older male. In other words, a majority of prostitutes were incest victims. (This does not mean that a majority of incest victims become prostitutes.)

Taking young middle-class prostitutes and looking back to their childhoods, Glazer has concluded: "When a child is left with an abuser, her options are few. She develops defense mechanisms. One way of coping is to disengage, to withdraw from that parent, sometimes to the extent that the child will 'leave her body' during the abuse." To whatever extent it is mastered, the numbing often comes in handy later. It did for Amy.

Finding an *older* male is a common trap for the abused girl. "The picking of older men obviously speaks to either deep attachment to or deep disappointment with one's father," says feminist psychotherapist Judith Klein, whose New York practice includes many abuse victims. "This girl is trying to redo her relationship with her father, or with the older male relative who abused her. To fix it. To correct it. Initially, it may work—and she feels powerful."

But that power is deceptive. For the men who are most eager to be corrective daddy stand-ins to clearly vulnerable girls are most often *looking* to exploit them, Dr. Diane Glazer has found in her work with middle-class prostitutes. This man typically initiates his lover/prey into dependence, then submission and exploitation. While thinking she is getting the relief of a "good" or "exciting" or "different" man, she is really getting a man who, under the guise of love, pushes her behavior in the direction of more risk, less self-esteem, and more debasement.

Nevertheless, says Lucy Berliner, M.S.W., director of the Sexual Assault Project at Seattle's Harborview Hospital and one of the country's most noted child-sex-abuse authorities, abuse during childhood *can* be overcome—and the path to such a man isn't necessarily inevitable. "If a child lives in a family that is loving and supportive," Berliner says, "even a pretty horrendous experience— like being abducted and raped—need not change the course of her life forever. The single most important way that long-term negative effects of abuse can be avoided [and many clinicians think emotional abuse is worse than sexual] is if the child was believed and supported."

But what if the person who believed the child most is suddenly taken away from her? What if that cherished and vital support vanishes overnight?

♦ ♦ ♦

3

Lost Girl

♦

Grandma died of cancer when I was eight and a half. I thought it was the end of my world. I cried and cried for months. I'd visit her grave in St. Charles Cemetery in nearby Farmingdale, and throw myself on it. I would bring gifts for Grandma to the grave and bury them there. (My mother would make a follow-up trip to dig them up, so the next time I came to the grave, they wouldn't be there—and I could think Grandma had received them.) Really, it wasn't normal, that grief. Grandparents are supposed to die—before parents, certainly. It's in the natural order of things. But with the loss of my favorite relative, I felt alone in the world again. Suddenly there was no one to protect me from my father anymore.

So I would protect myself. I developed this personality: If you push me, I'll push back harder. Now, back home after school with my father, I was no longer the meek little girl, content to sit scrunched up on her bed. I had this fight-back quality acquired through my two and a half years with Grandma and Mary Lynn. They toughened up their little Amy. My dad and I now locked horns a lot and he would throw me off guard because he was erratic. Sometimes something I was sure would make him furious—like a low grade in math—he wouldn't be troubled by. "Just try harder," he'd say, and I'd walk to my bedroom, my mouth open in surprise. Another time, even a higher grade would make him mad. I don't know if it's so good for a young girl to be so wary of a parent, to try to fight him so much. But I felt I had no choice.

Another thing I had no choice about was moving. The family business was good so we moved from our house in Wantagh to a nicer, bigger, more expensive house in Merrick. Merrick is a more upper-middle-class community. It's Bubbleland. The families of the kids I'd be going to junior high school and high school with made in excess of $100,000 a year. Maybe I was just a little unsure of myself, moving there and starting Merrick Junior High.

I was a skinny, flat-chested thirteen-year-old who had never had a date and only wore a bra because the other girls did. I thought I looked god-awful (though when I look at pictures of myself now, I see that I was kind of cute). I wore my hair in a ponytail. My mother said things like, "Don't let a boy kiss you." I wasn't even allowed out of the house on school nights.

One Saturday morning, soon after we moved into the new house, I slept in while my parents went, as usual, to Stitch 'n Sew. My father was getting out more these days, which was fine by me. And my mother, by now, had a custom-upholstery business on the premises. We were having tile work done in the fireplace and the kitchen. As I reluctantly came up from under my blanket and out of my dream, my ears filled with what had come to be the familiar highs and lows of workmen's voices drifting up from downstairs—half in English, half in Italian; a cement mixer chugging; a power drill whirring. Determined to grab a few extra minutes of sleep, I kept my eyes closed.

But there was this *other* sound, too—of a person behind my closed bedroom door. It wasn't my mother or father, I knew. They didn't shuffle. Didn't stop and start moving so the hall floorboards creaked, then stopped creaking. They didn't *lurk*.

This person was lurking.

I had on a T-shirt. Nothing else. I sat up straight. The inside knob of the door turned, just like in a corny movie. A short, balding, unwashed man walked in. I recognized him as one of the workers. I had sometimes caught him staring at me.

He said something to me in Italian and then he was on top of me. He didn't take off any of his clothes and he didn't take off my T-shirt, which I held down firmly with both of my hands. He just unzipped his fly, and then, in my own bed, he raped me. It was horrible!

I didn't scream because I was terrified that the other workmen would come up and watch—or join him. But I did pound and dig my nails into his back to try to get him off me. It was disgusting. It hurt. I was too stunned and naïve to worry about pregnancy. To this day, I don't know if he ejaculated. (I didn't know what ejaculation *was* then!) But I was afraid—of my parents finding out and punishing me. I had a feeling I did something wrong. Have you ever been raped? By someone you realize had been stalking you with his eyes while you squirmed around self-consciously, trying not to notice? Then that vague, awful, confused secret guilt is something you know about.

I told a couple of my girlfriends, who said, "Don't worry, you can sleep at my house." I spent most of my time at those friends' houses when the workmen were there, until they finally finished the job. When I found out a friend's family had hired that same contractor to do *their* kitchen, I told her what happened to me. She was two years older than me, forewarned and tougher. So when that same workman grabbed her, *she* cursed him out. He let go of her arm in an instant and stayed out of her way until their kitchen was finished.

Last summer, [1992] when I became anointed the Long Island Lolita, this friend sold her little anecdote to the media—only she didn't say that I told her I was sexually assaulted by this disgusting man; she said that I'd "bragged" that I had "fucked the tile man." I felt doubly victimized: first by the rape, then by her lie about it.

But the ugliest mischaracterization of that incident comes from Joey's criminal lawyer, Marvyn Kornberg. This big loudmouth, whose legal technique is to scream over interviewers who are making valid points in my favor, gloats about my rape and uses it as "proof" that I enjoy sex with older men. He's even decreased my age at the time of this ugly forced encounter with the "tile man" (as everybody insists on calling him) to "twelve." Mr. Kornberg, if you think *any* twelve- or thirteen-year-old girl enjoys sex, or even is capable of having consensual sex, with an adult male, then you are a very disturbed and exploitative man. And if you think gloating about the violation of a girl that age is an appropriate way to score a point for a client, then I think we need more women lawyers—or more male lawyers who are also human beings.

I put that ugly incident behind me. Erased it from my mind. It didn't happen. (I didn't realize it, but numbing myself had become for me quite a talent.) I considered myself a virgin, like the rest of my friends. My mother and I didn't talk much about sex. She just said, "Don't do it." If she had said "Don't do it" *all* the time, I might have run out and tried it. But, because she didn't make a big prohibition out of it, I was in no rush. I waited until the time was right.

As for my father, I didn't talk about sex at all with him.

Fifteen was mostly the age when girls from Merrick, my new neighborhood, had their first sexual experience—if they had a boyfriend. At least that's what we heard. My four best junior-high friends and I were eager to be sophisticated, so we talked about boys a lot, on our weekends of mall shopping and our winter skiing trips to Stowe, Vermont. The five of us were all close friends: me, Debbi, Jennifer, Heather, and Jill. I can't speak for myself (or, let's put it this way: I don't want to brag), but they had beautiful hair. We all dressed in designer-disaster clothes: Big John and Lee jeans, tight shirts, Nicona boots, southwestern jewelry. None of our parents were divorced. But, somehow, I felt their families were happier than mine was.

Jennifer and I were the closest, and we had the most in common in another way—each of us had one Jewish and one Catholic parent. Her mother was Irish, her father was Jewish.) In the world I was living in now—where almost every single kid had two Jewish parents—I felt like a mutt. Religion was something we just kind of avoided in our house (as I said before, that was fine with me), and as a result I didn't have much exposure to either tradition. My dad made noise about how he wanted me to know about Judaism, but he never took me to a synagogue or taught me Hebrew. I had gone to Catholic church with Grandma a lot, but never with my mother. Thirteen was when all the bar mitzvahs came. Jennifer and I entered those temples feeling—strange. Like all the other kids knew something we didn't know about. Like, what *were* we, anyway? Like, suddenly—surprise!—the world has pigeonholes, and, guess what? You don't fit in any.

As we moved from junior-high to high school, I could see my friends dividing into two groups: Debbi and Jennifer used their brains and studied, while Heather and Jill were into the Grateful Dead. I heard they were also into pot-smoking. I wasn't into drugs—I *never* did drugs, and I never even smoked cigarettes. But I had stopped being that hopeful little girl who drew the picture labeled "Lawyer." Even though I was good in my art classes and hoped to be a fashion designer (I'm still hoping for that) I wasn't studying. I was drifting along on my own little track. Angrier than my friends. More wanting to leave home. More looking for the kind of shelter I had had with Grandma.

I was all messed up: in my own little world. That's the only way I can explain it.

Now all these girls are at good colleges—especially Debbi and Jennifer. And they all have nice sports cars. Sometimes I wish I could leave prison and go out and be with them again. Be appropriate. Conform to that life. But I've experienced so much, I don't know how I could go back there.

Surprisingly, Jennifer—who had been such a nerd in junior high, she overachieved to make herself the most popular girl in high school—was one of the first to lose her virginity. I remember when she came running back to tell us, "I slept with Jared! I slept with Jared!" She was only fourteen! And she was so virtuous. Hey, I thought to myself, how could she have gone from A to Z with nothing in between? How could *she* be ahead of *me?*

So, in my freshman year at Kennedy High, I got myself a boyfriend. His name was—don't laugh—Joey. Joey DiNardo. He was Italian (so what else is new?) and he was three years older than me and handsome and macho: five-foot-ten and a bodybuilder with very dark hair, a broad chest, even a moustache. He had a tattoo (like Aunt Mary Lynn's Jimmy), which my parents did not like. I didn't have anything in common with Joey DiNardo, but I thought he was exciting. I was still a little girl to him and I was afraid to sleep with him. I dated him for two months, and then he called me a "cocktease" and broke up with me. I was crushed.

On the rebound from Joey DiNardo, I made probably the only smart decision about a boyfriend in my life. I started going with a boy named Rob. Rob was three years older than me, more athletic-looking than Joey DiNardo, and much, much nicer. Rob is the kind of boy who does errands for his grandmother and leaves funny messages on his answering machine and means it when he says he is going to college (he's in college now), comes over with presents. My parents loved him. He practically lived at our house. He liked me for myself, not just my body. In fact, we dated for months before we slept together. A month before my fifteenth birthday, Rob and I started planning for the big moment of our first night together. We planned it for a week.

Rob's parents are wealthy and they have another house besides their house in Merrick. It was summertime, and they were at their vacation place. The only other person in the house was Rob's brother, whom Rob kicked out of the house. Rob sent out for pizza and we played Honeymoon. When I look back to that sweet night, I think: I should have stayed with him.

But at fifteen you don't really know what you're doing. We were pretty sloppy about protection, too. Sometimes we used condoms, sometimes we didn't. We used the Russian roulette method of birth control. Pretty stupid, huh?

By the time I entered tenth grade, and Rob twelfth, we were always together. Despite being such a responsible boy, he had a wild streak. (I could never in a million years be attracted to anyone who didn't.) We cut a lot of classes that year. I'd go to school in the morning, then cut and go over to Rob's house. We went to the beach or the mall together. At night, instead of studying, we'd be in my room, playing Nintendo. We played Super Mario Brothers until we dropped. We had it on Mute, and when my parents knocked we'd quickly hit Pause. Rob'd be watching soundless TV and I'd be poring over my history book by the time they opened the door and entered. We always put it over on them.

I was getting good at keeping things from my parents. The truth is, a parent can love you so much she never expects the worst. Another parent can be naïve to the possibility of the worst, even when his difficulty with love helped push you to it. So, all in all, it is easy to hide things from parents.

Rob and I made plans to stay together. He would start college, then I would start college. Then he would go to graduate school and then maybe we'd get married. I even looked at catalogs of engagement rings. Still, I didn't think I wanted to get married, even though my mother and grandmother had married young. I didn't know what I wanted to do.

My friend Heather was into James Dean. When I saw his *Rebel Without a Cause* poster on her wall, I ran out and bought myself one. I framed and hung the poster up in my bedroom because I liked James Dean's jeans, tight T-shirt, and cowboy boots. He's standing next to a motorcycle, which I think is cool. And he's got a cigarette dangling from his mouth, which I think is *not* cool—healthwise, anyway. But it was that blank, half-sad, half-angry look on his face that really got me. I could have been looking in the mirror.

During winter vacation of tenth grade, my friend Samantha ran into Joey DiNardo at the mall. He asked about me. Samantha gave him my new phone number. He called me and I made a date with him. "Okay," I said, as I slid my cowboy boots on over my blue jeans. "He's not going to think I'm a cocktease anymore."

I broke up with Rob to go back with Joey DiNardo. Then I broke up with Joey and went back with Rob. I was going back and forth between excitement and security. Tenth and eleventh grades were a time of confusion for me in general. I started forging my parents' signatures on my report card; I did my homework for one class in the class right before it. A tough girl in my class, Madeline Cioffi, picked a fight with me. The second time we fought, she broke my nose and dislocated my jaw. I was in awful pain and had to go through surgery.*

So here I was, on the brink of sweet sixteen: a class-cutting, report-card-forging, ashamed secret rape victim who'd been sexually abused as a little kid, still pined for her dead grandmother, fought like cats and dogs with her father, liked Nintendo more than homework, was a human Ping-Pong ball between two boyfriends, and now had a busted nose and a bent jawbone.

When I got my junior driver's license at fifteen and a half, my dad bought me a white 1989 Dodge Daytona. People make a big deal out

---

*Madeline Cioffi explained her attack on Amy, on TV's "Jenny Jones Show," by saying that Amy had passed an untrue rumor about Madeline's sister and "I never liked her" [Amy]. After sixth period one day, Madeline says she attempted to intrude in an argument Amy was having with one of Madeline's friends. "I was raged," she says. "I've always been a fighter." When Amy "moved me out of the way . . . I came back and hit her. I heard a crack and she hit the wall and that was that. I walked away."

Madeline claims that when Amy's father picked her up at school, "as he was leaving he made a remark to Amy but it was overheard by a parking attendant: that Amy probably did deserve it."

Madeline Cioffi was charged with misdemeanor assault and pleaded guilty to a lesser charge in juvenile court. The Fishers sued the Bellmore-Merrick School District for $1.2 million for failing to protect Amy.

of the fact that I got that car, but most of the kids in my suburb got their own cars when they got their licenses.

One night I was at a girlfriend's house and I wanted to sleep over. I got in a fight with my mom and my dad grabbed the phone out of her hand. He was in one of his moods. He threatened me: "If you come home, I'll beat the shit out of you."

I drove my Daytona back to my house, but I was afraid to go in and see my father. So I parked at the end of the block, knocked on a neighbor's door, and asked to use their telephone. I dialed Aunt Mary's number. "Can I sleep at your house tonight?" I asked her.

"Sure," she said. "What happened?"

She drove over and picked me up. I stayed with her two days, but she had to go to work and, well, she's a little wild; she couldn't really watch me. So she drove me to my great-grandmother's house. I stayed there for two whole weeks. My great-aunt Christie drove me to school and back daily. I would *not* go home. When my mother pleaded, I said I'd rather go live with a friend.

My mother cried and said, "Please come home." She said everything would be better. I went home. Where else *could* I go?

During the time I was away, my parents reported me as a missing person. As part of that procedure, my father filed a report with a local assistant district attorney, calling me "totally uncontrollable." I guess that's what I seemed to him. But he seemed totally dictatorial to me. So I guess we were even.

Those two frustrated words of my dad's, which he later disavowed when he called to retract the missing-persons report, would come back in spades to haunt me when another D.A.—Fred Klein—called them out like a rallying cry through the courthouse and got me slapped with a $2 million bail.

Isn't it funny? All of my life, my parents said many, many positive words about me, but the only ones the D.A. used, and the judge listened to, were those two: "totally uncontrollable." Rapists, arsonists, pedophiles who build torture chambers, parent murderers, child murderers, cop killers, Mafiosi hitmen—all of these dangerous people got lower bail than one teenaged girl whose father had once scared her shitless over the telephone.

Through all this, Rob was my comfort. The one person I could count on. Then one day I had a bit of a panic. My period was late. A whole month late. I bought one of those packaged drugstore tests. I stood very still in my bathroom while I watched the spot on the stick turn pink. I was pregnant.

The experience scared me to death. Aunt Mary Lynn helped me through it. Rob drove me, paid for it, and waited in the waiting room. But the effect on me was a big one. For a couple of months afterward, I wouldn't let Rob touch me. Even with protection. I was too turned off, too scared. I wanted Rob to understand. Instead, he got mad.

Right after Memorial Day 1991, while I was still smarting from Rob's inability to deal with my feelings, I backed my Daytona out of the garage, not noticing how close I was on the left. I heard a loud crunch. The sideview mirror was lobbed off. Shit! I thought. My father will kill me.

I brought the car in for an estimate. Maybe Rob would help me pay for it. I chose the garage that my father had brought it to last Halloween: a huge auto service place in Baldwin called Complete Auto Body & Fender Inc. I had gone with him then and my father had schmoozed with one of the mechanics, but I hadn't paid much attention.

I drove in, wearing extra-large sweatpants with KENNEDY COUGARS printed across the butt, a sweatshirt, my hair in a ponytail, no makeup: a sixteen-year-old hiding her fourteen-year-old body.

I got an estimate on repairs—$800—from one of the owners.

Then the other man, his brother—a big, husky guy with a friendly smile in a tight T-shirt and blue jeans—came up to me. "I've seen you before!" he said. "You're Mr. Fisher's daughter! Remember, Bobby?" The big, friendly man turned to the first one. "This is Mr. Fisher's daughter." Then, to me, he said, "We don't get too many pretty girls around here, so you remember them."

I told them I was nervous about my father finding out that I had caused the damage.

The friendlier one—who had introduced himself as Joey—had a solution. "Park your car in the lot. We'll *tow* it in. We'll tell your father someone hit it."

The next day my father and I both came in, together, to talk to this man, Joey Buttafuoco, about how much it would cost to repair my "sideswiped" car mirror. Joey said a big booming hello to my father and to me, like he hadn't seen either of us since October.

41

Nobody would have dreamed I'd brought the car in for a secret estimate the day before. He made a big fuss about my father, like he was a prized customer—a friend, even. My father, who had no idea I'd caused the damage, was distracted and flattered. When my dad turned his head, Joey winked at me.

What I didn't know was that, when I'd come into the shop with my father last Halloween, Joey had said, out of the corner of his mouth, "I'd like to fuck that . . ." When he'd found out that "that" was the daughter of the customer standing next to him, Joey had apologized.

Somehow, that remark hadn't bothered my father. He dismissed it as a compliment. Stitch 'n Sew was in a Spanish neighborhood, and when I walked by with my father, some of the guys would cat-call at me, so I guess he was used to it.

Now Joey and my father and I sat in the Complete office, my father charmed by Joey's expansiveness. Then and later Joey's attitude would be: Go easy on her, Mr. Fisher. She's a good kid. You want her to love you, don't you? I have a daughter myself. I could tell that this man—loose and macho like Mary Lynn's Jimmy, but with more of an edge, a hint of danger—was a very good father. That he could, and would, help *me* with *my* father.

He was the kind of father *I* would have wanted to have.

4

True Love

Despite being charmed by Joey, my father thought $800 was too high to fix a sideview mirror. But the mirror was electric, Joey explained. He'd have to take the whole door off to do it right. Still, my father took the car to another body shop, which offered to do it for $200. "They're not going to do it right," Joey warned. "They won't give you new parts. It'll buckle." Sure enough, that's what happened. My dad brought the car back to Joey.

From what two of the TV movies said about me, and Joey's accounts, you might believe I kept crashing my car in order to get close to him, but the truth is the opposite. Joey delayed on making the repairs and my father was a perfectionist. Every time we came in to pick up the car, in June 1991, it was mysteriously not ready. But since we were there, we'd come into the office to talk to Joey anyway. Or, we'd get the car home and my father would say, "The molding's not right. Bring the car back to Joey." I'd bring the car back to Joey. Then I'd talk to Joey. The two men, my father and Joey, were doing this little dance with each other and I was almost the conduit, the link. Later, when Joey told me I should join "this great guy Paul Makely's" gym, it was the same thing all over again. I don't know anything about psychology, so I don't know if it was competition, or male bonding, or sizing up, or two men tossing a girl like a football. What do *you* think it was?

When I'd go and sit in Joey's office, we flirted—innocently. He definitely tried to impress me. On the bulletin board behind his desk he had a picture of himself flexing his muscles. Surrounding him sat his arm-wrestling trophies. "Once I wrestled with Sylvester Stallone, and I won," he said. He talked about his Cigarette racing boat. I had never even been on a boat. Oh, I'd walked onto a docked boat because my mother did decorating work on them. And I'd been on a tiny speedboat. But a real racing boat? Never. It seemed glamorous.

The boat, he told me, was named *Double Trouble.* That was the same name he'd pinstriped, in baby blue, onto his car, a black Cadillac Sedan DeVille with black limo tint. He walked me around his car with a kind of goofy pride. It had a boom box and a stereo system, just like a Wantagh or Levittown teenager's.

My father also drove a Cadillac, but I could as easily imagine *him* decking out his car as wearing Timberland boots, dancing to club music, and getting a tattoo. "You took this beautiful thirty-thousand-dollar car and turned it into a . . . kid guineamobile?" I asked Joey, amazed.

"Yep," he said. "I call it my guinea gunboat."

This guy is three years younger than my mother, I thought, but he has the maturity of a sixteen-year-old! I couldn't decide if it was very weird, or very cool.

By the end of June, it was kind of clear that Joey couldn't keep my car any longer. The sideview mirror was definitely fixed and he had pinstriped "Aimee" on the side. (That's still the way I prefer to spell it.) He had heard me tell my father I wanted a stereo system. We had devised a plan for payment. I would do a week of secretarial work at the electronics firm where Mary Lynn was a secretary, while she was on vacation, and my father would match my pay toward the system.

I worked the week before summer school started and got my $225; my dad matched it—and then some. Now I could get my stereo system. Joey had an idea. Since both my parents were working at Stitch 'n Sew, I would drive to Complete Auto Body after summer school, and Joey would take care of my car—have it brought to the stereo installer, Audiotronics. The car would be left there, and he'd drive me home.

Joey even called my father to ask his permission to drive me home. My father said yes. He thought Joey was a great guy. A courteous gentleman.

That was Tuesday, July 2, 1991. The beginning of it all.

Right when we walked out of Audiotronics, the flirting started— but in that tense, undefined way, when you're alone together in a new situation one of you put you in.

I thanked him for offering to take me home and he said, "Well, if you were a two-hundred-pound whale, don't think you'd get this ride."

"You mean you wouldn't like me if I was ugly?" I teased, as he opened the door of his decked Caddy.

"Absolutely not," he said. Then he said, "You're beautiful. That's the only reason I'm doing this."

Beautiful. No boyfriend had ever called me that before. I always tried to get that word out of Rob, but he withheld it. "Do you think I'm pretty?" I asked Rob.

The best I got back was, "Well, I wouldn't date a dog or anything."

As Joey drove us to my house, I didn't realize I was in the presence of a master sweet-talker. Let me tell you—they are dangerous.

Joey had a stretchy Ace bandage on his right arm. I asked him what happened and he said he tore a ligament lifting a car. *Lifting* a car? I was impressed. I snapped the bandage as he drove. Looking back now, it is obvious to me what all of this was leading up to. But I honestly did not know that back then. I didn't think. I didn't have a sense of cause-and-effect. I bet other sixteen-year-old girls know what I mean. People call you "seductive," as if you have power. But *you* feel you have *no* power. No power at all. You're just going blindly along on tools you picked up. But, if you'd ever been given a choice, those might not have been the tools you'd have chosen.

When we parked in front of my house, Joey asked for a tour. We went inside. The house had just been finished in European modern, so I was proud to show him around. My little dog, Muffin, followed from room to room. Joey asked for something to drink. I gave him a soda.

He asked to see my room. I led him upstairs.

What does a thirty-five-year-old man with an eight-year-old daughter feel when he walks into a room full of Teddy bears? If Joey was uncomfortable when he was confronted by my eight Gund

Teddies propped around the room, he didn't show it.* (Later he would buy me three more as presents.)

Here is the room Joey saw: gray walls (I had just painted them myself). White carpet. White Formica desk and dresser, with little etched mirrors. A print of Floridian colors—peach, blue, green, yellow, baby pink—in the curtains and matching sheets. A stereo rack system, phone, answering machine. My Teddy bears. My James Dean poster. A painted Native-American cow skull from a reservation I had recently visited and planned to do volunteer work at. My room was as spare and uncluttered as a furniture showroom. I was proud of it and kept it very neat.

I had a fish tank by my bed, with a pet salamander in it. I showed Joey the pet, and I felt the weight of his body behind me. All of a sudden, he pushed me on the bed by the tank. He was on top of me and kissing me. He was overpowering. He had his hands all over my face, my eyes, in my hair.

Still, I thought the kissing would stop. That's how it was with dates with boys my age. But it didn't stop. Joey threw me on the bed. He started taking off his clothes. I thought, Uh-oh. What did I get myself into?

I remember him telling me, "It's okay, I'm clean." I thought he meant he had no diseases. Then he clarified it: "Don't worry, I had a vasectomy."

I thought, Oh, God, I guess that means he wants to have sex with me. "I don't really think I should have sex with you," I said.

Joey just looked at me. He was on top of me. "I don't have sex," he said. "I make love."

Yeah, okay. What do I do now? I thought. So I just went with it. I remember lying there and not doing much—feeling uncomfortable because I thought he was judging me. I didn't feel like I was as good as he was. I was embarrassed about my body. But he put his hands all over me, as if I were beautiful. Then he said, "You're beautiful,"

---

*During the media attention after Amy's arrest, a call girl who had worked at a Manhattan house of prostitution called Nassau Homicide. During a personal interview with two detectives, she described Joey as a former customer and outlined his distinct preference for young prostitutes, youthfully dressed. Detective Martin Alger believed that the woman clearly knew Buttafuoco, though her information was not considered relevant to the investigation.

but in a much softer way than he had when we'd crossed the street an hour before. He kissed me on my forehead and stroked my eyelids and touched my hair real slowly.

It was an emotional, romantic kind of kissing, not like anything I had ever experienced. Joey DiNardo, who had gruntingly called me a "cocktease"; Rob, who had conceded I wasn't "a dog or anything"; they were unromantic, loping, groping boys. *This* was a whole different thing.

Everything changed after that. I was completely in love with Joey Buttafuoco. There was no turning back.

That afternoon my father drove me to Joey's body shop so I could pick up my car. I knew it wouldn't be there; I just wanted to see Joey again. As my father sat talking to Joey's father, Caspar Buttafuoco, the crusty old man who owns the place, Joey and I got in his car—supposedly to drive to Audiotronics. But we started kissing instead. Suddenly, there was my father—pulling his car around. I ducked. It's amazing he didn't see me. Joey and I laughed. He *loved* getting away with stuff.

"Hey. Tonight," Joey said, stroking my face. "Meet me here. We'll go out."

I told my parents I was going to Rob's house and I tore over to Joey's shop. I expected dinner, a movie—but I got take-out and the Freeport Motor Inn & Boatel. This would be the first of many motel dates with Joey, every one of which I remembered and told the police about.*

---

*When interviewed in early December 1992, Detective Alger and his superior, Detective Sergeant Dan Severin, said they are "positive" of the motel trysts between Amy and Joey. "Time and again, Amy would give us an exact day and time," Alger says, "and we would go to the motel and, sure enough: There was Joey's registration *for* that day and time. Joey signed his name, work address, and even gave his full driver's license number on most of the registrations. We had thirteen motel receipts in all. We sent them to the FBI; their handwriting specialists confirmed his handwriting on eleven of them." The motel clerk filled in the other two.

Despite this, and despite the manager and desk clerk at the Freeport Motor Inn & Boatel, declaring that Joey was there, Joey and his attorney, Marvyn Kornberg, contend that the receipts were faked, and implied that the manager, Chris Creamer, and the clerk, Paul Fischer, lied, perhaps at

I had never been to a motel before. Once we got inside, Joey was all over me with compliments and kisses. "I can't take my hands off you," he said. "You're beautiful," he said again. There was an intensity to the way he said it that made me believe him. I had on a pair of light-colored jeans, a big Champion sweatshirt, and Timberland boots. As he undressed me, I felt proud of my body for the first time in my life.

Joey made me feel sexy. I had never felt sexy before. I had never really thought that I would.

"I'm going to get you new underwear," he whispered, taking off my little-girl cotton briefs. Sure enough, that was the beginning of my transformation. In the weeks to come, I received silk G-strings and push-up bras from Frederick's of Hollywood. There isn't a piece of fabric close to my body that didn't come from Joey Buttafuoco. Or that I didn't buy because of his image of me.

The self-consciousness I had had when we'd made love on my bed that afternoon didn't return. With my two young boyfriends, I had always felt like a shy little girl. Now I felt totally desirable. And unafraid. After the abortion, I couldn't imagine being touched. Sex seemed risky and scary. Now, because Joey had told me about his vasectomy, I stopped worrying.

Joey was just so affectionate and emotional and loving. Touching, touching—all the time. "I'll give you a massage," he said. "I'll braid your hair."

"*You* can braid hair?"

"Sure, I can braid hair."

I moved my little body, spoon style, against his big one. This husky man who had lifted up a whole car worked his fingers gently into my hair; earnestly crisscrossing strands. I went to the motel bathroom mirror. "I never knew a man could do a French braid!" I must have looked amazed.

He laughed, like I was a little kid. "You're a trip," he said. "Where did they grow you from?"

Eric Naiburg's behest, and that the FBI handwriting confirmation was the work of arbitrary "experts" and therefore meaningless.

Today Chris Creamer says that what Marvyn Kornberg is saying "is not true and Marvyn knows it isn't true." Paul Fischer confirms today, "I checked Joey Buttafuoco into the motel approximately eight to ten times."

Then he put on a baby voice. "Come to Joey," he'd implore. That was a voice, and a plea, I would hear many times.

We made love again. Joey was amazing. He could do it six, eight times a night! I would get tired first. I never knew men could do it that much. I always thought, from movies and everything, that there were—you know, limits.

Joey went in the bathroom and immediately flushed the toilet. He always played this game—he called out to me, where he tries to race the toilet; see if he can finish peeing before the water stops swirling around the bowl.

Now who's the little kid? I thought, lying on the bed, laughing.

Joey turned on the motel radio and set the knob to K-Rock, the classic-rock station. He gave me a serious look and took my wrists in his hands. "I'm going to teach you good music," he told me. "We're gonna play Name That Song."

The game would be our motel staple. A song from the 1960s or 1970s would come on and he'd stick his finger out like a game-show master challenging a contestant.

"That one!" he'd order me.

And I'd jump up and say, "Grace Slick!" Or: "The Allman Brothers!" Or: "Led Zeppelin!" Or: "Van Morrison!" Or: "Janis Joplin!" The more I did it, the better I got.

He'd leap up and say, *"Ver-y* good! You're learning!"

It was getting toward the end of the time I could spend with him before my parents expected me home. Joey sat me on his lap and surprised me by saying, "I love you."

I *love* you? That was too much! This guy didn't know me. "You don't have to say that," I said.

"I'm not afraid to say it," he said. "In time you'll feel that way, too."

"But you're *married*," I reminded him. I didn't get it. He had a picture of his blond wife in his office. He had said, proudly, that she'd once posed for the Spiegel catalogue. He had told me and my dad about his kids.

"Our marriage died years ago," he said. "She doesn't even like me. We just live in the same house and have children.* She's a

---

*A woman who worked in the Buttafuoco home during that same period claims Mary Jo told her that she and her husband had sex "'only once every four or five months.'"

devout Catholic. She doesn't believe in divorce."

Now he started what would be a constant string of complaints and regrets about Mary Jo—how all she did was stay home all day, even though the kids were now old enough for her to work; how she would start taking college courses but never finish them; how he was out busting his butt; he wanted *her* to do something to make money. "I want *her* life," he said. He told me how she was vain—she'd had a nose job—and inconsiderate: He had gotten a puppy for the kids. A yapping little shih tzu. He loved the mutt, loved the way it shimmied up to him when he came home. One day, while he was at work, Mary Jo gave it away because it was too much bother. This upset him. Couldn't she take the time to train the dog, since she was home all day? "She will die for that," he said half-kiddingly, I guess, but with a very straight face.

He told me that he and Mary Jo had met in Massapequa High, that they'd hung around in the same crowd, but that he had been in love with another girl, a friend's girlfriend. The other girl was Italian. Mary Jo was Irish. Joey's father was always saying, "Marry your own kind—an Italian girl."

As Joey stroked my back on the motel bed, he told me the rest of the story: Joey didn't think it was right to steal his friend's girlfriend, so he started going with Mary Jo and then, after high school, they married. But he always regretted not having stepped in and taken the girl he really loved.

That girl and Joey's friend married. So did Joey and Mary Jo. Still, both marriages didn't keep Joey and the woman from having a secret affair. That affair lasted for years. Then, a few years ago, after they'd had three children, the friend left his wife. Joey had stepped in and got very, very serious about this woman he'd always loved. He was a substitute father to her children, giving them birthday presents, buying them bicycles. He even considered leaving Mary Jo for her. Then he changed his mind and stayed with Mary Jo. Still, he was glad he had spent that time with the girl he had loved.

By the time Joey and I drove back to Complete, and I got my car and drove home, my head was full of Joey: this big, smooth-talking, sexually masterful man with a full-blown life and a past and regrets and secrets and mysteries. I'm sure every sixteen-year-old girl who has found herself with an older married man knows what I mean.

It's like walking from a black-and-white movie with tinny sound on a tiny TV screen to a big Technicolor epic on a huge screen with Dolby wraparound.

He pushed everything else out of my life.

The next night, the doorbell rang. It was Rob—leaning in, angry and hurt. He had called earlier and asked me what I'd done last night. "Gone out with my girlfriends," I answered.

"Oh, did you have fun?" he asked.

"Yeah, I had a great time."

"Yeah, well, what was your car doing at Complete Auto Body?"

Dead silence.

Then we'd started fighting. When I'd see him next, it would be either to win me back or continue the fight.

I slammed the door in his face.

I went upstairs. Joey called. There came a banging on my window. Joey could hear it through the phone. It was Rob's fists. Rob's face. He had scaled the side of the house and gotten onto the roof. He was leaning down, banging on the window, screaming for me to open the window and let him in.

I explained to Joey, "It's my old boyfriend."

"You want me to come over and bust him up?" Joey asked.

"No," I said. "I can handle it."

Rob kept pounding. Finally, he just went away. At the time, Rob's contorted expression seemed to register insult and anger.* But now I wonder: Could it have been some kind of a warning, instead?

Joey and I started seeing each other every other night. He would pick me up, in Mary Jo's Jeep, and take me for candlelight dinners. One night he said, "I've got a surprise for you. Wait for me down at the marina." The marina was two blocks away from my house, at the end of the street.

Telling my parents I was going to Jennifer's, I raced out of the house at 6:30, wearing cut-offs, a tight T-shirt (I was showing my body more now; Joey inspired me), and a sweatshirt. I went to the appointed place, waited until I saw the *Double Trouble* chugging up,

---

*Rob was extremely loyal to Amy after her arrest, steadfastly resistant to exploiting her or even talking to the media. Until he moved away to college early in 1993, he kept in touch weekly with Amy's mother.

shooting foam on either side. As he cruised in and lifted me on board, I felt like Grace Kelly with Bing Crosby in that old movie where they sang "True Love."

We made love on the boat. Joey let me steer while I sat on his lap. We steered, naked, in the moonlight, with the waves lapping, with Joey touching me, kissing me, flattering me.

Later, in the cabin, I studied Joey's body. It was very hairy. He had two moles on the inside of one thigh. I asked him why he had such short pubic hair. He said, "I cut it." I asked him if the scar on the left side of his back was from his vasectomy. He laughed like I was a little girl.

"Then was it from a fight?"

"Can't tell you."

But he did tell me that he had a gun; that he'd once had a very bad cocaine problem. That was why he never touched a drink now—never smoked, either. He told me there were other things about his past he'd share with me—one day.

"What? *What?*" I tickled him until he coughed it up.

"I was a street pimp."

"You *were?*"

"They were just a bunch of dumb niggers," he said, sloughing it off. "They made me a couple of bucks on the side. It's no big deal."

I hated his racist language. Still, his exploits were intriguing. I never knew anyone who did things like that.

"Did you ever kill anybody?" I asked.

He gave me a mysterious look and said, "You do what you have to do."

One day, we drove past a marina and Joey waved at a guy on a boat and the guy waved back. "That was John Gotti, Jr.," he said casually.

"Wow!" I said. "You know him?"

"You're a trip, little girl," Joey said again. "And you're *my* little girl." He moved his finger over my lips.

We went on the boat a lot—from 6:30 or 7 P.M. till 11. Once I got upset that all we ever did was have sex. "Is that all you want me for?" I asked him.

"How could you say that? You don't really believe that, do you, sweetie? I love you," was his answer. Then he'd say, "Fine. We won't have sex anymore. We'll just go out."

We did that a couple of times. We went out and got something to eat, then drove around and parked by the duck pond and talked. I opened up a lot about my father, how critical he was of me.

"I'll take care of it," Joey said. And then the next day, he would call my dad at Stitch 'n Sew, and loosen him up. "How's everything, Mr. Fisher? How's Amy? How're the cars?" It *worked*. My dad got nicer! He dropped in on Joey at Complete now and then.

In the motel rooms, we'd dance. Then he'd push me. And keep pushing me. I'd say "Oww . . ." like a little girl.

He'd say, "What? You can't take it? Why don't you fight? *Fight!*" He'd push me back and make me angry and then when I hit him he'd say, "Good!" He wanted to see that feistiness.

Sometimes it felt like we were Bonnie and Clyde.

Later, we were lying side by side. He took my hand and kissed the tips of my fingers. He said, "We're beautiful."

His eyes roamed upward, at the motel room ceiling. And then he started telling me about his childhood. He told me that his mother died of cancer when he was eleven* and that he had very complicated feelings about her: guilt, love, anger. He had an older sister, an older brother (Bobby), an older half-brother, a younger sister. He said he was abused by his mother as a child and that both of his parents were very strict.

Once, he said, lying there rubbing my hand up and down his chest, his mother gave him change to go around the corner and buy a loaf of bread. When he got to the store, he forgot about the bread and instead bought two big packs of Sugar Daddies candy. He was sitting on a neighbor's lawn, eating the candy, when his mother came out and saw him. "She dragged me all the way home by my hair," he said, "and she beat the hell out of me." He shook his head. "I was just a *kid*."

"Did you cry?" I asked, thinking of myself, biting my lip, reciting D-E-V-E-L-O-P.

"Not since then," he said.

He lay staring at the ceiling, this man who was—all rolled up in one—my lover, my teacher, my father, and now also my twin brother.

---

*Other accounts maintain that Joey's mother died when Joey was four.

5

Twin Survivors

◆

Meet me out front." Joey spoke in a whisper that Sunday morning. He was calling me from home, something he rarely did.

I dressed quickly and ran out to wait. He came in the Caddy. Mary Jo and the kids were sleeping in. He was restless. He'd been up since 6:30. He was going to do his Sunday-morning thing.

"I'm taking you here 'cause I feel close to you," he explained, as he made a series of familiar turns. In moments we were at the gates of St. Charles Cemetery.

"My grandmother is buried here," I said. "This is where I went and cried my eyes out and buried toys when I was eight and a half."

"My mother's here," he said.

We parked and Joey took a bouquet of flowers from the backseat and we walked through the rows of granite slabs and crosses.

I didn't want to go to Grandma's grave; I would have bawled, and I didn't want Joey to see that. I followed Joey to his mom's grave. LOUISE BUTTAFUOCO, the headstone read.

I sat down Indian style. Joey rocked back on his heels. I pushed my hair back against the wind. Joey's eyes misted.

After a couple of minutes of silence, Joey spoke.

He felt so guilty when his mother died, he started coming here regularly, to talk to her. There were so many unfinished issues from his childhood, and she'd died before they could talk them out.

I said I knew what he meant about unfinished issues. I told him how close I was with my grandmother, how I saw her as my protector, that when she died, I felt my protection was suddenly snatched away. In my own cockeyed way, I had to go and protect myself. Joey said I was lucky; at least I'd had only good feelings toward my grandmother. It's easier when that person dies. The break is clean. On the other hand, he had real *bad* feelings about his mother—so now, by going to her grave, he tries to make it up to her. But it will always be too late.

Sometimes I feel that way about my father, I said. As unhappy as he made me, he *is* my father, and I love him, and if he died I would be crushed.

We talked about the way both of us were abused as kids. Joey was abused in a lot of the same ways as I was—and yet there was a difference. He didn't feel misunderstood, he said. He just didn't want to have the shit kicked out of him like it was. I was never physically hurt by a parent the way Joey was, but I felt belittled, the victim of an erratic temper—always afraid.

We talked about how we had reacted to those childhoods in totally opposite ways. He snapped back from the abuse by always wanting to be liked, surrounding himself by people. Being the life of the party. I reacted by turning inward. I told him that, although I had friends, I always felt alone, separate, like I didn't fit in. It wasn't just in Mandalay Elementary, when the compliments kids gave me rolled off my back as I sat there dreading going home from school; it was now, at Kennedy High. Debbi and Jennifer and Heather and Jill and I looked and seemed alike but I knew, as I said to Joey, "If you put all our brains on the table and studied them, mine would be different." Actually, I had drifted away from those girls. My new friends were Michelle and Julie. What we had in common was that we didn't study. But even they were boring to me now. As I sat on the grass, talking to Joey, *all* those girls seemed so young. The ski trips, the clothes talk, the gossip about sex with tenth-grade boys seemed like years, not mere months, ago.

But at least I'd *had* a childhood, Joey said. Joey felt he'd missed his childhood altogether. His father was strict—an old-country self-made man. A hard-ass. From the age of eight, Joey used to get out of elementary school and have to go straight to work at the gas station his father owned then. At 3 P.M., while all the other kids were biking home for cookies and cartoons and ball playing, he was dropping his dimes and quarters into the bus token box. He was the only eight-year-old on that bus. I pictured a little Joey: stocky, with his funny face and smashed-in nose, sitting on the worn seats between old men and ladies who couldn't afford cars or were too old to drive them, while blocks away his father checked his watch and waited for him to appear. At the same time, I remembered a cocky, footlose Amy, pulling cousin Tommy across Wantagh Avenue to the bowling alley, while Grandma, singing Italian as she cleaned her stove, didn't know that we, or her quarters, had disappeared. My eight-year-old self felt sorry for him.

"I never got to be a boy," he said. "They made me be a little man." Maybe that was why he acted, at thirty-five, like such a big kid—with the '70s music and the decked, pinstriped car.

He said that though he had once cried when his mother beat him after the Sugar Daddies–buying episode, he never let his *father* see him cry. And his father spanked him a lot. I told him that after the hot-chocolate incident, I, too, never let *my* father see me cry; that my aunt Mary Lynn had taught me, by example, how to stay cool and stay tough. And wear tight jeans.

"We're both survivors," Joey said. Sitting on that lawn, surrounded by row after row of tombstones, nothing seemed truer. We seemed like the only two people alive in the world.

"Tell me about your drug habit," I asked. There seemed no forbidden subjects.

Still, Joey hesitated. He had gone from having a heavy coke habit to being so clean he lectured other people to stop smoking. Going back and talking about it was like sticking your toe back in, I guess.

"I started doing drugs when I was ten," he confessed. Ten?! Even I, who liked to think of myself as a girl James Dean, was shocked that he'd started so young. "Smoking pot, later dropping acid." Acid. That was a word that went with the music he listened to. "One pill makes you larger, one pill makes you small": I'd named that song—*"White Rabbit!"*—during one of our times in the Freeport Motor Inn.

When he was eleven, Joey said, he and his buddies used to go to the train station at 6:30 on Friday night and meet the returning commuters. In those days, the Long Island Railroad tickets were different than they are now. Today, the tickets are punched, so you can't ride the train more than one way. Back then, I guess, the railroad was less concerned about fare-beaters. You got a stub good for a return trip before midnight. That's the last thing those tired commuters wanted to do.

So when Joey and his friends crowded around the train steps and asked the returning commuters if they had any stubs they weren't going to need, the commuters gave them up. Then Joey and his friends got on the Manhattan-bound train and rode into the city and scored drugs.

When they got back, they'd get high in the deserted field around the train tracks. Then they'd go to the underneath part of the Massapequa train station and give themselves the scare of their lives. "There's this little platform right there, where the train turns," Joey said. "That's where we all stood: stoned out of our minds." He pulled a notepad and pen out of his pocket and drew a train track curving at a right angle. At the start of that right turn, he cross-hatched in a little area, tucked in the corner, behind the track. "If you stood on this platform, it looked like the train was coming *right* at you, would smash right into you and run you over. Then all of a sudden, at the *very* last minute, so close you could touch it, the train turned. Man, it was better than the wildest roller coaster."

He sat staring off, as if back to that point in his life where he went from being a too-grown-up boy to being a too-young druggie. Then he snapped back to the present. "Time to go home." It was family day. Sunday. We stood and brushed the grass off our clothes.

One Thursday night in the middle of July, Joey said he was taking his kids to a church carnival in Massapequa. "Come down, bring your friends," he told me. I went with two school friends, and the three of us talked to Joey while he put his kids on rides.

It was very segregated—the men all together, the women in a little group with the children. Only Joey was playing Mommy that night. Joey said his wife would be at school. Joey seemed to like to show me off in front of the men. While his children were safely on the rides, and his buddies there, he put his arm around me. But the minute he saw the women and children coming, he removed it and his face turned serious and he wouldn't introduce me to them. (Later, Joey said he said he got a lot of static at home for having been seen at the fair talking to a young girl.)

It didn't occur to me to feel used. Or to feel insulted that, around the women, he acted like he hardly knew me. Our secret affair was exciting to me. And I felt flattered that he wanted to show me off to his friends. Soon, Joey would really take advantage of my acceptance of being exhibited, exploited. Even then, I wouldn't feel it. There was a great deal that I would start learning not to feel. But perhaps I'd really had that skill for a very long time.

Mostly, Joey was a wonderful father. Watching him, at that fair, touch and kiss and play with his kids, I thought: I never want my children to go through the pain that I went through.

Sometimes, though, the selective feeling Joey had about his children bothered and confused me. As good as he was to his own two kids—and as good as he was with the children of his secret high-school love and her ex-husband—there was another child he rejected: his illegitimate son, Donny, who lived in Florida. Donny was Joey's son by yet *another* high-school girlfriend. (Joey must have been quite a stud in high school.) The girl had chosen not to get an abortion, and Joey was going with Mary Jo by then. He continued to send child support—though with a lot of griping—even all these years later.

"How come you don't have Donny's picture here?" I asked him one day when I visited him at Complete and looked at the collage of pictures he and Bobby had of their children. If I were the forgotten child, left out of my dad's picture collage, I would be heartbroken.

"Ah, the kid's a little redneck. I have nothing in common with him," Joey said. He told me that Donny wanted to come up and visit him and work at Complete, but that he'd said no. I pictured the kid reading the word in a letter: "No."

"How can you be so *cold?*" I blurted out. "He's your *son.* He wants you to want him."

Maybe the reason I had such strong feelings about Joey's rejection of Donny was that Donny was exactly my age.

Joey did tricks with my head about age and size. Sometimes he called me his "little girl," his "baby," "little angel." Other times, he said I had the maturity of a thirty-year-old. At the same time, he was obsessed with me being little; he wanted me to get skinnier and skinnier. He also said I was his chance to start over, to have a second life. Lying in bed, he would say that he wanted to get his vasectomy reversed. He wanted one more child. Just one. A little girl. He *always* said a girl, never a boy. "She'll have your eyes," he said. "She'll look just like you." Being his girlfriend, being his child, being childlike, being his chance to regain his youth, having his child, having a child that was just like me—sometimes I got confused about my role.

Certain moments stay in my mind, they were so perfect. He gave me heavenly massages, and I manicured his nails. We were each other's geishas. Once, lying in bed with him, he circled my open eyelids, so gently I could barely feel the pressure of his fingers, staring into my eyes the whole time. His face was serious, almost regretful.

"Why does this feel so right?" he asked.

But those moments also scared me. The emotion was like a deep pit I thought I would never climb out of. I tried to toughen myself. "Aw, you'll break up with me," I said. "I predict, in six months you'll let me go for some other girl."

"Never predict," Joey said. "Anticipate. To predict is negative. To anticipate is positive."

Today, that line sounds like a bad fortune cookie. Or something a gigolo would say in a movie. To my sixteen-year-old ears, it was philosophy. Poetry.

Other times, those first few weeks, Joey said things that were a little too ominous to be poetry. When I asked him if I could ever spend a whole night with him, or if he would ever leave his wife, he'd say, "Shh! Patience." Did that mean he'd finally divorce her? I pressed. "No," he said. "But maybe she'll have an accident. Marriage is till death do us part. Sometimes you have to induce the last part." Other times he said, "Don't worry, soon she won't be around anymore. I cannot *stand* her."

He started talking incessantly about Mary Jo being out of the picture.

I confided about Joey to Mary Lynn. I talked to her on the condition that she wouldn't tell my mother. Mary Lynn did not like what she was hearing. When I told her about Joey's veiled promises about Mary Jo's demise, she put her head in her hand and shook it slowly. "He's either playing a game with you, Ame, or he's sick. Either way, he's bad news. Stay away from him."

I looked at my pretty, tough, sexy aunt, whose advice had been my gospel. For the first time ever, I wasn't going to listen to her.

About two weeks into my romance with Joey, I got blisters and a rash. When they didn't go away, I went to my gynecologist and had tests. I was diagnosed as having herpes.

Living at home and having your parents pay for your doctor bills, there was no way I could keep the presence of that disease from my parents. So I told them. And I told them I got it from Joey. My mother was upset. My father was furious. But his anger had a funny angle to it. "How could *you have let* that bastard touch you!" he shouted. What I heard from my father was: It's all *your* fault! You're a whore! You're garbage. And all of a sudden this man that he'd always been charmed by was a "bastard."

Weakly, I responded, "Joey loves me."

"Oh, really?" my father said sarcastically. "Joey loves you! I'll ask Joey how much he loves you when he's behind bars!" My father announced that he was going to report Joey to the district attorney for statutory rape.

I was so upset—about having the disease, about my father's anger at me, and about his threat to have Joey jailed—that when I was leaving a gas station the next day, I ran over a cement cinder block. I heard a *thump*. The whole undercarriage of my car was ripped out. Now I had four things to worry about.

I called Joey at Complete, but he wasn't there. Then I panicked and did something I'd never done, before or since—I called him at home. Mary Jo answered. I asked for him and she didn't even ask, "Who is it?" (I thought that was odd.) She just put him right on. As soon as he was on and he heard my voice telling him what phone booth I was standing at, he said, "I'm gonna send a truck down right away." Those words were so Mary Jo wouldn't suspect that I was more than just a regular customer.

He picked me up in his Caddy and we drove around, talking, for about forty-five minutes. He was very solicitous. He drove down Newbridge Road. Then he wanted to know where I went to summer school, so we drove by another school in the district, Mapham.

His voice was soothing and he was acting like he cared so much about me. He kept saying, "Don't you love me? Don't you want us to be together? If they arrest me, you'll never see me again."

Here I was, a kid with a scary disease I'd never heard of before, and he was focusing on himself. "Are you worried about going to jail?" I asked. "Is that it?"

"Nah," he said, kissing my hand. "I don't worry about things like that. *You're* what I worry about." Still, he told me I *had* to tell my parents that he didn't give it to me.

Sitting in the car next to him, listening to his Steely Dan tape, and him singing over it, I realized I was stuck. I couldn't imagine not being with Joey. He could not be out of my life. There was no question but that I would lie. "Then what about the cinder block? The undercarriage?" I asked. I would take the rap for the herpes, but who'd take the rap for the car?

"Say you went up on a curb to avoid a dangerous accident." He drove to a block where it could have happened and made up a whole scenario for me. Joey was a great liar. "One: Do what you want, just never get caught. Two: Never tell a person more than they need to know. Those are Joey's rules of survival," he said, so often I memorized them. Soon, I'd start living by them.

As we were driving down Merrick, we passed my mother. She recognized his car from the shop.

He stopped and called out, "No! No! No! It's not what you think, Mrs. Fisher!"

Her expression stayed angry. We followed my mother to the house.

"Make up a name," Joey ordered. "Any name."

Inside the house, Joey, the master showman, took control.

"Now let's all calm down," he said, moving his hands all around. "We'll all talk about this together, rationally."

Then I told my lie. "I had a one-night stand with a boy named Sal, who I met at a party. He gave the herpes to me." I didn't know any Sal. I was still a good little girl.

My father took Joey at his word. He believed my lie. My mother still believed Joey had given me the herpes, but she knew she couldn't prove it. She took my word that the affair was over.

Right after that, Joey and I started using the apartment he kept over Complete for our rendezvous. If I close my eyes I can still picture walking up those stairs until the clanking on car hoods and fenders faded away—up a staircase, then a little to the right, then up again. There's a landing. You go to the right and go through a door and enter the wood-paneled home gym: workout equipment and weight machines on sea-green carpeting. Then you walk through another door to the back and there's Joey's sexual playhouse. It's got a mattress with no sheet, a dark-wood headboard with the Superman sticker on it, a light-wood stand-alone closet, brand-new windows, some hand-me-down furniture. There's no radio, no TV, no phone. (If you want to make a call at night, you have to walk to the Amoco station next door.)

It was in this bare-bones room, ten months later, that Joey and I planned the shooting of Mary Jo.

If Joey didn't pick me up in his boat, I would meet him at Complete, where his friend Dave painted his custom cabinetry at night. Usually Joey's "helping" Dave was just an alibi for Mary Jo, but one night, when I thought we were going to go out to dinner, he was engrossed in painting. He stayed engrossed.

I waited. My stomach growled. "I thought we were going to go *out*," I said. Finally, when he continued to ignore me, I got so annoyed and frustrated that I threw a small piece of wood across the room. After all, didn't my spunk turn Joey on?

Not this time. Joey picked me up and slammed me against the wall so fast and so hard, I thought my head had cracked.

From that point on, we were playing by different rules.

The height of those new rules would come a month and a half later, right after I turned seventeen, on another evening at Complete. Dave was there that night, too. I'd quit a job to be with Joey; he had helped me get a new car and was making payments on it for me, but all of a sudden he stopped. I was stuck.

To solve my sudden problem, Joey opened the phone book and pointed to "ABBA Escorts." He said I should call them and try to get a job. He told me it would be fun, exciting work—dinners and interesting conversation—and *so* much money. He said that I wouldn't have to have sex with the men. I believed him.

♦ ♦ ♦

PART
♦
2

6

Joey Coco-Pops

♦

Last May, when the face of Joey Buttafuoco was splashed all over television in connection with his wife's shooting by Amy Fisher, numerous people looked at the screen and said, "I know that man!" Some of these people were neighbors and members of the Biltmore Shores Beach Club, right next door to the Buttafuocos' home, where handball, basketball, and volleyball courts, an Olympic-size pool, and a ninety-slip marina provided an idyllic weekend life for a membership of local residents, many of whom were, like the Buttafuocos, lifetime Massapequa residents who'd met one another in high school—or earlier. The Buttafuocos were popular members of the club. Mary Jo Buttafuoco, in fact, was club treasurer. On New Year's Eve 1992, a party from the club had spilled over into the Buttafuocos' living room, and club guests had slept on the floors and the couches.

Others who recognized him on TV were parishioners of St. Rose of Lima Church, where the Buttafuocos worshipped every Sunday. "It was in this church that Joey Buttafuoco and Mary Jo Connery had been married in 1977. It was here that they assembled for frequent communions and weddings of members of the large Buttafuoco and the larger Connery families.

Still others may have been customers of Complete Auto Body,

where Joey had worked ever since his father, Caspar Buttafuoco, a former race-car driver, mechanic, and gas station owner, opened it in 1970.

Then there was another group of people who recognized Joey Buttafuoco, when his face flashed on the nightly news, not as a family man, a beach club member, a churchgoer, or even an automotive mechanic. They say they remembered him in a different way—as a drug supplier to prostitutes and as a canvasser and revenue collector for a veteran escort service owner. In that other life of his, his nickname was "Joey Coco-Pops."

"Did street prostitutes here have knowledge of a 'Joey Coco-Pops'? Certainly. Did Joey Buttafuoco have some involvement with them? Yes, that's a possibility," says Nassau County Homicide Detective Martin Alger, who handled the arrest of Amy and the case's entire investigation.

Detective Sergeant Dan Severin: "We got numerous anonymous calls from prostitutes from Long Island and all over, saying they knew Joey."

The Buttafuocos seemed to have a lot of cash. A woman who worked as a weekly housekeeper in the Buttafuoco home until just before the shooting says she was always struck by the fact that "for a good hour or more, every Monday, Mary Jo would be sitting at a desk in the little corner area upstairs next to her bedroom, doing bank work and bookkeeping. It struck me as an unusual thing for a housewife to be spending so much time with, and when I asked her if she worked as her husband's business bookkeeper she said no, adding that the business was doing poorly. She was on the phone a lot and once I heard her saying, 'Joey wants me to get this thirty thousand dollars in the bank before noon.' I thought, 'Wow, she's got a lot of money. No wonder she was able to hire me.'"

Clearly, the money could have come from any number of sources, including her treasuryship of the beach club.

Indeed, this housekeeper, a local married woman with a pleasant face, was struck by the disparity between Mary Jo and Joey in terms of social presence and style. "She was always well dressed, well groomed, nicely made-up, trim, and really quite dignified. And she was an excellent mother. He was—well, he had these big lizard-skin boots and wide black belts in his closet and he kept a gun in his drawer. And once while I was working he came home during his lunch hour and he kind of followed me from room to room, asking personal questions. I had the uncomfortable feeling he was coming on to me. I could never quite put them together as a couple. She seemed so much better than him. When she told me that they only had sex every four or five months, I wondered why she even wanted to."

Two people have signed affidavits asserting that they knew that Joey Buttafuoco had a drug-selling and/or procurement relationship with streetwalkers. In addition, three veteran escort service owners in Queens and on Long Island claim, in no uncertain terms, that they had encounters with Joey Buttafuoco in his capacity as an associate of their business peer and usually friendly competitor, Lorraine Wurzburg. As the owner, first, of Allure, and, later, of ABBA escort service, Wurzburg, like the other three borough-escort-services entrepreneurs, belonged to a unique, closed little world with its own business procedures, ethics, and rituals.

"Escort service" is prostitution "lite": Prostitution gone high-tech and modern. No swarmy pimps, no girls shivering on street corners, no lavender-fetid brothels. Escorts are independent practitioners who pay their agencies a fee, much as any other service sellers pay their agents, for clients, bookings, and both legal and physical protection. The escort service is the offspring of three recent phenomena. One is the sexual revolution of the 1960s, which nudged the once clearly frowned-upon calling of prostitution under the tolerant rubric of "swinging" and which launched the escort industry's prime source of advertising, Al Goldstein's *Screw* magazine, twenty-five years ago. The next is the overwhelming crisis of serious victim crimes in most big cities.

Coping with this high-priority crime, police departments' vice and public-morals units have become manpower-strapped stepchildren, able to perform routine sweeps on public-nuisance streetwalking, but rarely bothering their more respectable, unobtrusive, and elusive prey—the escort services, which have trebled in volume under the cops' encouraging lack of interest.

But the phenomenon that most affected—and made distinct

—the escort service industry was the information revolution. Through a network of cable-TV ads, phone lines threaded from one apartment to the next and terminating in hidden switchboards, computerized telephone information banks, car phones, cellular phones, pay phones, beepers, and portable credit-card terminals, sexual services can now be explicitly advertised, telephonically ordered, caller-identity-checked, promptly and safely (for all parties) filled, and paid for in full—sometimes all within ninety minutes. Like EMS workers on marathon runs, some escorts can do six or eight calls a night before crashing.

Technically, under the euphemism through which they advertise, escort services are legal. It is not against the law to sell nonsexual companionship for, say, dinner parties and special occasions. Taking this surface legality literally, owners of the most enduring New York agencies file their businesses as "entertainment services" and wouldn't dream of courting tax-evasion charges by not filing promptly with the IRS. They also have credit-card accounts under their own agencies' names. More cautious or nervous owners, including those of the flourishing "Oriental outcall" agencies, prefer to pay to use the credit-card terminals and imprinters of small legitimate businesses—florists, laundries, car services—and they pass along the expense to their plastic-paying customers. (In Los Angeles, where it is illegal for escort agencies to operate by credit card, a call's price is often jacked up from $250 to $350 an hour for the card-using client.)

What's hidden in the AmEx and Visa charge slips, the Yellow Pages ads, and the 940 and 1099 forms, is the fact that it's *sex* that is being sold. It is a misdemeanor offense to be a prostitute, and it is a felony in most states for anyone or any agency to employ two or more prostitutes. (In New York, it is a D felony, which can land the employer a one- to seven-year jail sentence.) Sophistication is therefore required both in fending off untoward acts by the competition (here, protective cover by organized crime is essential) and in evading the police, who, though they don't pounce on these agencies, are likely to mount periodic undercover operations. Still, the businesses thrive. Escort services fill more than twenty-five pages of ads in the Manhattan phone book alone.

But Manhattan services are elite and small-scale compared to the volume business of the "borough" services, the name given to non-Manhattan-based services, which serve Queens, Staten Island, Brooklyn, Long Island, Connecticut, and New Jersey.

"Manhattan escort services are like gourmet shops. We're like twenty-four-hour-a-day supermarkets," says Phil, a twenty-five-year veteran of the business who co-owns three borough services and has seen many others fade and get busted while his have flourished.

Here's the difference: Manhattan escorts operate decorously —even leisurely. The girls are paged in their own apartments. Much like office temps, they take only those calls they want, *when* they want. They rarely travel out of Manhattan, are not accompanied by drivers, and split their $300-an-hour fee fifty–fifty with the agency.

Borough services, on the other hand, work on a volume, twenty-four-hour-a-day, immediate-on-call basis. "We station drivers all over the boroughs. We can move girls a lot faster and we're cheaper," says Phil, whose clients have included well-known newscasters, publishers, lawyers, attorneys, and stockbrokers. "If you call a Manhattan service from Jersey and ask for a girl, she'll arrive in an hour, with the call costing three hundred dollars. If you call us, we get her there in half an hour, and it's two hundred." That two hundred an hour is split not two, but *three* even ways: among the service, the girl, and a key third party absent in the realm of the Manhattan services—the driver.

A borough service escort starts her shift when she gets picked up at her home (or, as is often the case, her residence hotel) by her driver. Each girl must be on call until she finishes her shift eight hours later. The driver drives the girl to each customer's house, apartment, hotel, or place of business, sits outside while she's on the call, and provides for her safety during the call. She can beep him on an emergency code if she's on a call where the customer's behavior has turned questionable or dangerous. Between calls, driver and girl spend a lot of time in all-night-diner parking lots. The Flagship Diner in Kew Gardens, Queens, is a particularly popular parking lot for these purposes. Together, escort and driver kill time, fight boredom, play poker, exchange life stories, drink coffee, occasionally fall in love (one driver and girl recently married, quit the life, and opened a restaurant in Florida)—all the while waiting for the beeper to summon them to the diner's pay phone, there to call the agency to find out where the next call is. Six hours of work, a rarity on weeknights but likely on weekends, nets the escort $450.

The driver, who can make $700 to $1,500 a week for six days of work, comes to his profession often by way of carefully planted word of mouth. A trusted local liquor dealer, building security guard, or shipyard foreman might know a responsible fellow who's looking for work. He is checked out more scrupulously than the escort. When tight-ship agencies are hiring, the prospective driver's ID is run through a police computer. The top agencies have friends in high places—at the PD, and at the phone company. No one with a suspended driver's license, unpaid moving violations, or criminal record is hired. The driver provides his own car, and it must be in good running order, with no irregularities, such as broken lights or windshield wipers, for which a cop could pull him over. The driver must also know how to finesse a suspicious cop at a lonely stoplight at four in the morning. Playing the nervous husband cheating on his wife with the somewhat provocatively dressed woman seated next to him is a good way of giving the heat the satisfying feeling that he's made you sweat about *something*.

The driver is not just a bodyguard and chauffeur, he is also the collector. It is he who comes in at the end of a call and collects the fee—always when it's a credit-card call; sometimes, if the owners do not trust the girl, even on a cash call. This assures that the money will get to the agency first (after which, the split is made and the girl and driver are paid). With credit-card calls, this also assures that the girl does not have the customer's full name (as displayed on the credit card), and therefore is not able to look up his phone number and contact him directly, cutting out the agency.

Borough escort services are brutally professional.

Sometimes, aside from these other functions, the borough driver is also part-independent entrepreneur. He may have a side business selling condoms, lingerie, and sex toys. Owners like Phil and his partner, Larry, don't mind this. But if he has a side business selling cocaine, he's out on his ear in a minute. The fastest way to get busted is to have drugs in your driver's vehicle.

"We let our drivers and girls know," says Phil, "that we'll pay their legal fees if it's a prost bust. If they do anything stupid like drugs and get pinched, they're on their own."

Still, even the most stringent agencies have an ambivalent relationship with cocaine. There is nothing like it to drive up a $200 call, hour by hour by hour, to a $1,000 one. Some borough agencies know adjunct drug dealers who will sell to the girl, or who work standby—ready to be beeped by a girl on a call, to sell to the customer. Sometimes a call will be booked with the customer's code-worded request "for candy" or "to party." The girl and the agency owner benefit from the higher take from the longer call—and on a good night a dealer who works calls exclusively can make himself $200 from the girls and their clients alone. But because of the very incriminating complications that drug-dealing lends to the escort business, most of the drug sellers, if they're smart, don't stir the pot any more than they have to. They get in, make their sales, and get out—unobtrusively.

One day in 1990, however, Phil and his partner, Larry, assert that they started hearing about a particularly meddlesome dealer who was doubling as a competitive agency's canvasser. The guy was so pushy he was causing a fellow agency, Allure, to violate the cardinal rule of the business: No service poaches another's merchandise.

Allure was the latest agency owned by a woman whom Phil knew only as Rita. Rita was a former prostitute and fellow veteran service owner; she had opened her first agency in 1980. (Even those who have owned escort businesses in the same area for years often do not know one another's real names.) All Phil knew about Rita was three things: one, she ran a relatively small operation; two, in the past at least, she had always done business the right way. She advertised Allure in the *Village Voice* and in the Yellow Pages; the third thing about Rita was this: She was the only operative who could keep a business open in Nassau County, where, the joke among the borough agencies went, the cops went around busting services because they had so much time on their hands. Rita often bragged that she was untouchable—that her boyfriend was a higher-up in the local police department. Others thought she was simply a very shrewd operator.

But her alliance with a drug-selling adjunct who did not know the rules was *not* shrewd. "There's a guy, works with Rita, hanging around the Flagship parking lot, bothering the girls, giving Rita's cards to the girls," Phil remembers one of his drivers reporting with great annoyance.

When Phil asked the disgruntled driver what the guy looked like, he says he was told, "Husky. Italian-looking. Curly haired. Looks like a weightlifter. Looks like a Wiseguy."

A few days later, another driver called Phil's partner, Larry, and, Larry asserts, made the same complaint. This driver described the meddling driver as "a coke dealer, looks like that comedian, Jay Leno." The fellow went by a nickname, the driver said. "Joey Coco-Pops."

The partners let it pass until a third complaint from a driver came in. When they asked the two drivers what kind of car the guy drove, they were told that he drove a different car each time he came to the parking lot. Once he arrived in a Bonneville convertible; another time a Q45; a third time, a Mustang. Phil recalls, "I said to Larry, 'What is this guy, a used-car salesman?'"

Larry says, "We figured the guy owned a car service."

The partners were getting annoyed. Pestering the girls and the drivers was very bad news. An agency didn't want its good drivers to be hassled into quitting. Worse, trying to poach the girls was simply not done. It was one agency's way of skimming another's merchandise without paying their fair share of overhead. For advertising was not only the means by which services got customers; it was also the way that they got girls. And advertising was costly: A small ad in the Yellow Pages went for $230 a month; a dollar-bill-sized ad cost $600. A *Screw* ad with good placement and incidentals was close to $1,500 a week. The *Village Voice,* apparently torn between feminist political correctness and sheer revenue hunger, jacked up the listing price it charged for other businesses to a whopping $1,600 a month for sex services. Channel J, the local cable sex station, charged $2,500 a month for forty to forty-five weekly viewings of a thirty-second spot. (Despite the fact that the channel is blacked out on the cable boxes of the TV's in 50 percent of Manhattan hotel rooms, it's considered the best advertising of all.) Thus, ad overhead ran to $9,000 a month, more than a quarter of the monthly gross.

By using a third party to try to hire away girls, an escort service owner ditches part of his or her overhead. This had to stop. "That guy comes around the Flagship again, beep us immediately," the partners instructed their drivers.

One winter day in early 1990, Phil and Larry were beeped and told that Rita's canvasser–medication supplier, "Joey Coco-Pops," was back at the Flagship. They rode out in one car. Another car followed, in which rode three extremely husky men who often acted as enforcers.

"When we got to the parking lot," Larry says, "the guy was there—talking to the other driver, milling around. We didn't really waste a whole lot of time. We fingered him."

Phil: "We took him to the side, started telling him, 'We don't like what you're doing. It's not a proper way to conduct business. If you want girls, do what everybody else does—advertise. Things could happen to you if you keep this up.'" The three husky men stood, conspicuous but silent, against the car they'd come in. "The guy got a little nervous. He said, 'Oh, I'm sorry, I didn't know, I didn't realize.' All he was doing was mentioning the agency to the girls for extra work. He copped a plea."

The two men left, as did their car full of henchmen. Joey Coco-Pops never returned to the Flagship Diner parking lot.

Two years later, in late May, Phil was watching the 6 o'clock news. He did a double-take. He reached for the phone and called Larry. "Check out the eleven o'clock news. Tell me if that guy, the husband of that woman who was shot, isn't the bird that we grabbed at the Flagship."

Five hours later, Larry called Phil back and said, "Yeah, that's him. *No* doubt about it."

Lynn is another borough service owner, now semi-retired. She is attractive, affable, and seemingly well adjusted. Her clients included sports, music, and Broadway stars, as well as judges and financiers. In 1987, she struck up a telephone friendship with Rita. There weren't very many women borough owners then, and women like Rita and Lynn, who not only owned services but had been escorts themselves, had common experiences that none of the male owners could share.

"Rita and I knew how grueling the work could get—the long hours spent in diner parking lots. It's not for every girl—some of them crack up. To survive the knowledge, which you get from the business, that people are basically liars; to be able to enjoy the work and never get emotionally thrown; to be able to hold on to your money—there aren't that many of us who have done it. Rita was one. I was another. She was a very careful, intelligent woman. A sharp businesswoman. I liked her. Our phone calls were mainly about business, but sometimes we talked about other things. Her cats, for example. Rita was a cat person."

Lynn had apprenticed at the arguably better-run chief competitor to "Mayflower Madam" Sydney Biddle Barrows's Cachet agency. Rita had put in time at another choice house. The two women knew how to diversify their selection: hiring a certain number of tall girls, a certain number petite, a certain number busty, a variety of blondes, blacks, Hispanics. All of the girls had to be standouts, as well as well spoken and intelligent. Like Phil and Larry, Lynn got the occasional medical student working summers to rack up tuition money, but mostly she drew attractive but live-for-today girls with nebulous goals who, if they weren't careful, got hooked on the money and kept themselves otherwise skill-less, ending up in their thirties relegated to the burgeoning phone-sex services.

Unlike these girls, Lynn and Rita had learned the business ropes and saved their money. They got themselves "rabbis" with Mob connections. They became entrepreneurs. They taught their girls, from firsthand experience, how to "get into a call"—make it through the hotel lobby without being stopped by security—and how to "hold on to the call": push the client for additional hours. "If a girl couldn't consistently keep a call for five or six hours, the better agencies would let go of her."

According to Lynn, Rita was smart enough to keep moving— "she said she had advertised under several different names over the years"—and to keep complications out of her operation. "She was higher-priced than most of her borough competition —one hundred fifty dollars an hour, while everyone else was one hundred. She took cash only; no credit cards. She was very,

very meticulous with checking girls out. You needed two pieces of ID with date of birth—driver's license, passport. *Never* would she hire anyone under eighteen. None of us did. She ran a small shop. And, as I recall, no daytime. Sometimes she didn't turn on her phones until five, booking ten to forty calls a night, like I did—which broke down to five or six calls per girl."

Both women kept their phones well hidden. Some agencies pay rent on two apartments, one as a phone-jack decoy. Others ingeniously thread their wires, from jack to line to phone, through three separate commercial or residential spaces, paying a usage fee for each venue. Others pay off phone company employees to have bills listed with decoy addresses. This won't stanch a bust, but it does buy an agency time if a bust is imminent—the owners have a couple of hours to overwrite their client list on their computer's hard drive (separate backup discs are kept in undisclosed places) before the cops enter the premises. Spilling your list, especially if it includes respectable and powerful men, is the kiss of death. Well-connected owners can even get their phones listed in an adjacent area code. (Rita had a Queens—718—area code on phones that should have carried the Nassau County code, 516.)

Both Rita and Lynn were particularly attuned to screening calls—on two levels: first, to root out the police; second, to root out dangerous or unpleasant customers. Rooting out the cops wasn't especially difficult. Before accepting a call, escort bookers check out the man's identification. His name has to be verified by a listing with telephone information in the city he says he lives in before the booker will go any further. (Unlisted numbers are all right. Nonlisted names are not.) The best escort agencies have directories that list policemen's names. If a would-be client doesn't have a phone listing, he is closely grilled: What sales conference did he say he was in town for, and where was it convening? What airline and flight number did he come in on? If his information doesn't check out, his booking is not taken.

Cops almost always rent hotel rooms for incipient busts—and tend to have giveaway habits: They are specific about how the girl is to get to the room (under the clock and left at the registration desk to the elevators) and *un*specific about what kind of girl they are looking for—blonde, black, redhead, it doesn't matter. Legitimate customers are just the opposite. Policemen need corroboration to arrest prostitutes, and bookers demand to know exactly how many men are going to be in the room—and they verify the identities of each. If a girl gets to a room on a one-man call and two men are there, she's out the door fast. Party calls booked in hotel rooms are red flags.

Back in 1987, neither Lynn nor Rita booked party calls— even at private houses, or at conventions. Hotels with bad security were nixed. ("You'd rather risk having your girl get escorted out than not have a security man there if you get in the room and need one.") They lived by the escort service golden rule: *Never* let a girl be outnumbered in a room. Two men with one girl was out. Two girls with one man was fine. Girls working for either woman who dressed "too promiscuously" were told to come in for a dress-check before they went out the next night. Men who made off-color remarks or sounded loutish or strange were refused bookings. "You used your instinct, and Rita and I both had good instincts." Both would demand that new bookers train and observe for two to three weeks before they were allowed on the switchboard.

Given all they had in common, when Rita called Lynn one day in 1989 and proposed a bit of subcontracting, Lynn was amenable. Rita serviced only Nassau and Suffolk and she was starting to get calls for Queens and Brooklyn. Would Lynn help her out and split fees? Lynn accepted. A couple of times Lynn sent girls out. "In these cases, the girl was responsible for sending Rita her share, in a money order. At Rita's request, the money order was made out to 'Lorraine Wurzburg,' her real name."

But since times were bad for the business (the collapse of the bull market in 1987 pulled down everyone's take), and since Lynn was still young enough, sometimes *she* did the calls for Rita. In these cases, Lynn would deliver Rita her share of the fee—in cash, through a middleman.

"Have your driver drive you to the Flagship Diner parking lot," Lynn says Rita instructed her. "You're going to meet Joey Coco-Pops."

Lynn did this several times in 1989.

Her remembrance of Rita's point man, who collected her cash

in the parking lot, was that he was "a wisecracking, manipulative type of guy, a snake, a player. He'd say, 'Hi, how ya doin'? Can I get anything for you?' implying, certainly from his name, cocaine. He wasn't dealing for Rita. That was his own sideline operation. He was looking to make a few bucks here and there. But he was collecting for Rita—at least he was in my case."

Lynn says that Joey Coco-Pops was a known figure in the Flagship parking lot.

"Other drivers and girls who knew me would say, 'Oh, you're here to meet Joe? Joey Coco-Pops? Tell him I said hello,'" Lynn reports.

After the shooting, Lynn, too, saw Joey Buttafuoco on TV.

She says, "I recognized him as Joey Coco-Pops. His face hadn't changed, except his hair now seemed to have a touch of gray in it. It was him, all right."

After 1989, Lynn remembers being puzzled that her phone relationship with Rita was losing its amiability.

"Something was different. She seemed pressured. She no longer stayed on the phone as long. My conversations with her were starting to border on the unfriendly because she had other things to do. I asked her once, after I made a call for her, 'Is Joe going to pick up the money? Do you want me to come out to Queens?' She'd say, abruptly, 'No. Just send me a money order.' I'd say, 'Is there a problem?' She'd say, 'No, no, no, he just can't make it.'"

Lynn does not know what caused the change in Rita's attitude—ill health? Personal problems? (If it had been business failings, Lynn would have heard.) But the normally extremely careful service owner—the "unbustable" Nassau County survivor—became sloppy. On November 29, 1990, two of her girls were arrested in a setup pinch by the Nassau County vice squad. Sergeant Darius Perry, who ordered the undercover operation on Allure, took a look at Wurzburg's client list ("no prominent names popped out") and arrested Wurzburg, one driver, and two prostitutes, "who were heavily into drug use and were definitely not *Playboy* centerfold types."

Wurzburg posted her own $20,000 bail and paid an $18,000 fine in February 1991. Such desk appearances are how most prostitution busts are routinely dispensed with. What is unusual about that bust, however, is this—all records of it have vanished. The subsequent revelation of Amy Fisher's employment by Wurzburg led intrepid investigators—in the media and in private investigation—to search the usual files where such records are kept. The Wurzburg/Allure/ABBA file is conspicuously absent.

Soon after the bust, Lorraine Wurzburg was back in business, now calling herself "Lacy" and "Lily." She named her new agency ABBA, thus positioning it at the top of the phone book escort listings.

Lynn, Phil, and Larry lost track of her.

Then, and before—as ABBA and as Allure—Wurzburg's phones were answered in her home, at 2569 Grand Avenue in Baldwin. When Wurzburg was raided by Nassau vice, her deterioration from the intelligent, affable person with whom Lynn liked to talk to a distracted loner was evident in the house's eccentricity. Mannequins, busts, wig stands, and dolls were propped around a Victorian-furnished parlor, giving the room the effect of a Disneyland brothel in effigy. The cats that Rita had spoken to Lynn about seemed to be in control of that parlor. In early November 1992, months after Amy Fisher was arrested and her association with ABBA escort services blared over the news, Lorraine Wurzburg would die in that room. Her sudden death, in her fifties, from "natural causes" went uninvestigated.

She took her secrets to the grave with her.

The house on Grand Avenue where Lorraine Wurzburg lived and operated her escort service phone lines is three-quarters of a mile from Complete Auto Body. Three other people link Joey Buttafuoco to this house.

A Grand Avenue resident, Bobby Whitestone, a welder, says he saw Joey, whom he knew from the neighborhood and later recognized on television, coming out of the side entrance of that house "three or four times" in the winter of 1991–1992. (At this point, Amy had already become a prostitute, although she was now working on her own more than through Wurzburg.) Several other times Whitestone says he saw Buttafuoco's car parked on the side street, right around the corner from the entrance to the house. Whitestone says, "Joey would drive whatever car was in the shop that week. Mostly I saw him in a Lincoln or a Caddy with limo tint."

A young man named Anthony Saciolo was more detailed and specific. A former employee of the Amoco station next to Complete Auto Body, Saciolo is now in state prison for bank robbery. In August 1992, he wrote Eric Naiburg from that prison, saying he was voluntarily coming forward because Amy's portrayal "as someone who did this for the hell of it" and Joey's self-portrayal as an innocent contradicted his own experience with the man as "a cocaine dealer and probably a pimp, or at least [he] offered a girl to me like a pimp would."

Saciolo's letter prompted a visit, on August 19, from private investigator Richie Haeg, who was assisting Naiburg in preparing Amy's defense. Haeg found Saciolo "very credible" and, after intense questioning, determined that Saciolo had nothing to gain, or no score to settle, from making his statement. Saciolo's remarks harken to a point in time—pre-1987—when Joey Buttafuoco admits he had a bad cocaine problem. (In 1988, he spent twenty-eight days in a drug rehabilitation program at the South Oaks Mental Health Center in Massapequa.)

When portions of the statement were leaked by the press and printed in *Newsday*, Saciolo feared that he would endure hard going with fellow inmates for being a snitch. Apparently for this reason, when contacted by Nassau Homicide, Saciolo recanted his statement and denied ever having signed it.

Nevertheless, it is reprinted here:

During the period of the summer of 1987 to approximately February–March of 1988 I was employed at Neil's Amoco Gas Station located on Merrick Road in Baldwin, New York. Next to the station is Complete Auto Body repair shop. I recall meeting a male named Joey Buttafuoco, whom I thought was the owner of the body shop.* He would check

---

*Prior to his drug problems, Joey Buttafuoco and his brother, Bobby, bought out their father Caspar's business partner; Joey was indeed a co-owner of Complete. By the mid-1980s, however, Joey's drug use had taken its toll, and he apparently sold back his share of the business to his family and became an employee.

the auto-body shop at night. During the first or second week I was working at the station when I met Joey. I was in the station office with the lights off. I was using cocaine when Joey came in.

Joey saw the cocaine on the desk. Joey asked me where I bought the cocaine. When I told him I get [sic] it from Far Rockaway or in the city [Manhattan] he asked me how much did I buy at a time. I told him I sometimes get "eightballs" [an eighth of an ounce] for $150. Other times I bought the cocaine by the quarter ounce. . . . Joey offered to sell me cocaine and said: There's no need to go all the way into the city. I'll get you whatever you want at a cheaper price.

From that point on, Joey came to the Amoco station every Friday night. I bought cocaine from Joey at least twice a month and sometimes more than that. . . . His prices were in fact less than what I had been paying. Joey charged me $130 to $140 for an eightball, compared to the $150 I had been paying. Joey sold me a gram of cocaine for $60 to $75, compared to the $90 to $100 I had been paying in the city.

The quality Joey sold was even better than what I got from the city. I never contacted Joey. He came to the station and I told him . . . how much weight I wanted. Joey would then go out to his black Caddy with the smoked windows. The car had spoked hubcaps. When Joey would come back into the gas station office, he would give me the cocaine and I would pay Joey.

One night after he sold me some cocaine, Joey asked me if I had a girlfriend and I said, yes, I do. Joey said if I ever wanted to go out and party with someone different, he could fix me up with an agency in town [Baldwin]. When Joey spoke of an agency, I figured it was a large house down by the water with girls coming in and out.

I walked every day to and from work. I saw Joey's black Cadillac parked by the Stop sign at the Fenway and Grand Avenue. The car was there so often, I thought Joey lived there. The house where Joey parked in front of was in the newspapers.*

♦ ♦ ♦

Another person who says she met Joey in his drug-selling days is a young woman named Kenya Lyons. Kenya was a teenaged runaway who had rolled from one bad scene to the next. She left streetwalking to marry a drug dealer; after she left the dealer, she went back to streetwalking, with dealing on the side, on notorious North Franklin Avenue in Hempstead.

It is not a pretty life. Huddled in doorways and perched against cars, the Franklin Avenue girls—some white; mostly, like Kenya, black—sell blowjobs for $20 to get base and crack to smoke. Often they just roll their johns; get them into motel rooms, even doorways, grab their wallets out of their pockets when their pants are down, and split. The Hempstead vice squad patrolmen know the girls by first names, and the girls who are in and out of jail several times a year know the cops. Two detectives, Puma and Haacke, are so legendarily feared that their names, slightly mispronounced, have become generic terms for the fuzz. "It's Boomer and Hackett! It's Boomer and Hackett!" goes the warning cry when *any* two white cops in a squad car cruise by. The girls duck into liquor shops and vestibules as if dodging bullets.

When Kenya was last arrested, for drug selling, in late spring 1992, she caught a glimpse of the upper-tier television screen from her Nassau County Jail cell. A familiar face passed over the screen. Kenya bolted up—just as Lynn, Phil, Larry, Bobby Whitestone, and Anthony Saciolo had. "Oh, shit! I know that nigger!" she said. "Hey, Stephie, look!" Another North Franklin Avenue girl, a few cells over on a prostitution bust, knew him, too. "Hot damn, what they got old Joey for?" Kenya asked, with a snort of just-deserts.

"It ain't him they got," someone else called out. "It's the girl."

*   *   *

*Identified as Lorraine Wurzburg's house, housing the ABBA switchboard.

Today, sitting in the visitors' room in the upstate prison to which she is confined, Kenya Lyons says she has learned her lesson. No more drugs. No more hustling. Forthright, engaging, and seemingly motivated, at twenty-five she's completed her high-school equivalencies and is going for in-prison college courses. "I'm damn lucky I escaped AIDS. I want to become a substance-abuse counsellor and I want to get my two children back"—her mother has been raising them—"and finally be the mother they deserve." She shakes her head. "This life, once you get in it young, it's hell getting out. But you *have* to get out or it will kill you."

It was when she first tumbled into that life that she met the "big, stocky man, with black hair that goes back, named Joey. He had on jeans and a polo shirt, dark shades. He came to my house, where I lived with my husband, to buy an eighth of a key. He was a friendly guy. It was, 'Hey, Joe, how ya doin'? What's up?,' when he came in the door."

After she left her husband, Kenya says she ran into Joey again. She was a little surprised at the context. He would cruise around North Franklin Avenue—first in a Corvette, then in a white Cadillac with tinted windows. Many of the girls knew him, she claims. "Some said he was a mechanic.

"He would get out the car, stand on the corner, and talk to a couple of these girls, and they used to give him money." This surprised Kenya even more. His selling drugs was one thing. His buying sex from these sorry girls didn't make too much sense. "Then he started coming constantly. At one point, he was on a corner and these two Italian guys kept driving by and they stopped right in front of Joey's car and they said, 'Hi, Joe, What's up? Are you all right? Are you straight?' He tried to ignore them. I think he was working for them." Then it dawned on Kenya, she says: This Joey guy must be a pimp.

One night, Kenya found herself freebasing with Joey at the Courtesy Motel, the hostelry of choice for the North Franklin girls and their johns.

"He got high and he started talking a blue streak. How he had his own business as a mechanic. How he was bored with family life. He said, 'Yeah, I got this side business; your friends are my girls; they pay me. That's why I'm able to take you to this hotel and treat you like this.' "

82

Kenya was feisty.

"Well, don't do *me* no favors," she recalls saying. "I've got my own drugs."

Indeed. Now it turned out that Joey wanted to buy from *her,* Kenya says. She also remembers several more of these encounters—at the Courtesy Motel and the nearby Capri. She says she charged Joey $50 for sex and sometimes he gave her extra money to buy cocaine.

"There were times when he didn't have enough money for drugs and he asked me to offer sex on the street to get enough money for his drugs. I refused." Kenya also claims Joey had deals with some of the other girls, including Kenya's friend, a white streetwalker named Lenore.

Eventually Kenya stopped peddling sex, restricting her merchandise to drugs. She has said, in a sworn affidavit, that several times in the spring and summer of 1989 Joey drove her to Baldwin and parked in front of a house on Grand Avenue that "he said was an escort service where he said I could make some money supplying and selling drugs." (This is the same period of time during which Lynn claimed she met Joey, as Rita's collector, in the Flagship Diner parking lot.) Kenya noticed that Joey "could go in there and get money any time he wanted . . . I waited in the car and he went to the door and a thirty- or fortyish white woman would let him into the house. Joe was usually in the house ten or fifteen minutes." Other times, Kenya had friends drive her to "Joey's garage" with the crack that he ordered from her the night before.

Shortly after this spate of trips, Kenya was arrested on a drug charge and served a year in prison. When she returned to Hempstead in the early 1990s, she learned that two girls she had known were now off the sidewalk, working escort, "dressing up, wearing suits." Joey was still coming by North Franklin, still talking to the girls in a manner that suggested "he was controlling them." She stayed away from him.

But it is a night in 1987 that sticks in Kenya's mind most when she thinks of the man she first met with her husband. Kenya was in a North Franklin store when she heard Joey and her friend Lenore fighting outside on the street. Joey seemed angry at Lenore. From the gist of the conversation, Lenore had cut him out of money she owed him. "I came out of the store and saw Joey punch the shit out of Lenore," Kenya claims. "He just punched her in the face. She fell down. And she stayed down.

"I ran over and picked her up. Joey was saying, 'I've had it with that bullshit. She knows what she did.' I said to him, 'Yo, Joey, you better cool out. If Boomer and Hackett come by, *you're* going to jail, not Lenore.' "

Last May, right after Kenya Lyons made out Joey's face on the upper-tier TV screen through her Nassau County Jail cell bars, Amy Fisher was led onto Kenya's tier on the attempted-murder charge: scared, shell-shocked. "Girl," Kenya said, using the words she had wanted to use on that long-ago night to her white friend Lenore, "why *you* in this jail and not him?"

Amy shrugged and shook her head. After they talked a bit, Amy realized that Kenya had indeed known Joey. (Amy: "She even knew about his Corvette!") They became cellblock friends.

At one point, the twenty-five-year-old ex-streetwalker squinted, confused, at the seventeen-year-old ex-escort. "Tell me something," Kenya asked, "how you got pushed that low by that scumbag? How he work that shit on you?"

Amy's answer follows.

♦ ♦ ♦

7

Lady Mobster

◆

I'm a big fan of Danielle Steele's. When I was in the Nassau County Jail, in between finishing my twelfth-grade coursework so I could get my high school diploma, I read three of her books. I've read a couple in Albion, too. Love sounds so dramatic and romantic, the way she writes it. In real life it's not.

There's a woman here at Albion who has two teeth in the whole front of her mouth. Her boyfriend punched all the others out. (He couldn't dislodge the molars in the back.) There are a lot of women here who got AIDS from their lovers or pimps, or from the needles they used or from men they sold themselves to on the street. In Bedford Hills, the maximum-security prison I was in for a week, there are many women who finally killed the husbands or boyfriends who had battered them and their children for years. Whenever I feel down, I just look around here and remind myself: I'm a lucky one. I got off easy.

Still, even though I'm not physically wrecked, what happens in my mind is what scares me. I just follow people I'm attracted to. People just get this *hold* on me. Ever since I was a teenager, the minute one man popped down, another popped up. Whoever it is, I get mind-controlled. I *think* I'm strong and tough, but then an attractive man comes along and I turn to Jell-O. (Sometimes it can even be a girlfriend, as you'll soon see.) I try to be sexy and please that person and be smart and do everything they want. I'm theirs for the taking.

Joey did that taking the best. Joey was like Mr. Gaunt in Stephen King's *Needful Things*. Did you ever read that book? I sat down in Nassau County Jail and opened it and read it straight through. It reminded me of the past year of my life. In the book, Mr. Gaunt is a man who has the power to affect people's minds until they fling mud at each other and fight and kill each other. In the book, "Needful Things" is the name of the store Mr. Gaunt owns. In my life, *I* was the person that Joey owned; *I* was that needful thing.

Why am I so needy? How can I stop being that way? I go up to the scratched-up mirror in the prison bathroom (we're not allowed hand mirrors; no glass, nothing sharp) and I stare at myself and say, "I'm not going to do anything wrong anymore. I'm not going to let someone else get that hold. *I'm* going to be in control." Prison is a hard place to make that vow. As I write this, I've just been threatened by another inmate. People's power is even harder to control in here than out.

What's it going to be like when I'm out again?

Here's what it was like in the months before I went in.

"You know, I had a near-death experience once," Joey said to me one night in August, when we were dancing in the little love nest upstairs at Complete. There was no radio, no tape deck in that bare little room with the big bed. Still, lack of music didn't keep Joey from swooping me into his arms and hugging me and dancing with me, body to body, cheek to cheek.

It was when he was on drugs, he said. He almost died from an O.D. Or, rather, he *did* sort of die—he passed out. It *felt* like death, he said. And then he came to.*

---

*A less spiritual description of Joey's brush—or brushes—with death during his former drug-taking days was described on "Geraldo," on February 12, 1993, by former Complete employee Paul Bluin, who claims to have known Joey for fifteen years. According to Bluin (who was once convicted for misdemeanor drug possession), Joey's prodigious cocaine consumption often led him to compare himself braggingly to John Belushi, the difference being that *he* succeeded in staying alive. Bluin also stated that Joey stole from the Indian deli owner across the street from Complete, threw rocks over the repair-shop-yard fence to an adjacent building and insisted that Bluin drive him and other workers to the city to frequent a Manhattan brothel. Bluin complied.

Looking up at his face—my cheek pressed against his big chest—as he talked, I was intrigued and impressed.

"You learn something from that," he said, pointing his solemn face down at me, like a teacher. "You learn that life is a beautiful thing. Live it, make the most of it. Live life on the edge"—he kissed my nose—"and hope you don't fall off."

Live it on the edge. I liked that phrase. It was dramatic. I asked him what he meant. He told me that since he realized, from his near-death experience, that he only has a small time to exist on this earth, he's going to make the most of it and do everything for himself."

That sounded a little more selfish than dramatic. But— standing there with my body pressed against Joey's, following him in the dancing he did so well—I didn't think about the distinction too much.

Sometimes, when we danced like that, Joey picked me up and whisked me around. Sometimes I stood on his feet and he danced *for* me. Once he kiddingly taught me that dance—the lambada— that all the late-night comics made fun of. I always followed. Joey always led.

One night it was clear that instead of dancing we were going to do something else. We walked up to the love nest and Joey said, "I have a surprise for you." He took out a pair of handcuffs.

First, I was a little bit shocked. But he said, "Relax. This will be a trip."

Joey laid me down on the bed on my stomach, pulled my two arms up over my head, and snapped the handcuffs on. I couldn't move. We made love that way. It turned him on, me being so passive and all. He must have felt the attitude that was developing in me: total trust. If I was on top of a building and Joey was on the ground yelling "Jump! I'll catch you," I would jump.

Joey was so sexual, he could go on much longer than I. When I was exhausted and couldn't do it anymore, he would jerk himself off and, like a kid with a squirt gun, spray his semen around the room. He made me watch. I didn't like watching, but *he* liked it when I watched.

Watching was a big thing to Joey. A turn-on. "Come on, why don't you do it with so-and-so?" He'd name a friend of his. He'd be holding me and touching my hair while he asked me. "Why don't you two do it," he'd suggest in a soft, sexy voice, "and I'll watch?"

"No!" I'd say. To a sixteen-year-old girl, that sounded just . . . weird. *Rob* never asked me to have sex with his friend. I would have thought he was nuts if he had! "I only want to do it with you," I said. "I love you."

"I love you more," he said. Then he took my hands in his, clasping them, keeping them warm. "You know," he said, like a teacher pronouncing a golden rule, "you have sex with your body; you make love with your mind." He waited for it to sink in. "That means you can be in love with someone but have sex with someone else, as long as you keep your mind out of it. You just never kiss them. And *never* give them oral sex."

The importance of that little lesson didn't register immediately, but it would—soon enough.

One by one, Joey would ask me to do certain things. I always said no.

"Come on. Why don't you let me have another girl join us in bed sometime?" he said one night, rubbing my back.

"No!"

"I've done it before."

Another time, when we were in his car, going to dinner, he leaned over and popped a sticky little candy in my mouth—as an "appetizer."

On the CD player, the Steely Dan song "Hey Nineteen" was going:

> *The Cuervo Gold, the fine Colombian*
> *Make tonight a wonderful thing*

"Where'd you get this?" I asked. It wasn't like a candy you bought at the movies or at a candy store or anything. It was sort of sickeningly sweet.

"At a Korean massage parlor," he said. "The girls put it in your mouth while they massage you."

"Do you have sex with them?" I asked, not thrilled.

"No, but they give hand jobs."

> *Oh, we can't dance together*
> *Oh, we can't talk at all*

I slapped him on his leg. He grabbed my hand and rubbed my fingers. "Aw, come on. *Come* with me there."

"No! I don't want ladies giving me a massage and rubbing me in my sex organs! Men, either."

"Sure you do."

"No!" I was proud at how much I resisted.

Please take me along
As you slide on down

That song is supposed to be sung by a man who feels uncomfortable because he's with a girl who's nineteen—three years older than I was. But in my life with Joey, it was he, the older man, who was making the younger girl "slide on down."

Joey didn't give up on me. "You've got such a great body," he said one night, when I was sitting in front of him in my silk push-up bra from Frederick's and little lace-bordered black thong-back panties, so my cheeks showed. He traced my body with his hands, trying to make his fingers meet around my waist. Thank God, the Acu-Trim is paying off, I thought. I was breaking out in sweats from taking it. A couple of times I had to grab onto tables when I was walking, I was so sure I would faint.

"You know, you could make a lot of money as an exotic dancer," Joey said. He translated: "A stripper."

"Yeah, sure." I made a face. "Like I really want to do that."

"Hey, no, baby, really." He had that come-to-Joey look. "I've got friends, they dance at this place on Eleventh Avenue in the city. Goldfinger's.* Great money, babe."

"No!" I said again. "I am not going to undress on any stage and have men leering at me."

"What bothers you about it?" he wanted to know. He was looking at me like he really wanted to talk to me seriously about this.

"What bothers me is, dancing nude on the stage in front of hundreds of men bothers me! I mean, God forbid somebody I knew saw me. I would be mortified."

---

*In January 1993, the *New York Post* reported that "fellow patrons of the Eleventh Avenue flesh parlor [Goldfinger's] now report that, around the time that Mary Jo was in the hospital and Amy was in jail, Joey sought solace in the club's dark-glassed VIP room, where sisters of mercy with names like Bunny, Tiffany, and Chanel personally consoled him."

"Okay, so it's the public part that bothers you."

"Yes."

"Like being behind closed doors where no one knew your identity wouldn't be such a big deal."

"I don't know," I said. I had never thought of it before. "Yeah, I guess there's a difference."

He let the subject—and the distinction he'd made me see—pass. Temporarily.

I was never aggressive with Joey when we made love. I was afraid to make the wrong move. I was never quite comfortable. I was always nervous about the way I looked and the way he would perceive me.

Once, when he was undressing me, he just stopped.

"What?" I asked him.

"Nah, I'm not in the mood."

"What?" I was acting mad to cover my insecurity.

He pointed to my panties. I wasn't wearing the sexy ones he bought me. I had just thrown on a pair of old ones.

"What, you can't do it because I don't have the right underwear?"

He sort of shrugged.

In my mind, I was thinking, Well, he's just punishing *himself* by that pickiness. But in my heart I thought, Uh-oh, did I do something wrong?

We didn't make love that night, and I was gearing myself up to pick a big fight with him the next day. But when I came by the shop the next day, he was on the phone, soaping up my father. No one could soap up my father like Joey could. No one could *save* me from my father's anger like Joey could.

I needed Joey too much to be angry at him.

Soon he would help me with my father even more. And I'd need him that much more because of that help. Looking back now, I see what a setup it all was—what a trap. It started with me witnessing something illegal he was doing to a car.

"See that car?" Joey pointed to a red Ferrari one night when we were driving around Massapequa. "One of these days I'm going to take it. I've just got to find somebody to sell it to."

"You steal cars?" This was news to me.

"I'm talented," he said, throwing me a look. Then he explained to me how it works.* Complete Auto Body specializes in Caddies and Lincolns. Joey drives around town and scouts where all the good Caddies and Lincolns are. Say, for example, he passes a delicatessen, and there's a white '90 Lincoln parked in the lot, in the owner's spot. He passes the delicatessen on three or four other days. The car's still there. He looks and sees what color interior it has, what features it has.

Now, say a customer comes in with a practically totaled white '90 Lincoln. The insurance adjuster will come in and give an estimate on the damaged car. Let's say the adjuster estimates the repair work at $7,000 and says, "Yeah, we'll pay it."

Okay. Now either Joey or one of the two guys he works this scheme with will go out and steal the deli owner's Lincoln from the delicatessen parking lot. They'll drive it back into the shop. They'll give *it* to the customer. The customer thinks the Lincoln is *his* repaired car. Joey will also give the customer $7,000 worth of repairs, which the insurance will pay for.

The only thing is, Joey and the guys didn't *do* any repair work. What they did was sell the customer's wrecked Lincoln's *parts* for $20,000. So he's made $27,000 and the customer's got a good-as-new car. And the deli owner gets reimbursed from his insurer for the stolen car. Joey said he does this a lot.

Several nights I'd be at Complete Auto Body when the garage door went up and the guys would drive a new stolen car in. Then I would watch a very interesting process, one that takes great automotive-repair skill: the changing of the hidden VIN numbers.

VIN means Vehicle Identification Number. Every car has one. When somebody buys a new car, the automaker, to make the car traceable in case of theft, attaches a little metal tag with the number and sometimes also the buyer's name on the car engine. Most people know that.

But the automakers also do something else, which a lot of people *don't* know. *I* didn't know it until I saw Joey and the guys taking the door of the stolen car completely apart. The automaker also slips a little card with the VIN number in the inside part of the door, where the window slides up and down.

I watched as the guys took the door completely apart, as if the

---

* In the investigation following the shooting of Mary Jo Buttafuoco, Nassau Homicide found no indication of illegal "chop shop" operations by Joey.

door was a triple-decker sandwich and they were opening it up, and then scratched out the VIN card and changed the number. Don't ask me how they did it. As Joey says, they're talented.

"See, if you ever want a new car, baby . . ." Joey said.

I loved what an outlaw he was.

In a whole different way, I was about to become an honorary outlaw myself.

◆ ◆ ◆

In mid-August 1991, Amy took a job at Jean Country, a popular clothes store in Massapequa's Sunrise Mall. Like most suburban malls, the Sunrise is not merely a self-enclosed community center and town square but a virtual stage for the ongoing play of young life. It was there that Amy had spent a year of weekends, shopping with her friends Jill and Debbi and Jennifer and Heather for sophisticated clothes. It was there that Amy and Rob used to go on mornings they cut school. It was there that Amy's friend Samantha had bumped into Joey DiNardo over Christmas vacation 1989–1990, prompting Amy's reunion with him, the first boy who broke her heart. And it would be there—three months hence—that Amy would come with her mother, to shake off the sadness of her breakup with Joey Buttafuoco.

Within these weatherless bubbles of artificial ease—the clothing shops, photo shops, shoe stores, bookstores, music shops, movie theaters, drugstores, and fast-food restaurants all lined up, open and welcoming, side by side—teenagers spent their weekends, spent their allowances, met and mated, got their first jobs. As malls organized suburban landscapes during the very same years that galloping recession, unemployment, and drug use were disorganizing suburban homes, it would strike more than a few social scientists as ironic that the more controlled and sheltered teenagers' public environments grew, the more challenged and chaotic their personal ones became.

Jean Country, which featured neat display cases and circular racks of jeans, pants, shirts, shorts, sweatshirts, body suits, flannels, and socks, was considered a good place for a girl to get a job. The store was hip; its manager was twenty-four, and the sales help got discounts on the clothes. The clothes the store featured were thought of as "Jappy," which is the term the mostly Italian-American kids from Mapham High in Bellmore and McArthur High in Wantagh half-admiringly called the more upscale, preppy clothes the Jewish-American kids from Merrick wore. Even if it meant working for minimum wage, it was cool to be seen working at Jean Country: doing the register, folding and tagging the stock, telling a customer that the jeans vest should hang over flopping shirttails for the trendy layered look.

Jean Country hired two other new girls besides Amy in mid-August: Lori DeSaro and Maria Murabito. Both were nineteen and a full year out of McArthur and Mapham Highs, respectively. Long-haired and pretty, the daughter of a fairly prosperous family, Lori had gone to junior college for a semester. Tiny, feisty, bubbly Maria had not gone to college at all. She lived in a more modest home than Lori; her father was the manager of a pizza parlor. But Maria was a natural social ringleader, and she was the kind of opinionated mother hen that other girls wanted as best friend. Like many South Shore girls, she had a verbal style that was half Valley Girl and half dead-end kid.

In no time, Maria organized herself, Lori, and Amy into a little group. Both older girls saw Amy as a natural little sister—still going to high school but wishing she were out, living in Merrick (a.k.a. Bubbleland; a.k.a. Long Island 90210), but eager to cross the tracks to where the kids had more attitude, hung out in hotter places, and had *two* Italian parents, not one. "Lori and I liked her *so* much," Maria says. "We wanted to protect her."

Lori said, "Amy was so trusting, so sweet."

Maria, who had a more knowing air about her than Lori did, was particularly struck by Amy's vulnerability. As the girls started taking her out to the clubs they frequented—Jams, Escapes, Metro 700, Industry—Maria could see that Amy's outer toughness was an act. "She was so believing. She was so weak. She had *no* temper. She was scared of spiders. She was scared of driving. Amy was the biggest dizzball in the world!"

Amy was constantly mooning over her older boyfriend, Joey. When she told Maria he was married, Maria batted her eyes with exaggerated incredulousness and offered a judgmental "Ex*cuse* me . . . ?" Who would want to put up with a married guy? Maria wondered. Young, full-of-themselves *single* guys were bad enough! But Amy just kept telling Maria how wonderful Joey was. One day after work, she offered to show Maria for herself.

Amy drove Maria to Complete Auto Body. "She walks inside,"

Maria recalls, "and she's 'Hi, Joey,' and he's 'Hi, honey'—and he'd give her little love pats and stuff. His brother, Bobby, is walking around with this attitude: 'I don't know *nothing.*' " But the fact that married Joey paraded Amy at the family business was not the main shocker for Maria. She was mostly stunned that the man cute little Amy had raved about turned out to be "old and ugly and gross. He was strutting around in California Hardware baggy workout pants and tank tops—like he's showing off his body! Like, give me a *break!* His stomach hung out over those pants. I'm thinking, Yeah, Ame, he's real good-looking—*not.*"

The next day at Jean Country, Maria recalls, "Amy was saying Joey was going to divorce his wife and start all over with her." Maria didn't know whether to worry more about Amy's guile-lessness, or Joey's jive. "He must've been so convincing, 'cause *no* girl in her right mind would believe that line."

One day, the two older girls sat their still-sixteen-year-old "little sister" down at the mall's Roy Rogers for advice.

Maria recalls, "Me and Lori said, 'How can you believe this stuff from him? Don't be re*tar*ded! Like, *dump* him! He's *old!* What *is* the big deal?' Amy's like, 'Oh, I *looove* him.' I said, 'Amy, you can do better. His looks is—forget-about-it.' And she's like, 'Looks doesn't matter.' Like she's hurt. I felt bad. I said I was sorry." For a while Maria backed off.

Better, the two girls thought, to try to get Amy's mind off Joey by trying to get her to meet someone else.

Maria had a Camaro with pinstriping that announced it as "The Lady Mobster." She loved the nifty line. "I got it—let's make a club: The Lady Mobsters!" she proposed another day after work. They'd finished their fries and Cokes and Maria was whipping her cigarette around as she talked in her high, staccato voice. Her ripply hair, pulled way up in a scrunch-band ponytail, sprayed out like a geyser on top of her head, beneath which her dark eyes danced. "The Lady Mobsters," she said again, sucking her cigarette smoke up her nostrils and then blowing it back out again.

To even out the club, the girls needed a fourth member—and, boy, did they ever have one—their friend Jane.

Jane, also nineteen, was a tall, shapely, swaggering high-school graduate who had white skin, red-painted fingernails, tumbling auburn hair, and high-peaked brows over eyes that could either beam flirtatiously or narrow sublimely in threat. She worked as a hair colorist at a trendy local salon, The Quintessential Look, but, like many noncollege-bound South Shore girls, the fairly humble position did not reflect a lack of wealth or clout in her family. In fact, Jane was not shy about bragging that the Brooklyn scrap-metal yard her father and uncle owned doubled as a surreptitious crematorium for victims of Mob rubouts.

Although, like the other two girls, she lived on tacos and burgers and was an ace Nintendo player, Jane managed to lift herself above the banality, to create a presence—in no small part helped by the full-length silver-fox coat she strode around in during the winter, and the state-of-the-art-equipped car her father bought her each year. By means of these accessories and a patina of toughness unshared by the guileless Lori and the spunky Maria, Jane held herself apart from her more accessible friends.

If Mary McCarthy had used as her locale the tract houses of Levittown in 1991 instead of the brownstones of Manhattan in 1945, Jane would have ended up as Lacey in *The Group*.

For a lark, Lori and Maria took Amy to Escapes for its campy "happy hour" after work. Even though all three were underage —especially the dazed-looking Amy—the doorman let the trio in because, Amy says, "We were cute." They sat in that smoke-filled room among large tables of teased-haired housewives in rhinestone-dabbed, appliquéd overtops and small tables where furtive-eyed accountants, repairmen, and engineers singly nursed straight Scotches. Three muscular G-stringed men took the stage and did a bump-and-grind over the amplified anthem of two female rappers:

> *Let's talk about sex, bay-bee*
> *Let's talk about you and me*

Amy thought it was a great goof. The Merrick kids would *never* do this! Then Jane sashayed in. The minute Lori and Maria introduced her to Amy, Amy seemed shyly impressed. Jane was cocky, sexy, bossy, tough. Kind of like a female Joey.

With Jane, Lori, and organizer Maria, Amy transcended pallid Bubbleland and plunged herself into a neo-guido life. *Guido* (pronounced "gwee-do") was the newest self-reference for the Italian-American youth culture. Guido took over where *Saturday Night Fever* left off, and used the recent convictions of Italian-American boys in Howard Beach and Bensonhurst, for racially biased mob-action murder, as a kind of up-yours justification and political ballast. (The defendants, a number of whom are now serving long prison terms, were viewed in their communities as martyrs to a "politically correct" double standard that punishes Italian kids for actions that black kids can get away with.*)

Guidos and guidettes had special ways of dressing their bodies, dressing their cars, and hanging out. It said something about the deep pull of Italian-American heritage (conveniently dovetailing with the popularity of high-bravado hip-hop and rap music) that girls like Lori, Jane, and Maria wanted to forsake the all-American image their parents had struggled to lead them to, and emulate instead the strutting Bensonhurst *cugines* (cousins) whose parents were fresh off the boat.

There were three guido/guidette hangouts on Long Island: Hempstead Turnpike in Levittown; Deer Park Boulevard in Deer Park; and Francis Lewis Boulevard in Queens. Kids cruised those strips on hot summer nights, parked in the empty lots and flea markets, opened their car doors wide. Leaned on the hoods. Made taco runs and came back. Still, those three hangouts were pale next to the Real Thing—Eighty-sixth Street in Bensonhurst.

To cruise Bensonhurst effectively—or even the other three strips—you had to have a "guidomobile": a Cadillac Seville, Lincoln Sports Coupe (LSC), Ford Mustang, Pontiac Trans-Am, Pontiac Firebird or Chevrolet Camaro. The back should be jacked up, the windows tinted, and it had to be outfitted with a

---

*The much-resisted possibility that this might be true didn't emerge until fall 1992, when a black defendant was acquitted, despite extremely strong evidence, for the mob-inspired murder of a young Hasidic Jewish man in Brooklyn's Crown Heights in 1991. No other members of that mob were even apprehended. By contrast, in the Howard Beach and Bensonhurst cases, involving mostly Italian mobs leading to black youths' deaths, justice was far-reaching and swift. Writing from Attica Correctional Facility after the Crown Heights acquittal, Bensonhurst defendant Keith Mondello noted the disparity in a letter to the New York media.

state-of-the-art sound system: tweeter, woofer, kicker box, 210 speakers. Sometimes guidos pinstriped their cars with sayings from songs, like "Can't touch this" or "For your eyes only." Guys hung "guido bows"—big, cheap-looking, ready-made bouquets of plastic ribbons and streamers—on their rearview mirrors. Girls were given their boyfriends' guido bows. Those who didn't have guido bows made do with foam-rubber dice. The parade of ornamented cars, sociologists believe, dates back to the parades of painted wagons of Sicilian farmers; the car bows, to the chivalric practice of knights hanging their ladies' scarves over their battle swords.

Bensonhurst guidos even had their own way of driving—the *"cugine* lean." The point was to lean so far to the right as you steered with your left wrist that your head was barely visible from the street. Hot-dogging guidos even propped their left legs out their car windows as they leaned and drove. If you managed that maneuver in your decked, pinstriped, back-jacked guidomobile—while the sounds of Bobby Brown's "It's My Prerogative" or Bel Biv Devoe's "Do Me" blared from your 210's—you were almost eternally cool. So cool that when other guys slapped you five and asked you, "'Sup?" ("What's up?"), you didn't even have to answer. You could just blow them off with a chin cock.

These were the kinds of boys The Lady Mobsters—well, three of them, anyway—wanted.

Guidos had two looks: either cardigans or tufted black Windbreaker-style jackets worn with baggy pants; or, for the more hotshot guys (and definitely the Bensonhurst guidos), suits and silk ties. Guidos were peacocks; they slicked back their hair, wore earrings, cologne, and always lots of gold chains.

Guidettes wore boots and tight jeans in cool weather and, in summer, jean shorts and tank tops and high-heeled ankle boots and lots of bracelets. Guidette hair was ideally as high as possible. However, Maria, Lori, and Jane—and now Amy—were lazily flat-haired. "If someone didn't like it," Maria says, "it was, 'Oh, well . . .'" There was just so much a suburban girl would do.

Amy was fascinated by the inner workings of guidoism, and she liked the nights with the girls, cruising Deer Park and Hempstead. Still, her heart wasn't really in it. She never cared about those younger guys she met. It was always Joey, Joey, Joey.

Amy rhapsodized at work about how Joey had taken her out to elegant North Shore restaurants. In fact, she talked about Joey all the time. She'd be all set to go out with the girls, and then would cancel at the very last minute because Joey called and wanted to be with her.

This bothered Maria. Maria had backbone. She wanted Amy to have some, too. One night, when Amy came over to Maria's, Maria marched her out for pizza at Mama Gina's, near her house, and laid it out. "Look, I know you were sick of all the bullcrap with the young guys"—Amy had told Maria about the abortion with Rob, the back-and-forth with Joey DiNardo—"but these old guys can do it, too. Don't be blind! Joey's *full* of it. Him leaving his wife is a crock! He'll never do it! He's manipulating you."

"But I love him," Amy pleaded. "And he loves me."

Later that night, Amy and Maria picked up Lori. The three headed out for Francis Lewis Boulevard. They took Amy's Daytona—it was her maiden voyage with her real driver's license. "We almost crashed getting on the turnpike on-ramp," Maria says. "Amy was the *most* nervous, *most* scared, most *terrible* driver!" Suddenly Amy started up again, "about how Joey said he hated his wife and was going to get rid of her. 'Amy,' I said, 'get it out of your mind! He is *not* going to get divorced!'

"She says, 'I'm not talking about a divorce. I'm talking about something else. Joey loves me and he wants to try to get rid of her in a *different* way. And when it's done, he's going to get me an LSC.'"

Amy's boyfriend's shocking intention stuck in Lori's mind. Today, Lori confirms, "'Joey wants to try to get rid of her in a different way.' Those were Amy's *exact* words."

Maria turned and shot Lori a sharply worried look. Lori returned it. Who *was* this boyfriend of Amy's, a contract killer?

A few weeks later, in early September, Lori and Maria were driving to Amy's in Lori's '91 Geo Star. They were all going to go to Bensonhurst, hooking up with Jane there. On Hot 97, the girls' favorite radio station, the new hit, "O.P.P.," by the rap group Naughty by Nature, came on.

> *O.P. is for Other People's*
> *P is—scratch your temple.*

Everybody knew the last *P* stood for "pussy."

The song intercuts parts of the Jackson 5 record "ABC," the innocent song that had occupied the number-one spot the year Lori and Maria were born, with the rapping. Its infectious dual staccato made it great to drive to. "It's funny," Maria said to Lori, "we never hear this song except when we're driving to Amy's."

They didn't see Amy every day anymore; Amy had quit Jean Country. Maria, however, saw Amy in a different context now— and she saw more of Joey than she wanted to. Usually as often as twice a week, Amy would drag Maria along to Complete Auto Body with her. While Amy and Joey flirted, Maria sat on Joey's desk and called her friends from his telephone.

Amy ran out of the house when Lori honked. Maria thought Amy had "the best parents in the world, especially her mother." She never understood why Amy seemed so eager to escape them.

They stopped at Maria's to trade clothes. Maria's tiny house featured plastic-covered couches, shag carpets, faux-marble linoleum, smoked mirrors, statuary, a gilt-framed print of an English hunt scene, a bird in a suspended cage, a giant moosehead. The girls bounded through these improbable sur-roundings in their tight tops, cut-off jeans, and waist-tied sweatshirts.

Then Amy announced, "I quit my job today."

Maria bore down. *"What'd* you quit? You didn't *have* no job!"

Lori recalls, "That's when Amy told us that Joey had found her this job with an escort service. She said she only went out to dinner with the men and listened to their problems. But last night one of the guys wanted to have sex and she didn't want to, and the lady she worked for said, 'If you *don't* have sex, you're fired.' So Amy said she said, 'Fine. I quit!'"

Lori's and Maria's heads spun; they didn't know whether to

bawl out their dizzy little sister for falling for Joey's obvious snare, or to admire her for having rebuffed it. The latter reaction won, by a hair. They hugged Amy, and said, "Phew! . . ."

They didn't know that the last line of Amy's statement was her own purely wishful thinking.

♦ ♦ ♦

8

Teen Prostitute

♦

Even before Joey got me to sell my body, he showed me how to exhibit myself to his friends. Of course, I didn't figure this out until later. At the time, I loved being displayed as Joey's plaything. Even now when I think about that night at Paddy McGee's, I wonder, Was it so wrong? Should I have been insulted instead of flattered? All you seventeen-year-old girls out there with much older boyfriends, do *you* know when you should feel flattered and when you should feel insulted when your boyfriend is making a big deal to his friends that you're sexy? Don't you, in your heart of hearts, feel flattered *most* of the time that older men find you sexy?

All of August had been spent shedding my little-girl self for an image of excitement: going to those guido-scene parking lots and those clubs with Maria and Lori and Jane, hanging out till 2 A.M. It seemed amazing to me that just months before I was with Rob and with my babyish high-school friends, going to a diner and a movie, being home for 11:30 curfew. It was so *boring*. It was so far away. Now I was choosing excitement. And if excitement meant having a bunch of men laugh and scream while I was making love with my boyfriend, well, then, that must be part of it.

Here's what happened. One night at the beginning of September there was a party given by Joey's best friend, Dave (the one who did the cabinetry), for his nephew's twenty-first birthday. It was given at a restaurant, Paddy McGee's, on the dock at Long Beach. I invited Maria to come along. The guests—about fifteen friends of Dave's and his nephew's—motored in on two boats. Joey came in on the *Double Trouble.* It turned out that the nephew was very good-looking (though Maria did not agree): black wavy hair, moustache, about five-foot-nine, Italian (of course), very distinguished-looking in his nice suit.

One of the guys picked up a girl at the bar and took her out to one of the two boats. All the other guys were standing on the dock, laughing at what was going on down there. The big send-off the nephew was getting turned Joey on. He wanted that for himself. He's kissing me and stuff, in front of all the guys. The *Double Trouble* is parked at the dock (this is the last time we'd go on his boat for a while; his friends got drunk and crashed it later that night). Now, he figures it's *our* turn to go down there and have the guys laugh and cheer. What can I say? That's how guys do things on Long Island.

Joey had already been showing me off to the guys. I was wearing tight shorts and a tight shirt—I knew by this time to wear sexy clothes when his friends were around; he liked that. He would constantly put his arms around me and grab me and pick me up. If his friends perceived me as being sexy and fun and cute, it made him feel better. It made him feel like a bigger man.

So Joey pulled me onto the boat. We went underneath in the cabin, took off our clothes, and we heard the guys on the dock screaming and cheering and laughing. Then Joey stuck his head out of the hatch and waved, naked—and talked to them and called out, "Hey, bring her a drink!" (All his friends knew that *he,* as a recovering substance abuser, couldn't drink.) They came back with the drink and he took it and said, "Bye-bye," and popped back down again. And they were screaming and cheering.

When we came back up, I didn't feel humiliated—I felt special! All the guys who had been cheering and laughing thought I was sexy and pretty! It all sort of built up my ego.

Maria, when she found me, gave me a look like, I don't *think* so. (Poor Maria—I had just left her there.) She didn't want any part of it. She wanted to get the hell out of there.

♦ ♦ ♦

Maria recalls: "Amy and I were sitting on the dock at Paddy McGee's and Joey drove up in his boat and she said, 'Hi, honey!,' and he kissed her—in front of all those other guys. Joey said,

'Maria, how ya doin'?' He wanted to set me up with one of the guys. I wasn't interested. Amy and Joey took off—to go down in the hatch of his boat while the other guys whistled and laughed. I thought it was sort of disgusting. And I was left sitting there talking to some retarded twenty-one-year-old."

When Joey and Amy reemerged, Maria started complaining that she wanted to go to the club Industry.

As Maria has sworn in an affidavit: "So about ten minutes later, Joey walked us to my car. *He kissed Amy and said, 'I love you.'* [Emphasis added.] Then Joey said, 'Drive carefully.'"

In that same affidavit, Maria further declares: "Every time I was with Amy, which was every night during the warm weather and an hour during each day to go shopping, Joey would beep her. As I recall, he would beep her three times a day: around noon, around five P.M., and again at night. While we were out, she would go call him back."

A teenager having a beeper was not the big deal the media made it out to be. Although the beeper's origin as a device to help crack dealers wheel and deal gave it an outlaw caché, it and the car phone were becoming teen communications fads.* Throughout 1991, a lot of South Shore kids were acquiring both, and the two accessories heightened the constant communication of girl cliques.

One night, Maria and Amy were driving to Bensonhurst in one car, Lori and Jane in another. Maria remembers: "We beeped each other and called each other about ten times that night, just on the way in to Eighty-sixth Street."

Still, the origin of Amy's beeper was quite another story.

◆ ◆ ◆

I had gotten fired from Jean Country because I wouldn't take the rudeness. One day, one of the managers said, "Pick the fucking shirt up off the floor."

I turned around and said, "Pick your *own* fucking shirt up"—and walked out. No way was that man going to talk to me in that manner. I told Mary Lynn about it. She was so upset she wanted to go in and get mad at them for me. I told her, it's not worth it. But I hate that

---

*Beepers were not allowed at John F. Kennedy High. Amy's ability to use hers surreptitiously in the school relied on her habit of setting it on Vibrate, which made its beeping noiseless—and undetectable by her teachers.

attitude: You kids are only working for four dollars an hour. We can insult you; you're replaceable. Eventually Maria and Lori left Jean Country, too.

I looked around at a couple of other mall stores, but there were no jobs open. School was starting soon, anyway. And I was with Joey so much, he was paying for most of my entertainment.

Then something happened in early September that made me need a job. I had a head-on collision in the Daytona. The accident was the other driver's fault. I was going straight, and the other driver was parked at the curb. He moved into the traffic without looking. Boom! I smacked right into him. His insurance company agreed to pay 100 percent of my damage.

Joey towed in my car. It was about 50 percent damaged. To be considered "totaled" by an insurance company, a car has to be 80 percent damaged. "I don't really want this car, anyway," I told Joey. "What I want is a convertible."

So Joey, being Joey, took a hammer and smashed the transmission case. *Just* the case, mind you. He wanted to be able to salvage the transmission for his own purposes. He called the insurance adjuster to come back. "What happened here?" the adjuster said. "When I came before, this car wasn't eighty percent totaled; now it is."

Joey gave the guy a couple of hundred bucks not to say anything.

Then I went out car shopping and fell in love with a black Chrysler LeBaron. It was just eight months old, marked down from its original price of $15,000 to $13,000. I went and told my dad and he said, "Absolutely not! That's too expensive." Finally, after talking to Joey, I made an arrangement with my dad. I told him I would split the monthly payments of $400 with him—that I had gotten a job as a shampoo girl at the hair salon where Jane worked, The Quintessential Look. (I was starting to hang out with Jane, and was spending a lot of time in that hair salon, anyway.) My dad said fine. Little did he know that Joey had offered to give me that $200 a month to give to my father.

And little did *I* know that this new car I loved was my one-way ticket into a very ugly profession I wouldn't break free of until they put me in jail.

Two and a half weeks after I got the car, Joey broke the news to me—he was having business problems. He couldn't afford to help me out anymore with the car payments. "You have to assume responsibility for yourself," he said solemnly.

Great! I thought. Just great. I have a $15,000 car in my driveway, a thirty-five-year-old boyfriend who's supposed to be making payments, and a father who will be very, very angry if I tell him the situation. Plus, school has started. What kind of after-school job can I get that will earn me $200 a month?

I was sitting in Joey's office, pondering all of this, when he had a solution. "Join an escort service, babe," he said. "Here." He picked up the phone book. "There's even one here in Baldwin." He conveniently opened the phone book to the right page. He pointed to "ABBA Escorts."

"But aren't those sex services?"

"No, they're not sex services," he said, like I was naïve. "All that happens is men take you out to dinner at fancy restaurants. You meet interesting people and get all dressed up and you have dinner conversations with them. It's fun. They'll love you, babe. You're beautiful. You'll make a quick couple of hundred dollars a week to pay your father."

It sounded glamorous and exciting—like I was going to turn into Cinderella. But, was that really all there was?

"Did you ever use this service?" I asked Joey.

"No," he said. "But my friends have. Look, you're in good hands. My friends know them. Here." He wrote down the number. "Call them."

I went to Mary Lynn's house and told her what Joey had told me. "Amy," she said sternly, "that's a sex service. I do *not* want you doing that!"

Still, I figured Joey knew what he was talking about. I dismissed Mary Lynn's opinion. *She* wasn't worldly like *he* was. (This was the beginning of me choosing Joey over Mary Lynn: a dangerous choice. The forced rift would be complete in a few weeks. But I'll explain that later.)

So I called the number and a woman who called herself Lacy got on the phone and talked to me. Today I know that Lacy—who also called herself Lily—used to call herself Rita, and that her real name was Lorraine Wurzburg. After my arrest, a news team got a shot of her on the front lawn of her house (which is just down the block from Complete), saying, "I've known Joey Buttafuoco for twenty years. . . ." And Channel 4 televised a report, claiming that utility bills for ABBA were being sent to Joey's house.* But at the time, I had no idea "Lacy" knew Joey.

I was on and off the phone with Lacy for a couple of days before I was convinced that there was no sex involved. What clinched it was when I asked one of Joey's friends if *he* thought it was a good idea. Now, this guy isn't flashy like Joey—he's blond and wholesome-looking, like Barbie's Ken. He said, "Yeah, I've used that service. It's a good idea." He and Joey both boosted me. So I called Lacy back and said yes.**

---

*The report would prove highly controversial. After seeing it aired on the late news, Detective Martin Alger jumped in to investigate it first thing the next morning. He determined, as he reiterated when interviewed in early December 1992: "There is absolutely no truth in the report that ABBA's utility bills were sent to the Buttafuoco house." He and Detective Sergeant Dan Severin further believe very strongly that no relationship existed between Wurzburg and Joey, at least not at the time of Joey's arrest.

However, News-4 employees contend that the information-gathering, done by two separate private investigators *not* hired by parties in the case, met these important conditions: The sources had no axe to grind and were not in a position to know the significance of the address. Still, when the station retraced its steps in an effort to reconfirm the report, it was unable to do so. This, some News-4 employees are careful to imply, does not mean that the evidence never existed. During his January 1993 interview with Joey and Marvyn Kornberg, Chuck Scarborough said that after talking at length with the police, "there is no evidence [all emphases added] *that we can turn up* to support the allegations made in that report. The police have checked the utility bills thoroughly and there is *nothing that can be turned up* to support [News-4's] report. . . ."

When Kornberg then quickly said, "I'm glad that the public has been made aware that Joe Buttafuoco has absolutely no connection to ABBA whatsoever—thank you for clearing that up," Scarborough just as quickly responded: "Well, I didn't say exactly *that*. I simply said that we found no connection here. And we retract the report."

Subsequent to the telecast, Channel 4 station spokesperson Terry Doll clarifies that Scarborough's remark in the confusing heat of his exchange with Kornberg did not constitute a station retraction. "There was *no* retraction of the report," Doll says adamantly. "We stand by our story."

**To talk a girl over the age of seventeen into becoming a prostitute translates into criminal solicitation in the fifth degree—a violation as serious as jaywalking.

Joey had said, "Use a fake name," so I used Maria's. (Sorry, Maria!) Lacy hired me without meeting me, without checking my ID for my age. I know now how extremely unusual—how suicidal—it is for an escort owner to do that, and to hire a girl who is under eighteen—*unless* the person who is sending them that girl is someone they know very well.

Lacy called me with a customer the next day. I was to go to an office building at 10 P.M., in an industrial section of Mineola. It was cold; I remember I had been out with Maria and I ended up borrowing her coat. It was dark. I parked my new LeBaron in this big, almost totally empty parking lot and walked into a big office building. Most of the lights were off. Janitors were wheeling carts of cleaning equipment. If something weird happened and I screamed, would anyone hear?

I had the office number written on a piece of paper. I knocked on the door. This ugly man about fifty years old let me in. He was bald and scary-looking. I didn't think I should take off my coat—weren't we going out to dinner at a fancy restaurant, like Joey said?

But he said, "Take your coat off." So I did. He moved toward me and unzipped his pants. He said, "Give me a hand job."

I started laughing. I thought he was kidding. Was this the "interesting dinner conversation" Joey was talking about? But he just kept looking at me. Then he pointed to the jar of Pond's cold cream on his desk. He pulled his penis out.

I said, "Excuse me a minute," and I nervously dialed Lacy's number. I whispered in the phone, "Lacy, this man wants me to jerk him off! What do I do?"

"Well, *do* it," she said.

"But you told me this wasn't a sex service," I said.

"It's not," she said. "But if a customer wants you to do something, you *do* it or he won't call back." She clicked off.

I turned and faced the man. I realized I was all alone in this big dark office building, and my father was expecting $200 from my "shampoo girl" job in two days, and if I told him I didn't have the money because I got fired and it was my fault, he would scream at me and probably hit me and make my life hell and I would never hear the end of it. If I told him I was fired and it *wasn't* my fault—that they had fired me for no reason—he'd go into The Quintessential Look screaming at the owner. And he'd find out I

107

never had a job there, and Jane would also get in trouble. Then he'd want to know where I had been getting the $200 if it wasn't from a job, and I'd have to tell him "from Joey," and he'd put an end to me and Joey. And I didn't want to lose Joey.

So I took the Pond's cold cream and rubbed it on my hands. And I gave the man the hand job. I didn't think about self-respect or anything. I blocked out the mental hurt. I said to myself, I have to do this or I can't keep the things around me that I need to survive: Joey, my car, peace with my father.

When it was over, he wrote a check for $175. One hundred and seventy-five dollars! To have just turned seventeen and to have made $175 in fifty minutes—well, in my logic, I've been through so much worse than what I had to do to make that money.

So that's how it started. That's how I became a prostitute.

Soon I had my beeper, and, because I was dying to tell Lori and Maria something but I didn't want them to hate me for it, I said I started but quit. Then later, when they'd be at a club or the mall with me and my beeper would go off, I told them that I had my own private clients, but that there was no sex involved. They believed it, I guess. I always had the beeper clipped to my belt, on Vibrate. I'd feel it, look down, read the phone number, and if it was the service and I needed the money, I'd call and go. Later, when I had my own private customers, I memorized their phone numbers. (I have a photographic memory.) I called back the ones I wanted to accept.

Lacy would tell me what to wear and where to go. She asked me if I wanted protection and sometimes she sent a driver to sit outside. Mostly I chose to drive myself. I would wear tight short skirts, high heels, and crop tops. A G-string and push-up bra underneath. But no makeup. So I would look young, like I was. The customers said they loved my being young.

Most of the men didn't even want sex as much as just someone to talk to. They were sad, lonely men. I would come to their offices and they'd lock their doors and close their shades. I would meet them at motels. (I think I have been to every motel on Long Island.) The sex you could get over with fast, sometimes in five minutes. Most of the memories I have now are not of doing things to those men but of sitting and watching them do disgusting things to themselves: me stroking their arms, telling them how much I liked being with them, while they masturbated.

At the end of the hour, Lacy would phone (when I started out, she would do this at the end of each of my hourly calls), and the man would look surprised and say, "Wait—"

And I'd say, "Sorry, the hour's up."

If he wanted to extend the call another hour, I had to go through with it. (When I went out on my own, I didn't have to do that. I could keep my calls at one hour, no extensions.) I'd get the payment taken care of first. (Wouldn't it be horrible to have sex with these guys and then get stiffed?) I'd take either their check or cash. Other times the men paid by credit card. Lacy had an antiques shop she used as a front and I would use the shop's American Express account and run the card through that little machine. Just like at Jean Country. A lot of times at the end of the call the man would give me $50 or $100 extra as a tip. I'd keep that and drop the rest of the money, or the check or credit-card receipt, into Lacy's mail drop. And she would give me a money order, with my fee minus her commission. She trusted me so much (because of knowing Joey, I think) that I didn't have to come back with the money after each call. She would let me hold on to a couple of thousand dollars at a time.

I got good at telling the men what they wanted to hear. If a man weighs 300 pounds, you don't say, "What a great body you have." Instead, it's, "What nice, thick hair you have. . . ." After that first, forced hand job with the scary guy in Mineola, I learned that I could manipulate the call. If a man tried to take my hand and put it on his penis while he was masturbating, I'd say, "I'd rather just sit here and *watch* you do it."

He'd go, "Yeah? You *like* to watch?" His eyes would light up in surprise. (These men are so pathetic!)

I'd go, "Yeaah," like it was the biggest treat in the world.

They'd buy it. Being swooned over like that meant more to them than anything my hand could do. As a prostitute, you really have more power than you think. Those poor guys want you to like them; they want acceptance *so bad.* I was this sexy, young little thing walking in the door. If I said I'd rather watch them jerk themselves off than anything else—well, I could flatter them into keeping their hands on themselves and off me. I got myself out of some pretty creepy stuff with that line.

Not that I was doing that to be mean or cynical. I told them whatever they needed to hear to feel better. You just want to make them happy and get the fifty minutes over with so you can leave. When they'd ask me about myself, all I'd say is that my name was Maria and my father owned a pizza parlor. You learn to talk briefly and keep it so that they don't know anything more about you on day ten than they did on day one. If they pressed for more details, I'd say, "I don't want to talk about *me*—that's boring. You're *fascinating*. I want to hear about *you*." So they'd tell me about their marriages or their bad divorces or their businesses or their kids. Sometimes they took me to nice places for dinner or lunch. One of my regulars took me to a polo club. I let their talk go in one ear and out the other.

A lot of the men were doctors and lawyers, but I never thought they were bigger "catches" than Joey. Complete was the biggest body shop on the island. To my logic Joey was a very powerful man. I never thought these men were higher than him in any way at all. Besides, your average Long Island lawyer is *not* good-looking. (My lawyer's the exception.) I never felt any chemistry with any of those men. Once I was sent to this prunelike man at the Best Western Motel. We had straight sex with a condom. Later I saw his picture in the paper; he was a judge!

Sometimes I'd be sent to guys in their early twenties, who were just calling an escort service on a lark. After the first of those calls, I made sure to tell Lacy: I'm not taking any calls in Merrick! What if someone ended up being the brother or parent of a friend! Once I was sent to a personal trainer. After the sex, he gave me his card; he wanted me to come work with him. As he was paying me, he kept pinching the skin on my arm, from my elbow to my shoulder and back. "You only have six percent body fat!" he marveled. "Only *six* percent!" *That* turned him on more than the sex. Another man I was sent to didn't want to do anything but touch my feet and legs. Then there was that gross, 400-pound man from Long Beach I had to massage with the Jergens baby lotion. Thank God, he lay on his stomach so I didn't have to see his face. Thank God even more I didn't have to *massage* his fat stomach—or any place else but his back. He gave me $800 once. Just for a massage! Of course I came back!

After I left them I would go home and take a shower, even if they didn't touch me, even if I didn't touch them. After a month of escort work, I started to have trouble keeping my food down on days I had customers. After every call, I would go home and get sick. I lost even more weight than I'd lost on my Acu-Trim diet. (Joey liked that.) I was getting depressed in a way that I wasn't aware of. The work was revolting—and the fact that I felt I was suckering those men made me have contempt for myself. So those men were getting what they wanted. All *I* was getting was emotional scars and self-hate.

Joey gave me the rules, which he'd already sort of told me: "Don't *ever* kiss them. Always make them use a condom. Never give them oral sex." The kissing part was the most important—that separated having sex from making love. Joey had me believing it, like a catechism: "You have sex with your body, you make love with your mind."

I would go around thinking, I have two separate parts of me—the person who has sex, and the person who makes love. They never mix, they never mix, they never mix.

Making love was just for Joey. Just with Joey. The more I worked for the escort service, the more I realized how Joey was my prince. It was like banging your head against the wall 'cause it felt so good when you stopped. Those other men were whiny, wimpy, lonely, desperate—and here's Joey: this big, *built* six-foot-one-inch man who would say, when I came back from my calls, "Forget about it. I love you, sweetie." Being an escort made me *worship* Joey!

When I think about it now, it gives me the chills. *He* was making me—this high-school girl—play the role of a woman of the streets, coming to *him* for redemption. That's a little sick now, isn't it?

That's why he wanted to hear about those men much more than I wanted to talk about them. He kept asking; I started lying. Talking about the men, thinking about what I was doing; it got so painful. Listening to "Lyin' Eyes" made me sad and queasy. Forcing myself to remember, I feel that same bad way right now.

Still, I kept doing it. I can't even tell you why. The power of being seventeen and making $600 a week? I sure didn't need that much money to make my $200-a-month car payments. The control I had over those men? I used the defense mechanisms that I'd always used when I was hurt; I focused on something else and put the unpleasant thing I was doing out of my head. Maybe just *having* those defense mechanisms is why I could do it, and finding out that I *could* do it is why I *kept* doing it.* The psychiatrists think I became a prostitute because I was unhappy with myself and wanted to torture myself. Does that make sense? I don't know what makes sense anymore.

Eventually three of my customers became my regulars. They paid me directly. Lacy didn't know I had taken them. She'd call and I'd say, "Aaah, I don't feel like working, I'm feeling a little sick."

Finally, she called and asked, "What's up? You never want to work."

I told her, "It's not really for me. I'm not into that scene anymore."

I did still take some calls she got me. One was with an obnoxious man who lived in Levittown. I saw him three times: once through Lacy, twice on my own. The second time, he tried to talk me into doing S&M tricks with a whole bunch of men.

"I would never do that!" I said. "Not for two thousand dollars! I would not do that. I *can't* do that." What he was asking me to do reminded me of what Joey had asked me: the sex with his friends, the group sex, the stripping in front of the leering men at Goldfingers. Guys who would ask that made me sick.

Taking that horrible man as my customer—as you will see—turned out to be a very big mistake.

Having regular customers kept me from men who would make requests like that. I was making $600 a week on my three regulars, without having to give a commision. My main regular—I called him my Sugar Daddy—was a man who owned an electronics company. He was an easy $200, almost every single week. When I looked at my

---

*For many middle-class prostitutes who have been in the profession a long time, the question of why they have never left "the life" revolves around two things: (1) an addiction to the money (Where else do they think they can earn $150 or more an hour?); and (2) the psychological inurement to humiliation and exploitation that started early in their lives. "Joanne," a well-spoken woman who was raised in a middle-class home and has been working as a prostitute in a major U.S. city for eighteen years, says, "I have met well over a thousand girls in this profession and every single one has this in common: We all came from dysfunctional families—families in which there was alcoholism, sex abuse, suicide, abandonment, or something else very wrong."

wall calendar there was an *X* in the 5:30-to-6:30 P.M. spot on every Tuesday of the winter and spring.

He was a nice man—very rich, not bad-looking, about fifty. I would go to his office—the people there thought I was his girlfriend—dressed any way I wanted. Half of the time I just wore cut-offs and sweats. Sometimes he'd take me out to a nice restaurant and then we'd go back to his office and I would give him a hand job. He never wanted intercourse because he was married and he was paranoid—he said he didn't want to bring any diseases back to his wife. I didn't care. He was a sweet man, if a little pathetic. Sometimes he would look at me longingly and he would ask me questions about myself and I would just recite Maria's life. He had a son a year younger than me.

The second regular was a disgusting man who was one of the most prominent dentists on Long Island. He was thirty-seven, heavy-set, unattractive—and starved for attention. He was divorced and very, very lonely, and a coke addict. I would meet him about once a week at his huge house. He was a pig. I had sex with him only about three times. After that he had trouble getting an erection, so the rest of the time I would sit there in my underpants and bra and watch him masturbate. I would be thinking to myself, He's pathetic. This better end quick so I can get my $200 and be with Joey.

This man always proposed to marry me—every single week. After he masturbated, we'd sit and watch movies and then he'd turn to me and say, "You sure you won't marry me . . . ?"

I'd say, "Aw, you're too old for me, sweetie. You're thirty-seven. Tell you what, when *I'm* thirty-seven and you're fifty-seven, we'll get married, okay?" Joey taught me quick lines for everything.

The third regular—well, he was something else. You know how I just said I felt no chemistry with any of these customers? Well, this man was the exception. I was definitely attracted to him. He was a nice, dark, handsome Italian man who leased luxury cars—Lamborghinis, Corvettes, Cadillacs, Lincolns. He had called the escort service on a dare, as a joke. He was definitely not the kind of man who would need to use an escort service. Then he got me, and we clicked.

Most of the others I tried not to have sex with. Him, I had sex with. He always used a condom. And I kept to my golden rule of not letting him kiss me. But . . . with him, and only him, I could have crossed the line and fallen in love.

I was scared because I really liked him, and that was too confusing. I didn't want to have my life be like the movie *Pretty Woman,* where Julia Roberts and her customer, Richard Gere, fell in love and he proposed. As long as I kept my two lives *completely* separate, they made sense to me. One life was having sex with my customers; the other was making love—*only* with Joey. I couldn't bring this man into my real world. I couldn't. I mean, God forbid my parents and friends would learn what I did those three hours a week! I couldn't put them through it. Besides, he was too *much* like Joey. Italian. Well built. Worked with cars.

Except he was nicer than Joey. Classier, more of a gentleman than Joey. And single.

It scared me too much. It confused me too much.

So finally I said, "I can't see you anymore." I guess you can say I quit seeing him in order to stay under Joey's spell.

9

Slit Wrists

♦

So here I was by the fall of 1991. After trying, unsuccessfully, to convince me to have sex with his friend while he watched, to have lesbian sex, to be a stripper, and to be erotically massaged at a Korean massage parlor, Joey *had* succeeded in getting me into prostitution. He had paid off an insurance adjuster in order to get me a new car, the monthly cost of which kept me dependent on my prostitute earnings. He had gathered a bunch of guys around to laugh and cheer while we made love on his boat. And I depended on him to soften up my father.

He scared me when he slammed my head against the wall, and he scared and excited me when he handcuffed me before we made love. He made me tell him about my prostitute exploits, and he wouldn't have sex with me if I was wearing the wrong kind of underwear. And he kept talking about how he wanted his wife to be out of the picture for good. "Be patient," Joey would say. "She will have an accident. You can't do these things too quick."

I accepted all this without a second thought. By now, violence had gotten very exciting and glamorous to my little suburban mind, and the skill I had learned in my childhood—of blocking things out that were painful, even while they were happening—was something that, through my prostitute work, I was getting very good at. I had never met Mary Jo. She wasn't a person to me. She was just an obstacle to life with Joey.

Once, when we were out on his boat, I told Joey about Jane's father and uncle. I was hanging out at Jane's house as well as her hair salon now, and I'd always see those two short, funny-looking moustached guineas. I nicknamed them Mario and Luigi, because they looked like the Super Mario Brothers in my favorite Nintendo game. "Jane says they have this scrap-metal business and sometimes they melt down the bodies of guys who've been hit by the Mafia." Half kiddingly, to see what he'd say, I added, "You could get him to melt her body down."

But Joey wasn't kidding when he said, "No. With the body missing, I'd have to wait seven years to get the insurance money."

I was a little shocked at how ready and specific his answer was, as if he'd figured it all out.

I must have looked shocked to him because then he laughed and said, "Baby, I can't wait that long," as if he was half-joking, after all.

We were standing on the deck and the wind was whipping. But it was Joey's words, and not the wind, that made me feel a chill.

Joey knew I confided in Mary Lynn. He didn't like that at all. "Why can't you spend the night with me, ever?" I would ask him after we made love. "Mary Lynn says you're no good for me. Mary Lynn says you'll just hurt me.

Mary Lynn would give me questions to ask Joey: Why couldn't he divorce Mary Jo, if they had so little sex together? Wasn't it wrong to keep stringing me along? And sometimes our nights together would be like Twenty Questions: me asking him one adult-coached question after another. This annoyed Joey.

One night at the end of September when we were together in the apartment above Complete, he was talking about getting rid of Mary Jo—again. "How can you think it's okay to kill somebody?" I asked him. That question had come right from Mary Lynn's lips.

He could tell. He rolled over and stared at me and asked, "Did your aunt tell you to ask me that, too?" When I didn't answer, he said, "Stop seeing your aunts."

When I said, "No!" we had a fight. Then he got up and started getting dressed.

"Fine," he said, when I said what he was asking was ridiculous. (They're my family!) "I can't see you anymore."

I panicked. I couldn't imagine life without Joey.

"Okay," I said. "I won't see them anymore."

I stopped calling Mary Lynn and Alana to tell them my troubles, to ask how to deal with Joey. I didn't talk to them from October 1, 1991, until after May 1992. I cut myself off from an adult woman's perspective. At the same time, I started cutting myself off from the advice of friends close to my own age, too. (Not that I ever really listened to it.)

After that night when I mentioned to Maria and Lori that Joey wanted to get rid of his wife in a "different way" than divorce, Maria was even more skeptical of Joey than she'd been before. I could tell from the looks she would give when we were about to go out, Maria and Lori and me, and suddenly Joey called and I was out the door.

One day when we were at Maria's house, trading clothes, she said, "If you want to stay with him, fine—that's your business. But just realize what he's like."

She had met Joey and spent a lot of time around him, while Lori hadn't met him at all, I was more touchy about her opinion. "What do you mean, 'what he's like'?" I asked, getting defensive.

"He definitely seems the type who could do that—thing that he said," she explained. (The "different" getting-rid-of.) "He doesn't seem afraid of doing harm to people." Plus, she said, he always had a line. He put people on pedestals and gave phony compliments. Everything was "beautiful." I was beautiful, our relationship was beautiful, this was beautiful, that was beautiful. "Can't you *see through him?*" she asked.

Now I realize she was telling me that Joey didn't have a conscience. She was telling me that "Joey's rules of survival" were nothing I should be enamored of.

But then wasn't now. It stung to have Maria make me feel like a fool. I turned away from her. "I just don't want to hear it," I said.

It got so that Maria knew she couldn't keep a friendship with me and tell me the truth. So she—and Lori—would just sort of smile and let me do what I wanted. If they saw me really crashing into a brick wall, they would try to deter me a little bit, but they couldn't really stop me.

I didn't want to hear it. I didn't want to hear the truth.

* * *

Joey would get me out of school so I could be with him. I'd be in his office and he'd call Kennedy High and tell them I was sick and get me signed out. "Hello, this is Elliot Fisher," he would say, in a faked voice—and I'd be laughing noiselessly as I watched him. "My daughter has a fever." To the people in the attendance office, one male adult voice was as good as another. I thought it was great! As September turned to October, and October to November, he did it more and more. I'd beep him in the morning and he'd ask, "What's wrong today?"

And I'd say, "I have a cold."

Then he'd hang up and call the school.

By the middle of the first semester of senior year, I didn't have any friends left at Kennedy: No friends left at Kennedy. No Aunt Mary Lynn to get advice from. Maria knowing she couldn't dare tell me the truth. Me lying to my parents about working as a shampoo girl with Jane—and completely lying to them all about Joey. Joey lying to the school about being "Mr. Fisher." Me lying to Lori and Maria about what the escort service really was. Lying to Lacy about my private customers. Lying to *Joey* about my prostitution: telling him that being with those men was hot and sexy when it really made me vomit and hate myself.

Why couldn't I *see* how out of control I was spinning? I was not only doing self-destructive things; I was making it so that *nobody* knew enough about them so that they could guess the pain and confusion I was in. I would look at my James Dean poster. When I bought it, I didn't understand it. Now I understood it too well. No wonder he looks so lonely. I thought, as I dressed in my tight skirt and G-string to go to the pig-dentist's house.

I had this friend, Chris Drellos, who was kicked out of his parents' house in Merrick and was looking for a place of his own. Chris had graduated from Calhoun High a year before and he hung around with the same circle of friends that I had known through Joey DiNardo. Chris and I became friends. Chris was a real charmer. You could be real mad at him, but then he'd say something that would make you forgive him. I felt sorry for Chris because his parents kept kicking him out of his house. I could understand having tension with parents and feeling lost.

Chris and I were friends, *not* lovers. I wasn't even attracted to him.

My Story

He's not my type. We never went out on a date. No matter what you heard, we never had sex.*

It's upsetting when people make things up and they get believed. I know the story that Chris told is that I asked him for a gun and when he got tired of me asking, he introduced me to Stephen Sleeman. (Sleeman is the *real* liar! And he's admitted he's lied. But we'll get to *him* in a minute.) When I hear that story repeated, I just wish the two of them and I could be in the same room so I could confront them with the things that are not true.

Here's the real story about me and Chris Drellos.

At the end of September, Chris came over, all hangdog. He had been kicked out of his house again. Chris knew I worked as an escort—somehow it was safer to talk about it to him than someone closer to me who would be more judgmental, like Maria. So he knew I had a lot of extra money. He said he needed to get his own place right away. I told him I would go with him to look for an apartment and would loan him money for the deposit.

Why not be generous, with all the money I was making? I never thought of saving it. I bought my friends lunch and dinner, and when we went to clubs I always bought everybody drinks. So if Chris needed a loan to have a roof over his head, fine.

We went to a real estate place in Seaford. The lady there told us that three houses down there was a Chinese restaurant, and that the lady who owned it wanted to rent out the bottom of a house she owned nearby. The association was funny to me because Joey had told me he had had an affair with a woman who owns a Chinese restaurant.

Chris and I went to the restaurant and the lady showed us the

---

*Chris Drellos told police, through an attorney, that he'd had sex with Amy from May through August 1991, and that after August Amy "repeatedly," Drellos's attorney, Bruce Parnell, claimed, asked him to get her a gun. However, it must be noted that Drellos's lawyer, who was also Stephen Sleeman's lawyer, used this "information" to cut a profitable deal with the tabloid TV show "A Current Affair" and with the producers of one of three TV movies about the case. Detective Martin Alger says that while some of what both young men said about Amy's intent was worth examining (and that the whole issue of intent was something that would have been problematic for Naiburg, had the case gone to trial), Drellos's credibility as a trial witness would not be ideal and "God forbid you'd ever want to believe *anything* Stephen Sleeman had to say."

apartment. It was about $650 a month, which sounded reasonable. She said she would accept a $400 deposit to hold it. So I gave it to her, in cash. Chris was supposed to move in.

Two days later, after not hearing from Chris, I called his house. His parents told me he didn't live there anymore.

I had forgotten to write down the number of the house, so I went back to the lady who owned the Chinese restaurant and asked her, "Can I have the address of your house again, so I can see my friend?"

She shocked me. She said, "He never moved in. He came back yesterday and said he didn't want the apartment. He took back the four hundred dollars and left."

I felt very used. You don't take somebody's money and then use them and humiliate them like that!

Stephen Sleeman's lies were much worse. Stephen told the media I had sex with him. *Never* did I have sex with him! That lie angered me so much that I took a polygraph test to prove I never had sex with him. I passed with flying colors. He refused to take such a test. But he has admitted that he lied.*

Stephen Sleeman also told the media and the police that I went to Home Depot to buy an axe to chop up Mary Jo and the children. A complete lie! And he knows it!**

Here is the truth about Stephen Sleeman:

Toward the beginning of September, I took Chris out to dinner. I was in my feeling-sorry-for-him mood. He was out on his ear again, going from job to job, crashing at friends' houses. In fact, he had come to my house for dinner a lot. So I said, "I'm going to treat you to a nice restaurant dinner, Chris. Where do you want to go?" He chose Michael's, a nice restaurant on the water with good food. Chris had a friend who worked in the kitchen there, a guy named Stephen Sleeman. Chris and I went back and said hello. That's all I said: "Hello."

Stephen was the most god-awful ugly creature I ever had met: about five feet tall *and* five feet wide. He developed a crush on me,

---

*Not long after Stephen Sleeman's story—of Amy offering sexual favors in exchange for promises to help her shoot Mary Jo—surfaced, Lori DeSaro

just from seeing me that one night. He told Chris he had lustful feelings for me. Chris told me that Stephen said to him, "Wow, she's beautiful."

And Chris kept telling me, "C'mon, go out with him."

I said, "No."

Stephen started calling me and beeping me. I would never return his phone calls. He called constantly. He was one of the reasons I had my phone number changed. Then, finally, I decided to use him as a "gofer." Rob used to get things for me—a burger at McDonald's, a video: whatever I wanted. Joey wouldn't do that, so Stephen Sleeman filled that bill. After awhile, I figured he was a thoughtful creature. So we did become friends. I went to Friendly's with him once, Sizzler another time.

Around the middle of October, things were going badly with Joey. I was getting very upset with Joey's stalling, his not being with me. Every time I asked Joey when we were going to be together, I could tell he was trying to avoid an answer. He'd say, "We're gon-na take care of it. We're gonna be together. Be patient, we'll find a way . . ."

It hurt and confused me. I was seventeen years old. I didn't know how to be "the other woman."

I stopped being so trusting of Joey. For five months he had me in the palm of his hand. Maybe Maria was right about him feeding me a line. Maybe my prostitution had hardened me, made me more realistic about men using women and lying. Anyway, I wanted to see if Joey was lying to me. For this, I used Steve.

---

ran into Sleeman at a local 7-11. Lori says, "I walked up to him and said, 'Steve, why'd you lie about Amy? You know you didn't sleep with her.' He said, 'I know, I said it because I got paid for it'—and he walked away laughing, and I cursed him." Detective Martin Alger says Sleeman later admitted to him, as well, that he never had sex with Amy.

**Detective Alger says, "Sleeman didn't bring the axe-shopping story up until our third interview with him. If it was truthful, why did he wait so long?" Alger says that Mary Jo's use of the tale, which she inaccurately presented as truth, during her speech at Amy's sentencing, was an act of great irresponsibility by her lawyers and advisers. Sleeman, who also claimed to have Swiss bank accounts, was called a "pathological liar" by Eric Naiburg.

Most of the time it started with me calling Joey, asking him, "What are you doing tonight?"

"Oh, I'm tired," he'd say. Or, "Oh, I have business."

I didn't believe him. This was new, not believing him. I'd call Steve and say, "I don't believe him. Let's drive by his house." I always drove, but I needed the company.

Sure enough, his car would be parked outside. So, he was lying! The next day I'd get mad at him. "Why'd you have to make up excuses? Why couldn't you just tell it to me straight?"

By the end of October, I was really getting upset. Or maybe you could call it obsessed. There *had* to be more to their marriage than what Joey was telling me; he had to have *some kind* of relationship with his wife. Otherwise, why would he still be with her? Why would he be afraid to tell me he was spending an evening at home? When we first met, Joey had told me that she had been a model for the Spiegel catalogue. Maybe she was beautiful.

Suddenly I *had* to find out. And I couldn't bring myself to find out with my own eyes. So I asked Stephen to find a way to get a look at her. I thought he would just sit in his car and wait for her to come out of the house. But instead, he went up to her door with candy he was selling for Farmingdale High—for muscular dystrophy.

Let me tell you right now: The story Stephen told the media (which found its way into the TV movies) about hiding, at my request, in the bushes with a rifle in front of the Buttafuoco house? Well, the Buttafuoco house doesn't *have* bushes to hide in. Figure out for yourself how honest he's been.

What Stephen did do was sell her candy. "Oh, yeah," he said, "I got rid of a couple of bars." He gave me a blow-by-blow description of the whole transaction.

But I didn't care about their conversation about the candy. I only cared about one thing. "Stephen," I asked, "is she prettier than me?"

"No," he said. "You're beautiful. She's old, she's wrinkly. She has nice eyes but, you know . . ." He shrugged.

"Do you think she was *ever* prettier than me?"

"No," he said. "Never."

I felt good after that. But still, Stephen was pretty much of an idiot. I made a mental note that I would try to take a look at her myself.

♦ ♦ ♦

Amy's friends started to worry about her. Maria already knew she couldn't say anything bad about Joey's treatment, for risk of losing Amy. Now it was Lori's turn to notice what was going on. She recalls, "In the fall, Amy was always teary-eyed—always saying, "I really love Joey and he *says* he loves me, but he won't leave his wife." She was really hurt. She was starting to think he was playing her."

Quickly, things with Joey got worse.

In a sworn affidavit, Lori has said, "Sometime in November, Amy became very upset and was crying a lot. She said that Joey wanted to separate from her. One night in November I was at Amy's house with Maria Murabito. At around nine P.M. Joey called Amy on the telephone. . . . She was defending herself because she was going out with Maria and me that night. They were on the phone for about fifteen minutes and Amy was crying most of the time."

Lori saw Amy deteriorating, and it scared her. She wasn't sure that all those men beeping her as an escort was a good idea.

One night Lori asked Maria, "How can she do that?" Maria, who'd already been through the process of trying to argue with Amy, shook her head. "Amy, tell the truth," Lori asked her friend the next time they were together and Amy got one of her infamous beeps. "Are you having sex with those guys?"

"No!" Lori remembers Amy saying. " 'They're like forty years old. They take me out to dinner and dancing, that's all.' "

There was not much either Lori or Maria could do with Amy's airtight fiction. Besides, both girls had just acquired steady boyfriends—young men close to their age—who were taking up most of their weeknights and their weekends. They offered to fix Amy up, but the Hempstead Turnpike scene seemed to bore Amy, and guys her age seemed not to turn her on. What was actually happening was something else. Amy says, "Being a prostitute messed me up—it made me not want to date at all."

Meanwhile, as the two Lady Mobsters Amy had been closest to became more preoccupied with their own lives and more resigned to Amy's silent, stubborn decisions, the fourth and most charismatic member was moving in to close the gap: Amy was getting closer and closer to Jane. She spent more and more time at The Quintessential Look (where her parents thought she had a job as a shampooer) and at Jane's spacious home. Jane presented herself as someone who knew everything there was to know about murder and the Mafia and violence—and Amy seemed to love it.

Lori and Maria always thought Jane was sweet—*until* they introduced her to Amy. Then she started getting braggy, bitchy, and very hard-boiled. Did Amy just choose the wrong people, or did some people sense in her a vulnerability—a desperation to walk over the edge with a blindfold—that brought out their worst, most manipulative instincts? Maria and Lori didn't know. They hoped their little friend would be okay. They went on with their lives with their new boyfriends, but they wondered and worried.

◆ ◆ ◆

Things with Joey had been going downhill since September. By the end of November, something was very wrong between us. Right after Thanksgiving, I told him I wanted more. I wanted him to make a decision. I gave him an ultimatum on the telephone. I said, "I love you very, very much. I can't take this. Make up your mind! Come with me or stay with her. But if you stay with her, then I am leaving you."

He kept trying to have it both ways. "Please, don't make me make that choice. I can't leave right now. I can't do anything about the situation."

Under all those stalling words he was saying, I'm not ever going to leave her. Get used to it.

In fact, he started talking like he *wanted* me to break it off! Like my leaving would be a relief for him. "If you feel it's best for you, you can leave," he said, trying to sound so sensible. "I don't want to ruin your life. The ball's in your court. Sweetie, it's your choice."

I made myself feel I was being strong. I said, "I don't want to see you anymore!"

He said, "I'm sorry you feel that way." And that was the end of the conversation.

After I hung up, it hit me what happened. Yes, I had told Joey that I didn't want to see him anymore. Still, I didn't want it to go like it did. I didn't even expect it to go that way. I was devastated. I started crying hysterically.

I was alone in the house. The phone rang. It was my mother— calling from work. She heard me sobbing. "What's the matter?" she asked. "Amy, what happened?"

I wouldn't tell her.

"Do you want me to come home?" she asked.

"No, no, no," I said. "You don't need to."

I hung up, thinking she wasn't coming home.

I went into my bathroom and took apart a razor and I slit my wrists. I wanted to kill myself.

Minutes later, the front door opened and my mother rushed in and up the stairs and into my room (thank God, my father wasn't with her!), and she followed my sobs into the bathroom. She saw the blood on the tile floor. Then she looked up and saw my wrists bleeding. She was horrified! She led me to the sink and put my wrists under the faucet and ran cold water over them. Then she took them and looked at them. They were not deep enough cuts to require stitches. She cleaned them and wrapped them in bandages.

I told her about me and Joey, that I was in love with him. At the time, I thought I'd never get back together with him, so I figured I could be honest with her.

She was shocked. Yes, she had known we had had sex when the herpes thing came up (Joey had not managed to convince her of his innocence—he convinced only my father), but she figured that was long over.

Her shock turned to anger. She wanted to go down to Complete and confront him.

"No, no, Mom," I said. "The reason I'm so upset is, we just broke up."

Next, she wanted to call him up.

I convinced her to just let it die, for the sake of my mental health.

She knew she couldn't make a report to the police; I was seventeen. My affair with Joey could no longer be statutory rape.

Her attitude changed to one of protecting and consoling me. She wanted to take me to a therapist, but I said no—and she knew she couldn't make me go. (My parents have learned that they can't make me do—or not do—a lot of things.) So she just concentrated on giving me love and trying to make me feel better. She promised me she would not tell my father.

After a few days of consoling me, she changed to wanting to cheer me up. She figured the relationship with Joey was over—no use crying over spilled milk. My mom's the type of person who tries to make everything good and sweep all the problems under the rug. Her attitude is, If I have a smile on my face and eat my oatmeal, then everything's okay.

So she'd take me to the Sunrise Mall and we'd be in a store and she'd point to a boy about eighteen or twenty and say, "Isn't he cute . . . ?" But I wasn't interested. She thought if she could find me a young boyfriend all my problems would end—I'd be magically back to where I was when I was with Rob; us doing nothing more outlawish than playing Nintendo with the Mute button on when I was supposed to be studying history.

Could it be that those nights were only six months ago?

We had a Christmas vacation cruise to the Caribbean planned— me, Mom, and Dad. A couple of times before we left, my beeper vibrated and I looked down and the screen said 007: Joey's and my code. I was a really good girl—I didn't call him back.

Still, one night, right after the breakup, I talked Maria into driving me to Joey's house. We bought a bunch of big candy bars and, like Stephen had done, I pretended that I was selling for some school charity. I went to the door while Maria waited across the street in her Camaro.

I rang the doorbell and Mary Jo opened it and I said, "Do you want to buy candy," just like Stephen did.*

---

*In the version Mary Jo gave, and the one that found its way into the TV movies, Amy was tongue-tied; then she talked a reluctant Mary Jo (who

I got a good look—a good stare—at her. And that was good. I ran back to the car, with the two dollars she'd given me, and I thought to myself, I'm prettier! I was excited when I opened the car door. "Joey will be back!" I announced to Maria.

Maria didn't look thrilled as she gunned the engine.

Stephen Sleeman started asking me for money. He had a girl-friend but he didn't have a job and he wanted to buy her a Christmas present, so I lent him more money. He *promised* he would pay me back after the new year.

When he didn't, I called his house and screamed at his mother. I was really pissed! He had really hurt me a lot, and I did my usual: I got tough. It got so that I called and threatened him that if he didn't give me back my money, I would have somebody beat him up *so* bad his medical bills would cost him more than the money he took. His mother had her own sob stories. "Oh, I lent him a thousand dollars for him to fix his car and he didn't pay me back."

I told her, Sorry, that's not my problem. I just want my money.

Later, Steve claimed to the media that I had given him the money for him to get me a gun and that I had called his mother and gotten angry because he hadn't delivered. *That is not true.* I loaned him the money to help him—twice—and he lied to me and used me instead.

There were times during December that I felt strong—not used by anyone. I was sure I wouldn't take Joey back, even if he presented himself on a silver platter. There were days I just felt *so in control.* One day my mother and I were walking on the beach at Long Beach, talking girl-talk. She told me about boyfriends she'd had when she was my age, how hurt she had been by breakups. She said, "You can't center your life around a man." She sounded so full of conviction. My mother's very feisty and she proudly calls herself a feminist. (She thinks that what the district attorney put me through had a lot to do with my gender, and she was surprised and a little disappointed when women's groups didn't organize to protest the dropping of the investigation of Joey.)

I said, "You're right. I won't center my life around a man."

As we walked, my mother smiled as she talked about her days as a design student at Fashion Institute of Technology. I dreamed of

---

protested that the house was full of Halloween candy) into the purchase; then she ran off without saying thank-you.

being a designer, too. We had recently gone to Manhattan to see the Halston exhibit they had in the college's gallery. I was so impressed with it—especially by the dresses Liza Minnelli lent. I loved the school itself: a big dramatic building near the flower district in Manhattan. It had a beautiful library and dorms on a pretty side street. Hip-looking kids of all ethnic groups were walking around carrying portfolios. Calvin Klein had gone to school there. So had a lot of other now-famous designers. My mom had dreamed of a career like that when she was my age, and, though she got a little detoured by marriage and my birth, she hadn't done too badly. (She was doing custom upholstery work now—for the insides of yachts, even.)

I had definite talent in art, and design was the career I wanted. (It's the career I *still* want. And when I get out of prison I hope to pursue it.)

"You *can* have a design career," my mom said. I believed her.

As I walked through the cool sand next to my supportive mom—both of us hugging our chests in our big sweatshirts—it actually seemed that my messed-up life was a piece of deadwood I could toss out to sea till it sank to the bottom of the ocean.

10

Vixen

◆

After my parents and I came back from our Caribbean cruise—right after New Year's 1992—my mother needed some electrical work done on her car, so my father brought it in to Complete. My mother hadn't told him about the incident with the razor blades in the bathroom, and what I had confided to her right after. As far as my father was concerned, I hadn't seen Joey Buttafuoco since that horrible day in our living room when I "confessed" that a boy named Sal, not Joey, had given me herpes.

My father told Joey about the cruise and about what a good time I had. He also told Joey I needed an oil change for my car. So now Joey had an excuse to call me.

The phone rang one day. It was Joey, asking, "Is your father home? He said you needed an oil change."

He *knew* my father was at Stitch 'n Sew,* and he knew that phone number. So I knew he was really calling to talk to me.

"How are you? How was the cruise? Are you still mad at me?" he asked me. I felt myself softening. Then he said, "Bring the car in. I'll take care of the oil change for you."

* * *

---

*By now Elliot Fisher was well enough to be back at the store on a regular basis.

So I brought the car in the next day. Joey pulled me into one of the offices and he started getting very passionate. Not just passionate, but teary-eyed. It was a very hard-to-resist combination.

"I missed you," he whispered, and then he hugged me. He pressed me close to him and didn't let me go for about five minutes. Then he started to kiss me.

At first I pulled away. But he was insistent.

"I called you," he said. "Why didn't you call me back?" He seemed genuinely upset. "I love you," he said, and he didn't let go.

We got back together.

Joey and I were together almost every day straight, for almost a week. He took me out to dinner a lot. I tried to hold it in, but then I started again. "I really want to be with you forever."

His reaction was impatience. "Oh, here you go again," he'd say. "We have a good thing. Why do you always have to ruin it?"

Damn it! I thought. Why does he get all romantic and set me up to love him again, and then when I express my love and frustration, why does he get that way? I was angry and hurt.

One night in late January, I came home from an evening with Joey (I'd told my parents I was with Maria, of course) and my father suddenly decided 11:30 was too late to come home on a school night. Now, many other nights I'd stay out until 1 or 2 A.M.—and he wouldn't say anything. But this night he was in a particularly bad mood.

"What are you doing home so late?!" he screamed.

"Dad," I said, "it's only eleven-thirty." I was too scared to argue.

"You whore!" he bellowed.

I was afraid if I shouted back he would hit me. Besides, wasn't I just what he was calling me? I went up to my room and slammed my door, feeling angry, but also almost as afraid of him bursting in as I was when I was seven.

"You whore! You whore!" His words echoed in my brain. I had finally become what may have always, somehow, been expected of me.

Joey had joined this gym, Future Physique, and he started going there every night. Toward the end of January, he started talking me into joining.

I remember calling Joey on Friday, January 31, and saying, "I don't know anything about gyms. I don't know how to use the equipment."

He said, "There's a great guy named Paul in there. You'll like him. He works on Saturdays and Sundays. Go in there tomorrow and tell him you're with me. He'll train you. He's my buddy."

So I joined Future Physique the next day, Saturday, February 1. And that's how it started that instead of having one exploitative older boyfriend, I came to have two.

It turned out that there were two owners of Future Physique, Dave and Paul. Paul Makely. Paul was a friendly, handsome twenty-nine-year-old guy with longish hair and a moustache. As you now know, he is the person who "co-starred" in that fateful videotape for "Hard Copy." He was paid by them to goad me into going to the gym and to get me to tell him the six things I wanted before I went to prison—to get me to act like a spoiled brat while a secret camera rolled. When that videotape (which was spliced to remove all the parts where I sounded even remotely remorseful) was shown on TV, the district attorney decided, as a direct result of seeing it, to drop the investigation of Joey.

You also probably know that this entrapment—this incredible betrayal—by someone I trusted, at my most vulnerable moment, is what led me to try to kill myself with sleeping pills.

But to anyone who will listen, this same Paul Makely presents a picture of himself as the good guy who cared for me as a whole person, while Joey just wanted to have sex with me. Paul also tells people that *I* came on to him—that I stripped to my bra and panties when he was coming out of the shower, that he resisted my passes, that I gave him a hand job, that I forced myself on him while he protested.

He is flattering himself. He is lying. Paul Makely *came on to me.* And we never had our first sex that way. We had our first sex when he took me to the most expensive motel on Long Island, the Hollywood Motel, on February 6. (Like Joey, Paul also denied, until the bitter end, that he ever had sex with me. For a long time I bitterly thought, Is *every* older man who's ever used me going to insist, like Joey insists, that we just "had pizza together once"? If every tryst with these guys was a pizza slice, by now I'd be three-quarters tomato sauce and mozzarella.)

Paul and I had sex, and he became my lover. At first I was having sex just to get back at Joey. In some ways, Paul was very different than Joey. Joey's a smoothie, a sweet-talker. Paul doesn't have Joey's charm. Paul doesn't have Joey's ability to play with your mind. Paul is a little pushy and obvious sometimes. He says something and if you don't like it, tough. Joey tells you what you want to hear, how you want to hear it. Paul struck me as someone who would be safer on my emotions than Joey.

In a way, I was right. In another way—if you count the buttons he pushed, back to my own painful childhood—no man was ever more dangerous.

Paul didn't wrap himself in a mystique like Joey did. The first time Paul and I made love, he showed me his hair weave—where they sewed someone else's hair into his premature bald patch. He even laughed about it.

Paul didn't keep me on edge and make me feel insecure about my body and my sexual skill, like Joey had. I felt comfortable, but with that comfort, some edge, some attraction is gone.

I started having real feelings for Paul. I would meet him several nights a week at the gym, work out with him, help him clean up at the end. At first Joey didn't know. It was a little awkward, Joey still going to the gym. Joey would say, "Come down to the gym with me," and I'd make an excuse for why I couldn't go. I'd only go to Future Physique when Joey *wasn't* there.

Joey caught on to my affair with Paul around the end of February. At first he thought it was Paul's partner, Dave, who I was seeing. He started asking Dave twenty questions: "There's a new girl who joined here. Her name is Amy. Have you seen her? Have you talked to her?"

Finally I admitted, "You know I'm seeing Paul."

"What?!" Joey grabbed me. "Are you having *sex* with him?"

I told him yes, but I minimized the relationship. I made it sound like nothing. I acted puzzled by his jealousy: "But you *said,* 'You have sex with your body; you make love with your mind'—that's all I'm doing."

Joey wasn't buying it. When it came to my being a prostitute—fawning over him as a sexual king next to those poor slobs who paid to have sex with me—that motto was very handy. But Paul was a man Joey thought of as a peer. He wasn't degrading me as a whore; he was choosing me. *That* was different.

First Joey was shocked. Then he got pouty. He said, "Well, I can't go to the gym with you." He didn't want to go back there, ever again.

He was pouting like a little boy. So he joined a different gym: Maximum Fitness.

I was kind of flattered, though, because I was seeing both of them and Joey was trying to pull me back to him. Flattered but mostly very, very confused. It was much more than it had been between Joey DiNardo and Rob—these were grown-up men!

Paul didn't say "I love you" every five minutes, like Joey did. So Joey's hold was much stronger. But if I ended it with Paul, like Joey wanted me to, would Joey leave Mary Jo? Or would it be more of the same old agony?

It's hard being seventeen and having feelings for *two* older men—and two older men who were committed to other women. You see, Paul had a girlfriend, whom he lived with. They had a child together. He explained that he didn't love her and they weren't married and he didn't even sleep with her. But because of their child, he wasn't free to leave her.

Joey loved to rub this in. He told me Paul would never leave his girlfriend, and he told me Paul had been in trouble with drugs. Eventually, Joey stopped stressing this second fact.

One day Paul took me to his house to meet his son, Pauly. All right, I said to myself, maybe I can do a little detective work and find out if he's really telling the truth when he says he doesn't sleep with the child's mother. Paul has this really nice house on a lot of land in North Babylon. It's got all modern furniture. The outside is done in cedar. There's an in-ground pool in the backyard. I saw a picture of Silvana, the Spanish woman he lives with. She was dark and didn't seem so pretty. She worked as a secretary at Grumman (they make airplanes) and she wasn't at home in the daytime. Then I met Pauly, their little boy. What can I say? It was love at first sight. I took to the funny, open-faced little two-and-a-half-year-old, and he took to me, in an instant. It was like he was my long-lost baby brother.

I went with Pauly into his room. We plopped into his leatherlike floor beanbag chair and rolled around and watched TV. He was a spirited little kid, like me at his age. He had a mischievous glint in his eye. I could picture him soon grabbing quarters and sneaking across a wide boulevard, like I had done. I looked in his eyes and said, "I need you to help me out, Pauly." I could tell he understood, from my eyes, that this was important. "Show me which room your mommy sleeps in."

Paul was in the shower. Pauly took my hand in his little one and led me to a bedroom with a big waterbed. "Mommy sleeps here?" I asked. Pauly looked at me and nodded.

"Then where does Daddy sleep?" I asked him.

He took my hand and we walked into what looked like a spare bedroom with a twin bed in it.

"Daddy sleeps here—every night?" I asked.

He said, "Yes."

I believed him. And I admired Paul for staying for the sake of his son.

I took Pauly back in his room and we played and drew. I promised to show him Nintendo. His room had the Sesame Street toys and books my old room used to have, and the coloring books and the board games. Sitting in the middle of all those things, a quiet sadness filled me. I don't think you ever lose how you felt as a child in your room. It's there inside you always.

"Maybe we'll find some Smurf reruns," I said as I flicked on the television. I sat on the floor, my legs out in a wide V, and pulled little Pauly in front of me. He would be my special friend now. My little buddy.

As February turned to March, the other people at Future Physique got to know me as Paul's girlfriend. He used to take me upstairs to where the tanning room was—a balconylike space where you could see the whole workout floor. We used to eat up there. Even when he wasn't there or wasn't with me, I got special treatment from the staff. I didn't have to pay for drinks or to use the tanning bed.

By now I was working out with Paul until 9:30 several nights a week. Plus seeing Joey, my real love. Plus seeing my three escort regulars (and once in a while a customer Lacy would throw me). Plus seeing Lori and Maria when I could. Going to clubs and spending my prostitute money like water. (I saved practically nothing.) And I was seeing a lot of Jane. I'd go by her shop and she'd make me look beautiful. We'd rent video games. We'd drive in to Bensonhurst.

Jane liked to show off how tough she was for me. When she did my hair and face, she touched me and hugged me a lot. Jane paid a lot of attention to me and it made me feel good.

Jane is so pretty. Pretty people: I'm a sucker for them.

*   *   *

I saw the movie everyone was talking about: *Basic Instinct.*
Sharon Stone plays this sexy, gorgeous bisexual murderer. Michael
Douglas plays this cop who falls in love with her. I was so taken by it,
I saw it twice: once with friends; then at a drive-in theater, with
Paul. The sex scenes made me hot—like they were supposed to, I
guess. The second time I saw it, I wasn't wearing underwear—like
Sharon Stone wasn't, in the scene where the police take her in for
questioning.

She was very cocky and sure of herself in that scene. She made
those cops look like jerks.

She got away with everything.

I think Jane saw the movie, too, also probably more than once.

Paul, like Joey, had an over-the-store sexual hideaway. (I sure
know how to pick 'em, don't I?) Paul's was even more explicit. Forget
Joey's little Superman sticker; *Paul's* place would make your eyes
fall out of your head. Mirrors on the ceiling, on the walls, on the
door. One night when we were in there going through Paul's videos,
I came across a tape that looked like a labeled, self-made videotape.
I put it in the VCR.

"No," he said quickly. "Don't look at that."

"No," I said, my curiosity piqued. "I want to look at it."

And that's how I got introduced to Paul Makely's home movies.
There were all kinds of women writhing in sexual ecstasy. "I have
sex with them, and then I videotape them," he admitted.

"Well, you're obviously not very discriminating," I said, as one
ugly woman came on. She looked about fifty.

He asked me to let him make a video of me doing a little
striptease. I agreed to do it. What great shape I was in: one boyfriend
pushing me into an escort service, the other asking me to be in a
porn movie. And me going along with both of them.

Paul sold that video to "Hard Copy" for God knows how much
money. Made-up news of the "triple-X-rated tape" was all over the
tabloid headlines just as the ruckus from the TV movies was finally
dying down and I was trying my damnedest to settle in as a regular
prisoner at Albion. If you're a "celebrity prisoner," they make life
very tough on you. Other prisoners and the guards think you think
you're a bigshot and they single you out for hard treatment. These
things that Paul keeps doing to make himself money have hurt me a

lot. He's out there walking around. I'm behind bars, at other people's mercy.

In March, Paul took me up to Vermont. We went about three times. I told my parents about the trip, but they didn't know I was being sexual with Paul (though my father had suspicions). I just told them I wanted to go skiing.

We had fun. We'd go to Denny's for breakfast and drive right up. We stayed in a motel in Killington. Paul's friend Vinnie owns a place up there—Giuseppe's Restaurant. We went quad riding in Paul's all-terrain vehicle. We huddled around a fire, played in the snow. Paul was easier to be with than Joey. Paul was much more emotional. He'd keep everything inside—and then he'd start to cry. At those times I'd feel very, very compassionate toward him.

Paul suspected I was still seeing Joey, but I always denied it. We'd go through these sessions where he'd ask, "Are you seeing him?"

And I'd say, "No." And we'd repeat the question-and-answer until he decided to give up.

One night in April, Paul looked at me solemnly and asked, "Do you have something to tell me?"

I said, "No." What was he getting at?

"Are you sure?" he asked. Then he asked, "How come you always have so much money?" I was generous to Paul, as I was to all my friends.

"I've saved," I lied. "I have a bank account."

His solemn look persisted. "I know more than you think I know," he said. Then, like he was giving me the benefit of the doubt, he said, "I heard the craziest thing today. Somebody told me you were a prostitute."

That somebody turned out to be big-mouthed Chris Drellos, who had told a friend who also knew Paul. Paul had run into him at a gas station and somehow my name had come up.

I got very defensive. "Well, that somebody doesn't know what he's talking about!" I lied. "How could somebody say that?!"

He took my hands and acted like a teacher who's decided to be nice to the kid he's caught cheating. "You can tell me. I'm not going to leave," he said. "I just want you to level with me."

Well, I couldn't bring myself to level with him. "I used to do it," I said. "But I've stopped."

He chose to believe me.

Still, I guess he thought of me as this racy little thing. "Vixen," he called me. "You're a vixen."

The word stuck. That's how Joey thought of me, too. I guess. I smile and I frown when I think of it. *Vixen.* The trouble with me is that things other girls would be insulted by, or warned that they're stepping over the line by doing, I accept. *Vixen.* Where does it come from, that acceptance?

"You could never be loyal to me," Paul would say to his little vixen. He was testing me.

"Oh, really?" I'd tease back. "We could move to Texas or Arizona"—I had seen *Thelma and Louise,* so I thought of Texas—"and get married and everything will be okay." I was half-serious, half-joking. I didn't really want to get married, but I did want to escape my life. I quickly amended it. "No, Texas is too hot. Maybe we could move to New Jersey."

Paul cracked up, even though I didn't mean to be funny. I could tell it was one of those unintentionally funny things I sometimes say. The kind of thing that made Joey say, "You're a trip, babe."

Another time, I asked Paul to be my date at the Kennedy High Senior Prom. He laughed and said yes. Later he said he needed $2,000 to get his car's transmission replaced. I offered to loan the money to him. He accepted. I guess my prostitution didn't bother him so much that he couldn't benefit from the proceeds.

For all of Paul's nice-guy parts, he had a mean streak to him. People are complicated, aren't they? Joey's much slicker and sweet-talking and he believes in getting away with as much as you can in life. But he's not as mean as Paul could be. For example, Joey put my father on a pedestal—"How ya doin', Mr. Fisher!"—and made him feel great. All that B.S.-ing kept my dad from realizing that we were seeing each other. My father liked Joey, give or take the herpes event. My father was *snowed* by Joey.

With Paul it was different. Oil and water. Paul didn't even put up the pretense of charming him. My father did his usual routine—calling up Paul when I didn't get home until 2 or 3 A.M. on a school night and screaming, "I'll have you arrested for statutory rape, you bum!"

Paul knew I was seventeen—legal. He knew my father had no ammunition.

AMY FISHER

"Stay away from my daughter!" my father would yell.

"It's up to Amy if she wants to see me," Paul would reply, very coolly. And then he would just hang up on him. There weren't many more of those phone calls.

Sometimes Paul struck me. It hurt.

But Paul's rudeness to my father and his flashes of temper with me weren't what really pushed all my buttons—really drove a stake in my heart. What did *that* was another kind of meanness that I came to see in him. And that was his cruelty toward Pauly. That really killed me. He had no patience as a father. He punished that poor kid just for crying, for having a tantrum, for throwing his food—for things that all two- and three-year-olds *do*. He would make Pauly hysterical. It just ate me up inside. I *hated* it.

I always intervened. I pushed Paul aside and screamed at him and took Pauly into his room and soothed him and played with him.

Joey would *never* do this, I'd think. Joey is such a *man*.

Once when I was in Pauly's room with him, Pauly looked at me like he was hoping I could save him. You can see that innocent hope in a little kid's eyes. I felt powerful. I felt worthwhile. The feeling was good.

Now, if I could just hold on to it.

◆ ◆ ◆

PART
◆
3

11

To the Brink

◆

Amy didn't tell **Maria and Lori** that Paul was so rough on
his son. The girls weren't sure what to make of Amy's new
boyfriend, other than to think he had to be better than Joey,
because nobody could be worse. But one thing they had a
definite—negative—opinion on was the fact that Jane had all
but taken over Amy. In the process, Jane was snubbing the other
two girls and doing a full 180-degree turn in her persona.

"Before, Jane was a total sweetheart," Maria says. "All of a
sudden she started getting stuck up and bitchy." "Before, we all
used to go to lunch together at Taco Bell or Friendly's," Lori
remembers. "Me and Maria and Amy used to be really close.
And then Jane hung out with Amy for just two weeks, and
something changed, you know?"

Maybe it was the trips to Bensonhurst Amy was making with
Jane—trips that ended with them hanging out in the parking
lot of the Caesar's Bay shopping center, a stretch of cement
dramatically perched over the black water of The Narrows,
which separated Brooklyn from Staten Island. Maybe it was the
way Jane had taken over doing Amy's hair and makeup. Maybe
it was the reflected glamour of Jane's fur coat, her long
fingernails. Whatever it was, Amy was in Jane's thrall and Jane
seemed to be duly impressed with her evident power.

"Now Jane only called us if she wanted us to drive her to Brooklyn in one of our cars," Lori recalls. "She didn't want to drive her brand-new '92 Firebird into a bad neighborhood if she could get someone else to drive her. Maria and I felt used. One night Maria and I got into a fight with Jane over it. 'How come you just call us for our car?!' I asked. 'You've changed.'"

"I didn't change," Jane insisted toughly. "I'm just tired of people stepping all over me."

Maria and Lori couldn't remember anyone ever stepping on Jane. The two girls got into a fight with Jane, and Amy played peacemaker. Lori remembers: "She said, in this pleading voice, 'Come on, girls, we're all friends. No fighting.' You wanted to hug her, she was so sweet." But when tension increased, Amy stopped being so neutral. "When me and Maria got into fights with Jane, Amy always took Jane's side. Maria and I tried to tell Amy that Jane was a backstabber, but Amy wouldn't believe it. 'She's such a sweet girl,' Amy would say. We're like, *What?* You don't know the real Jane, Amy. You just know the fake Jane. Can't you see through her?"

For Maria, Amy's worshipful loyalty was troublingly familiar. She recalled having used that same line—"Can't you see through him?!"—about Joey.

Amy followed Jane as if she were her puppy. The more impressed and attentive Amy grew, the tougher and more full of bravado Jane seemed to become, as if she was cranking up her act—or some tendency inside her that had never come out before. Lori and Maria weren't sure which. Lori and Maria couldn't understand why Amy thought Jane was so pretty, and they got tired of Jane's bragging loudly to Amy about her father's Mafia connections. Even if it was true, the two wondered, why brag about it so much?

As winter turned to spring, Maria and Lori started spending more time with their boyfriends than with each other. When they did talk to each other, however, one or the other would ask, in a concerned, feeling-out kind of way, "How's Ame doin'?" "You talk to Ame?" Amy seemed to have too much on her plate. Between Joey and Paul and those escort-service guys who were always beeping her, how much could a girl handle? Having *one* boyfriend to mess up her head was enough.

Amy overdid it. When Lori and Maria took her to clubs, she

bought two, three, four rounds of drinks for everyone in their group. Maria, especially, whose family knew about budgeting, wondered how Amy could throw her money away like that. She'd stopped wondering how Amy *got* the money; she chose to take Amy's November explanation—that the men just took her out to dinner—with a kind of grudging acceptance.

Amy's transformation—from the eager, defenseless little sister they'd met at Jean Country to Jane's protégée and a girl with a secret life—was disconcerting. In certain obvious ways she'd outpaced her two older friends, and sometimes Maria wondered if it was losing her role as mentor that bent her nose out of shape. But in other ways, Maria felt even more like a big sister to Amy than ever, albeit an unlistened-to one. It took a pizza parlor manager's daughter from North Bellmore to see just how over her head the gangster-struck Merrick girl had gotten.

Amy was trying so hard to be a *cugine,* Maria thought, but at heart she was still a Jappy-dressed girl whose father watched the Financial News Network. To her, Bensonhurst was this exotic world whose ways she seemed to want to master to some ultimate degree. She didn't understand that the Eighty-sixth Street regulars were not glamorous toughs floating above the law. They were just kids playing out the last gasp of a stylized one-hundred-year-old Sicilian ritual before they married one another and settled, just like their parents, in Perma-Stoned buildings in Brooklyn or houses in Bellmore, Wantagh, or Levittown. Overnight, the girls would shed their tight, showy clothes. They'd stay funny and peppy and bossy. But they'd also get fat and frustrated.

On the way to that inevitable life—or maybe resisting it— Jane was turning up the volume on the toughest part of herself, for an awed audience of one. It sure seemed to Lori and Maria, at least, that Jane was putting on an act—and Amy was eating it up.

"You okay, Ame?" Maria asked one afternoon in late April, when Amy stopped over at Maria's house to trade back some clothes she had borrowed. Amy and Maria had traded clothes all through the summer and fall and winter, and now that Amy and Jane were so tight, *they* had started trading. Maria welcomed Amy's offer of the exchange; she didn't want her hard-paid-for

Umbro shorts and B.U.M. khakis to go riding around on Jane's rump. Maria's television was tuned to MTV; the "Wayne's World" guys were bobbing up and down in their car to the plaintive strains of Queen's "Bohemian Rhapsody." "Mama, I killed a man, put a bullet through his head," Freddy Mercury wailed, while Wayne and Garth smiled and goofed.

Amy said, "Yeah, I'm okay," but she looked to Maria pale and confused.

They switched jeans and tops. Maria felt a little ache. They used to do this all the time; now they did it rarely.

Amy's beeper beeped.

"Is that Joey?" Maria asked warily.

Amy shook her head. "He's at Jetsky's track meet."

" 'Jetsky'?"

"His daughter." Amy had this thing about Joey as a good father—as if it were both a sign of nobility and also, somehow, a big turn-on. Of all the things Joey was, Maria had to concede, that was probably the best thing about him.

Still, the more into his kids he was, the more *not* into Amy he had to be. Didn't her starry-eyed friend see that? Maria sucked her cigarette smoke up into her nostrils, shook her head forsakenly, and said, with exaggerated patience, "He is *never* gonna *leave* her." The "her" came out a pleadingly grunted *"huh."*

Joey was a sore subject between the two girls. He really had Amy whipped, Maria thought. She hated how her younger friend cried over that fat, old, married guy when she could have a young, single boyfriend with a great body, like Lori's Danny or her own Gio. Maria talked about Gio a lot—he was twenty-one and in the marines. She had Gio's guido bow taped to her bedroom mirror and was always pulling the picture of him— flexing his workout-pumped muscles—out of her wallet.

Amy's beeper went off again. "I gotta go," she said.

Maria narrowed her eyes. "It's not none of those escort guys beeping you, is it?"

"No," Amy lied. Little did Maria know that Amy called herself "Maria Murabito" when she was with her pig-dentist, her cute Italian car-leaser, and her nice-but-pathetic electronics magnate.

"I swear," Maria said, "if you're sleeping with those guys, I'll smack you in the head, I'll be so pissed."

Amy smiled. When Maria was like this, she was just like Grandma Vise. Still, Grandma Vise was dead; Mary Lynn was, by Joey's rules, verboten. And from the look on Maria's and Lori's faces whenever that beeper went off, Amy had half a feeling that they-knew-but-didn't-want-to-know what the nature of her services to her escort customers really was. And Jane? Jane *encouraged* Amy's raciness. Jane had become Amy's outlaw role model.

Amy knew in her heart that the prostitution, a hideous habit she couldn't seem to break, had already taken its toll. It had hardened her. It gave her days a constant undercurrent of cynicism, pain, and self-contempt well beyond her coping mechanisms. No wonder escort services didn't take girls who were under eighteen (in California, not until they were twenty-one). Apart from the penal-code hell to pay, underage girls were mental-health risks. Even with girls over eighteen, only those with damaged childhoods had sufficient desperation to seek the life—and a skewed enough sense of human relationships to accommodate it. And most of them gave up, or cracked up—or both.

Maria walked Amy through her ornate, shag-carpeted living room, and to her front door. The girls paused by the plastic-covered velveteen couch. Over MTV, Bel Biv Devoe's "Poison" had halted its instrumental backup so that Ronny Devoe could contemptuously brag: "Me and the crew used to do her. . . ." And the words echoed into the next room.

Sometimes, Maria thought, It's real tough being a girl.

"You going to Eighty-sixth Street?" Maria asked Amy.

"Probably. Later."

"Beep me. We'll meet up."

Amy said, "Okay."

But Maria knew Amy would be with Jane, and she and Lori really didn't want to run into Jane these days.

As Maria watched her little friend back her LeBaron out of her parents' driveway, she was tempted to open the door and yell "Be careful on the on-ramp!" Amy's driving was so tragic, especially when she had so much on her mind; and these days

Amy's mind seemed as crowded as the inside of a jumbo spin dryer.

But Maria didn't say anything. She figured she'd gotten bossy enough for one hour. Plus, Amy wouldn't listen anyway.

The next time Maria saw Amy it would be in the visitors' room of the Nassau County Jail.

♦ ♦ ♦

I was infatuated with Jane. I idolized Jane. She was so beautiful, so tough.

Jane had a *bop*. A bop is a tough-Italian way of walking. It has a sway in it. It says, I have it all together; don't mess with me. Her toughness was almost like a guy's. But at the same time she was so feminine—five-foot-six and busty. Now that it was getting warm, she had taken off the full-length silver-fox coat that she had sashayed around in all winter—she's such an Italian princess!—and she'd strut around the cars, showing off her figure in tight jeans and tight shirts. She was very volatile and animated, and her long red nails would flick up and down as she chain-smoked Newports and swigged from her bottle of Cisco.

Cisco is the locally bottled alcohol that all the Eighty-sixth Street kids drink. It comes in different flavors. Jane always drank berry. She calls it "liquid crack." I could never handle Cisco. The one time I tried it, I almost fainted. It must be 200-proof.

Jane always had the best hair—which isn't surprising, since she worked as a colorist and her mom was also a beauty operator. She had just dyed her hair eggplant and it looked great. I wanted that color for *my* hair. She would hug me and say, "Come by the shop and I'll make you so pretty." She was always hugging me, and she was always making me pretty: tweezing my eyebrows so they arched like hers; gelling my hair so it looked like hers; doing my eyes and my mouth. Jane was very protective of me. If somebody at Eighty-sixth Street said something snide to me—it didn't even have to be as strong as "fuck you"—Jane would give that person a narrow-eyed, deep, deep look and say very calmly, "Don't mess with my girl." I always felt safe after that.

Jane called me her "girl" a lot. In late April she had also started calling me her "wife." At times it sounded like she was trying to talk me into having a really intimate relationship with her. I don't think Lori and Maria ever caught on to that part.

The person Jane was most possessive with was her boyfriend,

Rocky. Rocky was gorgeous—he looked just like Ken Wahl in the TV show "Wiseguy." He had a brain the size of a chickpea (not that Jane cared). Jane was twenty and Rocky was nineteen. He was still in high school because he'd been left back. Every night we'd drive down to Eighty-sixth Street and to Caesar's Bay, where Jane would look for Rocky, and Rocky would betray her, and Jane would go after Rocky. It was a great little passion play.

The parking lot of the Caesar's Bay shopping center is on Bay Parkway, five blocks off Eighty-sixth Street. Caesar's Bay is a huge, L-shaped shopping area right on the water, where The Narrows flows out into the Atlantic Ocean. On the east side there's a Waldbaum's, a Radio Shack, a pizza parlor, a liquor store, and Trader Horn. On the west side, there's a big, domed tennis court. On the north, there's a bank and a Roy Rogers. And on the south side there's a Toys "Я" Us and the flea market. The flea market is basically a mall with dozens of kiosks and stores separated by curtained areas. The aisles are laid out with street names on signs hanging from the ceiling: Broadway, Fourteenth Street, Amsterdam Avenue: pretend-Manhattan. There are fluorescent lights and pop music playing over an intercom. A section by the entrance, "Vogue Plaza," sells clothes. Lots of guidettes—in spandex bodysuit tops, platform heels, and big hair—work the stands.

At night, when all the stores are closed up, Caesar's Bay turns into a whole different world: a place to hang out. There are hundreds of kids there, all very tough, very gang-oriented. Between the tennis court and the Toys "Я" Us, there's a small unlit parking area tucked away from the shopping center, right on the water. The steel railing is separated from the water by piles of large rocks. On the other side of the water you can see a line of dark yellow lights. To the right, the Verrazano Narrows Bridge, connecting Brooklyn to Staten Island, juts out over the water; the cars moving over it look like a slow parade of diamonds. When I'm locked into my solitary room at Albion at 10 P.M. (they put me in solitary—a small room with a mattress on the floor—after another prisoner threatened me), I sometimes remember, with a little pang, what those endless nights were like.

To get to Caesar's Bay, you first cruise Eighty-sixth Street itself, this big, wide, six-lane street that's the main drag of Bensonhurst. It's so eerie and glamorous—especially if you're used to the suburbs. The buildings are close together and old. The B-train track overhead is like a huge, low, black ceiling, cutting out the night sky. It's like being in a coal tunnel, so dismal and dark. If ever there was a gangster place, this is it.

Everyone would come driving in at 10, a half-hour after the stores were closed. (The pizzeria stayed open, like a lighthouse.) They drove through Eighty-sixth Street and down Bay Parkway in their decked guidomobiles. People were hitting on each other, making deals, making moves, slugging their Cisco, stealing one another's boyfriends and girlfriends and getting into fights about it, dancing on the street corner and in the parking lot to the turned-up sound systems playing club music. Everyone liked Hot 97. A couple of the kids played KISS-FM—98.7, the more black version of the same music. Me, 'cause of Joey, I loved the '70s sounds on classic K-Rock. But the Doobie Brothers and Fleetwood Mac did *not* go with the scene here.

Being down there in the middle of it all eased my pain. I could forget I was being jerked around by Joey, forget I was a prostitute. Down there, screwed-up lives seemed all right.

Take Jane and Rocky, for instance. Rocky would grab other girls and kiss them right in front of Jane. He didn't care if Jane saw; Rocky wanted to make it with anything that walked. Jane would bop over and smack Rocky. Or she'd smack the girl. Jane liked being violent. She loved making threats. "I know where you live," she'd say to those girls kissing Rocky. "I know where you *sleep.*"

Sometimes, if the girl Rocky had been kissing didn't seem scared enough, Jane would bop over to her brand-new '92 Firebird and throw open the door and fish out her baseball bat. Dangling from the rearview mirror, where some kids had guido bows and others (like me) had foam-rubber dice, Jane had an air freshener in the form of a Chippendale's nude male dancer—like the guys we used to see at Escapes. The poor little dummy would go pinging around like a yo-yo when she banged the bat out of the car. Rocky and the girl got in his guidomobile. They were *out* of there.

A lot of the Eighty-sixth Street kids were nicknamed according to their looks. Frankie Nose was this tall, funny guy—very built—with a big, weird nose. He had a brand-new Lincoln Mark VII, a $35,000 car. We used to see him at this hot Bensonhurst club where you had to be twenty-one to get in. (But we *knew* people.) Skinny Vinnie: well, his name is self-explanatory. Skinny Vinnie always wore a denim jacket with a picture on the back of Bugs Bunny wearing a leather jacket, carrying a chain and a gun. Other kids were down to earth—like Rory, a quiet, intelligent blond girl who was only fifteen and always talked about how she and her boyfriend were in love and were going to get married and that he would be a doctor. Nobody else on Eighty-sixth Street but Rory talked like that. Not many kids had their whole lives planned out like that.

Skinny Vinnie's best friend and Rory's boyfriend was a boy we all knew as Petey G. He was a skinny guy, so dark and curly haired he could have been Spanish or even Arab. Instead of driving a typical guidomobile, Petey G. was a little more original. He had a burgundy T-bird. Everybody else bopped around and talked real fast. Petey G. just leaned on his car, with his feet crossed at the ankles and his head down, nodding and saying little and letting everyone come to *him.* He had an older brother, Anthony, who was often at his side. Petey G. always dressed immaculately, mostly in suits, and he always smelled real good. He had gone to college for a year. People thought of him as a brain, even though he worked as a clerk in an auto-supply store. Petey G. was different—and very, very cool.

"'Ey, Petey G., Petey G., what's up? How ya doin'?" other guys would jump around, asking. Next to how still and cool he was, they looked like prizefighters warming up. They'd pat him on the back, talk a mile a minute, moving their hands and all. Petey G. would just stand there, looking at the ground, taking it in. What he was thinking, no one could tell. Then, when he felt like it, he just walked away. If you asked Petey G. a personal question, he'd say, "None of your business." Or: "Do I ask you about *your* life?" That shut people up.

A lot of kids at Eighty-sixth Street didn't like Petey G. They thought he was stuck up. Maria thought he was a geek. But he had a mystique about him, which you couldn't help but admire. *I* admired it, anyway. Just like I admired Jane's.

In the morning, after being out late in Bensonhurst, I'd drag myself out of bed and go to school. It was getting very bad, my cutting-school habit. I showed up for school only two or three days a week. If Attendance called the house, I would pretend I was Rose Fisher. "My daughter's got a temperature," I'd say. If I did that too much, I'd have Joey call in. He had his Elliot Fisher voice down pat.

I would lift myself out of bed in the morning and look at the clock—I had overslept first period: home economics. That was nothing. Who could sit in a class baking sourdough bread and making stir-fry at 7:30 in the morning and not get sick? But when I also slept through second period, Spanish, after a day that I completely cut, I would look at my wall poster and then say to myself, "I *am* a female James Dean."

I would get to school for third period. English. Our teacher was sick—something bad: cancer or AIDS—so we had a permanent replacement teacher, easier to push around. When I'd get a beeper call I wouldn't even bother to raise my hand and get the bathroom pass. I'd just pick up and leave.

Fourth period: economics. The teacher was a pushover. All he did was hand out dittos. Everybody would cheat: copy other people's dittos and hand them back in and the teacher would grade them as tests. I got an eighty.

Fifth period: sociology. Everyone called it Bullshit 101.* It was my bagel-and-soda time. I'd go to the cafeteria and get my bagel with ham, lettuce, and cheese, and a can of soda, and I'd bring it back to class. By the time I sat down at my desk, class was half over, so I figured I might as well eat. By the time I finished eating, sixth-period bell rang.

Gym was sixth period. I always cut gym.

One day after school in late April I went to Paul's house to play with Pauly. I heard the kid crying the minute I walked in the door. Paul had spanked him for wetting his pants and had locked him in his room. I hated when that happened! I cannot *tell* you what that did to me! To smack a *little kid?* "He's only three!" I screamed to Paul. "He can't help wetting himself! Why make the poor kid terrified! Why mess him up for life?!"

"Come on, Pauly, come on, buddy," I said softly, as I walked in his room and he toddled up to me, crying in big noisy gusts. "It'll be okay." I was three once. You can't help wetting yourself. So you spill chocolate milk—is that such a crime? When children are made to

---

*In fairness to John F. Kennedy High, its 1992 graduating class earned the highest percentage of Regents diplomas awarded to any school in New York State. Kennedy students score far above the national average on SAT scores. Ninety-seven percent of its graduating seniors go off to college, 75 percent to four-year colleges. And in fairness to Amy, attendance records indicate that her habit of cutting school was not as egregious as she remembers it.

think their tiny screw-ups are criminal, maybe that's when they grow up to commit crimes.

Paul had a really nice house and pool. Pauly had lots of toys. But I'll tell you something: He will not remember the pool and the toys nearly as much as he'll remember his father's slaps.

I held the poor, sobbing kid until he calmed down. I held him so long and close, I almost didn't know where the cries were coming from, his body or mine. When he finally stopped crying, I made a funny face. It took him a few seconds, but then his face lit up in a smile.

Tough little guy. Survivor. Maybe I could do for him what Aunt Mary Lynn had done for me. Maybe the lesson would take a little better the second time around.

I called Joey that day and asked if he could be with me. No, he said. He had to go home and oversee some workmen—they were checking the security alarm in his house. Because of the work he did, he could never be too careful. "And my children have to be safe," he said. "I want my children safe."

He's such a good father, I thought. The opposite of Paul.

My beeper started beeping. Two of my regulars: the dentist and the electronics guy. How did I get myself into this? Why can't I give this up? Trying to unravel the source of my decisions only made me more confused—like taking a loose thread and working yourself back into a big messy knot. If Joey was so wonderful, how come he started me with the prostitution, which made me feel like shit? If Joey *wasn't* so wonderful, then how come I wanted to be with him so much? If prostitution sucked, then why was I still doing it? How come I was so angry that I couldn't be with Joey—yet also felt I loved Paul? How could I love Paul when he hit me and made porno videos of all the girls he had sex with and—worse than anything— was so tough on his kid?

Every compensation I tried was worse than the thing it was making up for. Every reaction was worse than the thing I reacted against. Every time I turned around and did something else, I messed myself up more. My life didn't make any sense.

I closed my eyes tight and wished I could be back with my old friends—Jennifer and Debbi and Heather and Jill. That tame little life: the bar mitzvahs, the ski trips, the giggles about sex. "I slept with Jared! I slept with Jared!" They had taken three steps away from those old days, like normal girls. I had taken a hundred. They had nice cars and were going to decent colleges. I didn't know where I was going, and my cars had led me to hell.

After this, things started getting more intense. I'm going to try to remember, day by day, the week that changed my life. You'll also hear what the police detectives saw and thought. Remember, when you get to that part, those pea-brains who arrested me weren't on my side one bit. They wanted to nail me even worse than they did.

But they *still* said what they said about Joey's behavior and attitude—didn't they?

Watch.

12

The Shooting

♦

When I think about the days Wednesday, May 13, through Tuesday, May 19, it's like reaching back into a nightmare. No, it's worse than a nightmare. In a nightmare, you're a helpless victim of events. You're being acted on. In this nightmare, I was the actor. I planned and did these things. That fact is as much a nightmare for me today as the events themselves.

Tuesday, May 12 I called Joey from school and asked if I could see him that night, but he had something to do with one of the kids.

"When *can* we be together?" I asked. "I mean, really together."

"Patience," he said.

"Joey, you're so full of shit." I thought about what Maria had said. "You're never going to leave her."

"Hey. Ne——"

" 'Never predict. To predict is negative. To anticipate is positive.' "

"That's my girl. I love you."

"I love you."

"I love you more." He hung up.

Months ago, in the Freeport Motor Inn, he had said, "A marriage is till death do us part. Sometimes you just have to speed up the last part." On the boat he had said, "With the body missing, I'd have to wait seven years to get the insurance money. Baby, I can't wait that long." He had said that if Mary Jo was no longer around, if she had her "accident," he'd buy me an LSC or a Corvette. I didn't need those things. I needed *him*. The wonderful lover-father I idolized. To steady my life.

Fifth-period bell rang. It was bagel-and-soda time and I'd already slept through home ec and Spanish. The other day my registration form for Nassau Community College arrived. Registration was only one day: next Tuesday, May 19. They would really let a kid like me in? What a joke.

At 5:30 I arrived at the electronics guy's office. He was my easiest, steadiest customer—every week the same time. Locked door. Pulled shade. My cut-offs and sweats on the back of the chair as he unzipped his pants.

I think he figured as long as I just watched him masturbate, he could go home with a clean conscience to his wife. But what did he think when he looked past me sitting there in my thong-back panties and push-up bra and saw the framed picture of his teenaged son, a year younger than me?

Later, my psychiatrist at Huntington Hospital said I was abusing myself by my prostitution. But I didn't feel as bad about being with the electronics guy as I did with the dentist. Maybe that not-feeling is the worst self-abuse of all.

Wednesday, May 13 I drove from school to The Quintessential Look.

I walked into the shop and plopped myself down in a seat in front of the mirror at Jane's coloring stand. "Okay, do my hair like yours," I said. I had told Joey, on the phone after I had called him at the shop, that I was going to get eggplant hair. "You'll look beautiful," he said.

After Jane did the color—mine came out more purple than hers because her natural hair color was darker than mine—she and I went back to the little employee area in back. We unwrapped the bagels that I brought and popped open the spouts of our cartons of OJ. She peeled off her plastic coloring gloves, lit a Newport, narrowed her eyes, and started stomping around in a bop.

"I am going to kill her," she said. She was talking about the girl Rocky had been fooling around with the other night. "I mean it—I am going to kill the bitch. I am going to get a gun and blow her fucking head off."

"Very funny," I said. "Where are you going to get a gun?"

Jane got defensive. She gets defensive when you challenge her toughness. "What do you mean? I can't get a gun? I can get a gun!" she said, with her "yo" accent, throwing her hands around.

"Jane, don't you think you're overdoing it?"

"No! I can get a gun. You don't know too much, do you? Anyone can get a gun. You can get a gun in two minutes. They sell them in Brooklyn, they sell them on Canal Street in Manhattan. You just have to know how to get them."

As she was talking, I was looking out the window, kind of drifting off. I wasn't listening to her. The words just kept repeating over and over in my mind: If I could get a gun, if *I* could get a gun . . .

"Could you get me a gun?" I asked Jane.

"What?" I guess those words didn't sound right, coming from her little girl, whom she always protected.

"Yeah, I want a gun."

She kept looking at me, like I was blowing her mind.

"Why do you want a gun?"

"I just want one." I started lying and making excuses. "Just for protection, just to have one." Then I admitted it. "I want to shoot someone."

Immediately she asked, "Joey?"

"No. His wife."

She looked down, and when she looked back up there was a smile on her face. "For real?" she asked. When I nodded, she said, "Okay." But then, as if she couldn't believe what I was asking, she started in on her mother routine. Did I understand the consequences? Did I know how much trouble I'd get into if I got caught? "You could go to jail for twenty-five years."

I shrugged her off. "Nothing's gonna happen," I said.

"Did you tell Joey?"

"I'm going to tell him later today."

"You know, we could get it tonight."

"I'd need someone to help me do it, too."

"We can get that . . ." She was warming to the idea. "When it's over, and you get that LSC, you and I can drive down to South Carolina." Jane's family had a house there, with live-in servants and all kinds of animals.

"How are we going to get it?" I asked. "Who's the gun dealer?"

She said nothing for about thirty seconds, making me guess. And then she said, "Petey G."

That night, I went to meet Joey at Complete at 5:15, just as the other workers were leaving for the day and after the secretary (whom he fought like cats and dogs with) was gone. I was wearing shorts and a tight top.

We went upstairs and made love. Afterward, I rolled over on top of him, pointed my finger at his nose, and said, "I have a surprise for you. Bang-bang." At first he didn't get it. I just kept looking at him, my expression saying, C'mon, don't you get it?

Finally he lifted himself up on his elbows and said, "What? What, you want me to get you a gun?"

"No," I said. "I'm *going* to get a gun—tonight. And I'm going to shoot your wife."

He laughed. "You're a trip. Where'd they grow you from?" He was as disbelieving as Jane had been.

I told him about the afternoon's conversation with her. He started believing me. "We're going to Brooklyn tonight, to find Petey G."

"Don't tell him *one* thing about me," Joey said, making an air-slicing gesture with his left hand. As for Jane, Joey said, in his typical insinuating style, "You tell her to do the right thing. Explain to her the facts, what's going on. You know what to do." He pointed to his head. "You got it up here. I know I don't have to tell you how to be." What he was saying was, If Jane gets you that gun, Jane's in this as deep as you are, baby. She better fucking shut up about me.

I told him Jane doesn't scare easily.

Joey pointed in my face. "*Make* her scared."

Like so many times before, I felt we were Bonnie and Clyde.

"All right," he said. "How are you going to do this?"

I probably shrugged; the whole thing wasn't *real* to me. "I'll just shoot her. I'll just go out in the night." To me, shooting people was always about night raids by people in ski masks.

"No, no, no! Not when my kids are home. *Never* at night. You do it in the afternoon."

156

"In broad daylight?"

"Never, *never* do you put my kids in jeopardy."

"But there'll be people on the street."

He shook his head. "Everyone in the neighborhood works. It's a quiet residential neighborhood. And I'll be at work. I need to have people around."

Then he told me exactly how to do it.

"Go up to the door. When she answers it, don't even wait for her to open the screen door. Just shoot and keep shooting. Here. Like this."

He stood up behind me and leaned over and put his face next to mine and hugged my hands with his longer ones, making them stretch out in a shooting stance. He clasped his big hands over my smaller hands, pushed my palms together. His two big index fingers flexed together over mine in a silent bang-bang.

I turned. He forcefully pulled my face to him by my chin. He looked deep into my eyes. "You'd really do this for me?"

I nodded.

He looked at me and said, "I'll be able to live and breathe again." Then he said, "I love you."

That is what *really* happened, people. The indelible memory of all of those words is why I seemed so convincing (you saw my truthfulness; I know you did) when I stood up in Judge Goodman's courtroom before my sentencing and said, "When Joey Buttafuoco learned of my intentions toward his wife, he encouraged me."

I checked my watch: 7:45. I was supposed to meet Jane at her cousin's in Oceanside, forty-five minutes ago. As I got dressed, my beeper beeped. Ten minutes later it beeped again. I pictured Jane stomping around at her cousin's, flicking her ashes, going, "Where *is* she?"

I tried to hurry, but Joey wanted to keep talking. For some reason, he wanted to talk about Paul. I had told Joey a few weeks ago that I'd loaned Paul $2,000 to get his transmission replaced. All of a sudden he asked, "Did you get that two grand back from Paul?"

When I told Joey that Paul hadn't paid me back yet, he got very adamant, very upset, almost mad.

"Get it back! It's not right, someone who cares about you keeping your money. *I* don't take anything from you. I give, I don't take. Paul's a bum! Get it back!"

He was almost yelling. I couldn't figure out why he was going on about Paul and the money, but his tirade touched me and flattered me. Joey *is* the only one who loves me, I decided.

Then Joey held me by my arms and said, "We're gonna be together forever. Who is this guy? He's a nobody. *Get the money back!*"

Jane beeped for the third time; it was 8:25 P.M.

Since Joey knew Oceanside better than I, I followed his car to Jane's cousin's address. He honked and drove off. He was going to Maximum Fitness to work out.

That was the last time I ever saw my lover, Joey Buttafuoco. In person. Face to face. In my life.

Jane and I took my car down the Southern State to the Belt to Exit 5: Bensonhurst. The dice on my rearview were dangling along, as we switched stations from KISS to K-Rock (Jane's a classic-rock fan like me) and back. En Vogue was singing: *"Never gonna get it, never gonna get it . . ."* They were four tough, sexy girls who had it all over the guys—just like us Lady Mobsters were supposed to be.

When we got to Bensonhurst, Jane and I cruised around until we found Petey's car. I waited in the car while Jane went to talk to him. I watched her lean in close, talking right into his ear. He nodded, nodded—then looked up and signaled to me.

"You have something you want to talk to me about?" he asked as I approached.

"Yeah," I said. "Can you get me a gun?"

"Depends. What do you want it for?"

"To kill my boyfriend's wife."

He gave me a look: What, are you nuts?

I started explaining. He procrastinated in responding.

"Okay, forget it." I started back to the car.

"No, no, no," he said, pulling me back. "I don't care what you want to do with it. You want it, I can get it." I guess it was his Italian honor code.

I told him there was more to it than my getting the gun. I wanted him to drive me, to help me carry it out.

"Okay," he said, trying to figure out if he wanted to get involved, "but I'm going to need money for my expenses. I'm going to have to take a day off work."*

"How much do you want?"

"A thousand."

I shook my head.

"Nine hundred."

I shook it again.

"Eight."

"Deal." I figured the gun itself was probably worth less than fifty bucks, but how many idiots could I get to do this?

"Bring the money tomorrow night." Then he wanted to know about Joey. Despite my promise to Joey two hours before, I told Peter his name and I told him about Complete. "I'll check him out," Peter said in his best tough-guy voice.

I went to Paul's house after school to play with my little pal Pauly.

Pauly was having his nap, so I went into his room and lay down next to him, just like Mary Lynn used to do with me. He woke up. I smiled into his sleepy face, hoping I was reassuring him that the world was okay, like she had reassured me. But then something happened that stunned me—threw everything out of whack. All of a sudden, Pauly rolled over on me and started trying to kiss me. On the *lips*. I don't know, maybe I was overreacting but I thought: this isn't right! He was *three* years old! What was being *done* to this poor, hurt, tough little kid that he would try to do something like this?

"Paul!" I went looking for him. "Do you know what Pauly just tried to do? Do you *know*?" When I told him, he got mad and dismissive.

He said, "Why are you saying these things?"

I stood there and said, "That's not the way a three-year-old is supposed to act!" I thought Pauly's behavior was abnormal.

---

*When he was arrested on June 11, Peter Guagenti claimed he never knew what Amy wanted to do with the gun he was selling her. That statement, from which he never deviated, enabled him to be charged only with third-degree criminal possession of a weapon, not the far more serious conspiracy-to-commit-murder.

Paul's phone rang. He turned away and picked up the phone and started talking; ignoring me. I stood there, trying to talk to him. He moved away the the phone. I followed him, talking.

Finally, he just stood up and ordered, "Leave!"

I tore out of there, sad and furious—at so many things all together, I couldn't even figure out what. It all just seemed useless —everything.

That new song that they were plastering all over the radio— "Jump"—came on. Jane and I had heard it the other day. "Daddy Mack'll make you jump! jump! jump!" the kids sang. "Mack Dad'll make you jump! jump! jump!" The singers named themselves Mack Daddy and Daddy Mack. The singers were thirteen-year-old boys. Daddy Mack and Mack Daddy mean "pimp."

We took Jane's car into Brooklyn that night. We found Petey G's car. "Do you have the money?" he asked, when I opened the door and got in next to him.

"Yeah," I said. "Do you have the gun?"

"Not yet," he said. "Give me the money and I'll get it."

I took the eight hundred-dollar bills out of my wallet, but I didn't give them to him. "How do I know you're not just going to take this and run?"

"Here's how." He pulled out his wallet and opened it. Two neat rows of credit cards faced each other. "Pick out any one, and take it as collateral," he said proudly.

I picked a Citibank MasterCard. It had *Peter Guagenti* stamped on it as cardholder. From that moment on, I stopped thinking of him as Petey G. He was Peter. My business associate. We exchanged beeper numbers. I gave him directions to my house: the Belt to the Southern State to the Meadowbrook, Merrick Road to Hewlett Avenue to Berkley Lane. He said he'd leave early—he didn't know Long Island. So he wasn't such a been-around guy, after all.

I wanted to make sure Peter wouldn't back out at the last minute. "Why do you want to do this for me. Is it just the money?" I asked, trying to feel him out.

He said, "I'm not doing this for *you*. I'm doing it for me. When all this is over, I'll wait a couple of months and I'll walk into Complete Auto Body and talk to Joey, and Joey will hook me up nice."

Sure, I said to myself. If you ask Joey for a job in return for this favor you did, Joey will say, I don't know what you're talking about. Get the hell out of here.

On the way home, Jane and I laughed about how if she got on one side of Peter and I got on the other, and we squeezed, he'd squish like a marshmallow. I didn't want to do the shooting myself. I wanted to get Peter to shoot Mary Jo *for* me.

◆ ◆ ◆

In subsequent press accounts, Peter Guagenti was treated highly sympathetically. A paperback book on the case, *Lethal Lolita,* referred to him as "naïve"—entirely the opposite of the impression Amy got of him: a "frail young man" who "lived an unassuming life in his parents' two-story home in Bensonhurst." A *Newsday* report featured Bensonhurst neighbors expressing their shock that this "good kid" from a "close-knit Italian family" could have landed himself in such trouble.

For all the disingenuousness of these accounts, Guagenti, twenty-one, had, indeed, been an honors student—at John Dewey High School—and had for a short while attended Fordham University, expressing an interest in medicine. He had, however, a record for disorderly conduct stemming from a possession-of-stolen-property charge.

Guagenti's parents were themselves born and raised in Italy. Like a declining but still substantial number of Bensonhurst youth, he was first-generation Italian-American. His parents, Luigi and Carmelina, were hospital workers; his brother, Anthony, also an Eighty-sixth Street regular, was a transit policeman, and his sister, Christine, worked in the Manhattan district attorney's office. Peter Guagenti suffered a collapsed lung in the fall of 1991; his condition required surgery. His father died of a heart attack just before Christmas, throwing the family into deep grieving.

Peter was a working-class immigrant's son; Amy, a suburban girl confusedly perched between social classes, ethnic groups, and religious identities. He had a patina of macho over great vulnerability; she had already—riskily, combustibly—done the same thing in her own life. She found him charismatic, while the more knowing Maria found him "geeky," and others found him naïve. So they set off to impress each other, to work together.

They alone bought each other's self-fantasy.

♦ ♦ ♦

Friday, May 15 I was asleep when my beeper, on my bedside table, woke me. I looked at the clock—it was just after 8:30. I had overslept Spanish again. The number on my beeper screen was 007. Joey hardly ever called me this early.

I dialed Complete's number. "So did you get it?" Joey asked.

I sat upright, rubbing sleep out of my eyes. "Get what?"

"The piece. The thing." He was anxious.

"Not yet. But I'm going to. I gave the guy money. I took his Citibank card as collateral."

"Did you see it?" He had to know every detail.

"No, but the guy definitely has it."

"What kind is it?" It was almost like he was testing me.

"It's a twenty-two." That's what Peter said it would be.

"Perfect," Joey said. "When it goes in, it'll ricochet all a-round."

I wasn't exactly sure what this piece of technical information meant, but I didn't let on.

I wanted to hang up and get to school, but Joey pressed me with one more question. "Did you get the money back from Paul?"

The thought of that ugly afternoon yesterday made me cranky and depressed. In my head I disinvited Paul to my senior prom. "No, I forgot to even ask him for it. We were fighting. It's a long story. Don't worry, we broke up, anyway."

He asked, "Are you *sure?*"

"Yeah, I'm sure." I don't know if I was touched or confused by how much Joey was pushing to get me mad at Paul. (In case you haven't noticed, I don't think about people's motives or my own feelings. I just react.) If he was doing it to make me more dependent on him, it was working, I guess.

"See, I told you the guy didn't care about you."

"I know," I said. "I love you."

"I love you, too."

We hung up.

* * *

My Story

I was in English when my beeper vibrated on my waist. The replacement teacher was talking about *Beowulf*. I looked down: 007. "I've got to go to the bathroom," I muttered as I whipped out of class and to the two pay phones under the cathedral windows by the auditorium.

"What?" I asked, when Joey picked up the phone at Complete. I was slightly bugged by his pestering me. I had cut and walked out of enough classes already this year.

"I just wanted to hear your voice." A pause. "Did the guy call?"

"Not yet. Soon."

"Don't mention my name. Don't tell him anything about me. He doesn't know your last name, does he?"

I couldn't remember. I said, "No."

"Good." Joey didn't know that Peter was coming along with me; that I was trying to get Peter to *do* it; that Jane and I thought I *could*. If he had known Peter was coming along, or Jane knew what she knew, he would have been *furious*. And paranoid out of his mind.

My beeper vibrated. I looked down. It was Peter's beeper number. "It's him," I told Joey. "Should I call him back?"

"Yeah, call him back right now."

I looked around for another kid to get change from, and then I called Peter back at his store. The line was busy. I kept calling. Busy, busy, busy. Ten minutes later I finally got through.

"I'm getting it tonight. We'll do it Monday," Peter said. "Get the plates." That referred to a deal we had made. He would drive me only on the condition that I got another set of license plates to put over his.

Joey then beeped again.

When I called Joey back and told him, he sounded excited. He didn't want to know what day the shooting was planned for. "Surprise me," he said. He said not to call him afterward. He'd call *me*. "I probably won't call you for a couple of months," he said, "but it will be worth it in the end."

I slipped back into my seat just as the teacher was finishing talking about Chaucer.

Sunday, May 17 Jane and I decided we'd steal the license plates to put over Peter's in Garden City, a rich neighborhood. "It's Lollipopland," she figured. "People there aren't looking to be robbed."

We decided to see a movie first at the Roosevelt Field mall Loews. Jane had a friend who worked for another Loews—in Queens. She called him and we got free passes left for us at the door. On the way in, we started talking to the assistant manager.

"As long as I'm letting you girls in," he said, "how about you giving me a ride home?"

We said sure. The movie was *Lethal Weapon 3*. Near the beginning —just when the guy who'd botched the armored-car heist was pushed into the fresh-poured cement and buried alive as it set— Peter beeped.

I went to the pay phone and called him.

"I've got to take care of business tomorrow," he told me. "It'll have to be Tuesday. I'll meet you at your house after school."

We put off getting the plates for a night. We gave the assistant manager his lift back to Levittown, where he lived. "Come back and I'll let you in free again," he said, as we drove off.

Jane and I never made it back to see him again. But the homicide detective did.

Monday, May 18 Where to steal the license plates? We went into Brooklyn to hang out and check in with Peter. He said, "Don't take them from around here. There are cops all over Eighty-sixth Street."

We drove back to Roosevelt Field and cruised the mall parking lot, but Jane nixed that idea, again because there were too many patrolmen around. "I'd be embarrassed," she said, playing the tough girl, "getting busted for something as Mickey-Mouse as lifting plates."

We drove out of the mall parking lot and turned right on the first residential street. We saw a house with an old car parked outside of a one-story home.

"Anyone driving something like that," said Jane, "wouldn't notice his plates were gone."*

I agreed. Jane played sentry while I hopped out. Using the screwdriver I'd taken from my garage, I bent down at the front fender and unscrewed the plate. Then I did the same with the rear.

---

*Jane was right. The elderly couple who owned the car didn't notice their license plates were missing until, several days later, concerned fellow drivers honked at, and gestured to, them in the parking lot of a Pergament hardware store.

Those two rusty rectangles of red, white, and blue tin spent the night hidden in my car.

Tuesday, May 19 Today was the day.

It didn't seem real.

The whole thing was a mirage, a movie, a fantasy.

People don't want to hear this, but I wasn't nervous. I wasn't affected. I don't know how I could go through this whole day with as little feeling as I had. Maybe it's because my whole life I've been used to pain; nothing affects me anymore.

I overslept as usual. I threw on ripped denim cut-offs, a black T-shirt—and at the last minute decided to take my prized possession, a $400 black-leather jacket.

I got to school at 8 A.M. and got a late pass at the attendance office. I went to home ec, Spanish, then economics. I didn't know it, but by 9:30, just as I was struggling to stay awake during economics, Peter was already parked in front of my house; he had left Brooklyn real early—he was *that* worried he'd get lost on the parkways.

In sociology I had a conversation with Josh, a preppy kid, about registering at Nassau later. He offered to give me a ride at 2:30. I gave him directions to my house.

I had bad cramps from my period so I excused myself in the middle of English and went to the school nurse and got a note to go home. I called my mother at Stitch 'n Sew and we talked for a few minutes about my enrolling at Nassau.

As I drove down Berkley, I made out Peter's car, parked in front of my house. I pulled even with him. We both rolled down our windows. "Let me pull my car into the garage," he said, his face shadowed by a black baseball cap.

I opened the garage and he pulled in. I got the stolen plates out of my drawer and a tape dispenser from the kitchen. Peter put the decoy plates over his own plates with heavy-duty Scotch tape. He backed out into the driveway. Now we had to negotiate who would do what.

The whole time I was planning this, I never seriously believed *I* would be the one to walk up to the porch with the gun.

"You're going to do this, right?" I asked.

"Hey, wait a minute, that wasn't the deal," he said.

I kept pushing him to do it and he kept saying, No: *You.* Anyone driving by would have thought we were a regular girlfriend and

AMY FISHER

boyfriend, ruining a beautiful late-spring day by having a stupid
fight. I left it with him thinking I'd do the shooting, just to get him
to drive.

He took the gun out of the glove compartment. It was a Titan .25
semi-automatic. He showed me how it worked and he put it in my
hand.

Okay, I was thinking. This is real now. I have to follow through.
Joey will be mad if I don't.

"Hey, what are you doing?" Peter said. I must have been handling
the gun wrong. "You'll shoot yourself or"—this is when he grabbed
the weapon back—"you'll shoot my car!" (Sometimes, standing
here working my eight-hour shift in the prison kitchen, I say, If only
I'd accidentally shot his car. That would be it: no gun, no ride, a
furious Peter, no rest of the day.) After he took the gun away, he
looked at me as if I was a zombie and said, "Look, if you can't shoot
her, at least talk to her. Then you can just walk away."

Yes, talk to her. That sounded good. But what would I say? Joey's
plan had been: She opens the door, you go bang-bang-bang. I
thought a moment (something I rarely do, you can probably tell).
Then I went into my car and took out a collared, polo-style T-shirt
Joey had put on me after we'd made love two weeks before—the
now-famous T-shirt with COMPLETE AUTO BODY on the back. It was
size extra-large. I'm size petite, which is one below small. Joey and I
laughed when he put it on me; it looked like I was wearing a dress.
The shirt would prove I was Joey's lover. I decided to take it along.

We got to Joey's house. Then I got nervous and I made Peter drive
me around the corner while I tried, again, to talk him into doing it
for me. We drove back and parked across the street from the house.
He took the gun out and gave it to me. "*Please* do it," I told him, still
again. "It's no big deal." He was trying to convince me of the same
thing. Then he took his baseball cap off and put it on my head. "Just
do what you said"—meaning how Joey told me to do it. "Just walk
up and shoot her and come back. Fifty seconds."

I tucked my hair under Peter's baseball cap. I put the gun in my
jacket pocket, took the T-shirt, and walked to the small front
landing, with its two skinny wood railings on either side. I rang the
doorbell.

Mary Jo came to the door. I remember just staring at her for a
minute. She was a person, a human being. I hadn't expected that.

The moment I had waited for was here and I didn't know what to do with it. She looked at me through the screen door I was supposed to shoot through and said, "Can I help you?" I was so disoriented, I forgot why I was there until I felt the gun in my pocket. I had my hand on the trigger. I started to pull it out, but then the whole thing—this moment I'd planned for—suddenly didn't make sense.

I put the gun back in. "Can I talk to you for a minute?" I asked. I was leaning against the wooden railing. She came outside. I took the baseball cap off and my hair spilled out.

"It's not often that I confront a wife," I said. I told her that my name was Ann Marie and that my sister was having an affair with her husband. Using a phony name and turning myself into my sister—it was like using Maria's name when I was a prostitute; a way to be there, to not be doing what I was doing. *If I am very quiet, maybe I will disappear. Maybe all the pain of this will go away.*

She asked me: Where do you live? Who are you? What's your sister's name?

I forgot what name I made up for my sister. I couldn't keep up with the questions; I didn't expect so many.

She was like a teacher, or a parent.

I felt tricked up. I told her I lived in Massapequa, then another community, Bar Harbor. I didn't know what to say; I just wanted to get out of there. When I said Bar Harbor I was so nervous. I pointed in the wrong direction. I felt humiliated when she corrected me. I finally said Dolphin Court.

Then she did something interesting. She asked me if I was some other man's daughter. (In my nervousness, I didn't remember his name.) Was Joey having an affair with *another* customer's kid?

I showed her the T-shirt. "This is your husband's. He gave it to my sister," I said.

"Can I see it?" she asked. She looked it over and checked its size and said, "This isn't my husband's. It's not his size. You're lying. What are you doing here?"

And I was thinking, Joey *gave* that T-shirt to me. A week before, in the motel, after we made love. He *put it on me*. I was seeing Joey for a year; he was telling me he loved me. And she just dismissed my reality.

I said something to the effect of, "Well, you're not having sex with Joey."

She got all defensive. "*Who* told you that, your sister? I don't think so." Then she asked me, "Well, when does your sister see him?" she asked, like she was right and I was lying.

"Nights. At motels." I couldn't get many words out. I was stumbling. I was nervous. She was a powerful, angry grown-up, and I—I didn't know why I was there. I wanted a hug, more than anything else. I wanted to be forgiven—understood—for doing something stupid. Not punished, not dismissed.

Instead: "Who *are* you? What are you doing here?" she asked, as if I was some . . . nothing. Some pest. "Why are you saying this? My husband wouldn't do something like this!"

I started to get angry. I said, "Don't you *want* to know? Aren't you curious to know what a scumbag your husband is?"

She didn't want to hear that. She just cut the conversation short. She gave me a look of disgust and turned to go inside and said, "I'm going to talk to my husband."

I called out, louder, "Don't you *want* to *know?*"

She turned around and said, "Get the fuck off my property."

Fuck you. Fuck off. What you're feeling, what you know, it doesn't count, it isn't real. I had felt that from people for so long, and the only way I could triumph over it was to become tougher, much tougher, than they. To get myself numb and then lash out—that was my M.O. All those years of being terrified of being alone with my father, and my grandmother dying in the middle of rescuing me. All those years of my dad labeling me a bad kid, a dumb kid—"You will not get up from this table until you spell 'develop' "—when I didn't do anything wrong. Being raped by that creepy workman and thinking it was my fault. Being told I was just going out to dinner with the escort clients—and then having to have sex with them, and then, real fast, getting numbed to the sex, to those pigs, to the lies I would tell them and my friends and myself. Spending all my prostitution money, $600 a week: *throwing* it away. Going with Paul to get back at Joey. Going with Joey to get back at Paul. Letting myself be humiliated by both. Paul kicking me out of his house the other day. Joey's wife kicking me out now.

Half an hour ago, Peter had looked at me like I was a zombie and wondered if I could shoot her. Peter was wrong. It's not the zombies—the people who've been numbed inside—who can't pull the triggers.

Those are exactly the people who *can.*

I had been fiddling with the gun in my pocket the whole time we were talking, but when she said those words—"Get the fuck off my property"—I took the gun out. I hit her on the back of the head. Then I hit her a second time—harder than I expected. Harder than I thought I could. This second time, the gun went off. I was surprised to hear the pop.

The next thing I remember, she was falling on me. Then she was bleeding and screaming, lying in my lap.

I didn't know what to do. I panicked. I wanted to stop the screaming, so I hit her on the head two or three times. I dropped the gun. I dropped the T-shirt. I ran. When I got to the car, Peter hissed, "Get the gun!"

So I ran back and grabbed it. Even lying there—shot, bleeding— she had grabbed Joey's T-shirt. I yanked it out of her hand.

"I can't believe you!" Peter said, nervous and angry as I got in the car. "You were standing there talking to her for fifteen minutes! Someone could've seen you, could have seen us both!"

He saw Mary Jo bloody on the step, but I guess his desire to be a doctor escaped him. He gunned the motor and got us the hell out of there.

I was very upset.

Peter said, "Calm down. Don't worry. She's dead." I saw blood on my shorts and legs. I started crying. He tried to make me laugh. He said, "Come on, you're an old pro now."

Then he asked for the gun.

I gave it to him.

It was bloody.

"Where's the rest of it?" he asked. That's when we realized some parts of the gun had broken off and were left on the porch. "Oh, shit!" he said, fingering the gun as he steered us through traffic. "I can't use it again."

We stopped around the corner from my house. Peter took the plates off. I gave Peter the gun and the COMPLETE AUTO BODY shirt. He wrapped the gun in the shirt and put the package under the passenger's seat.

"I'll throw these away when I get to Brooklyn,"* he said. We both realized I was too bloody—my shorts, my sneakers, my socks, my

---

*Guagenti apparently decided to get rid of them earlier. Several days later, the police found the license plates in a sewer on Merrick Road, less than a half-mile from Amy's house.

black-leather jacket were all streaked. "Give me those, too. Take them all off," Peter said.

So I pulled off my shorts, sneakers, socks, and shoes, and he stashed them as well. I was left in only panties and T-shirt. I did *not* give Peter my black-leather jacket.

"Here, get yourself clean," he said, popping open his glove compartment and pulling out two packets of Wash 'n' Dri's. I smeared the tiny, sticky wet cloths up and down my bloody legs and arms.

Peter dropped me off at the corner of Berkley and Hewlett. "I guess I'll see you in a couple of years," he said as I got out of his car.

I walked to my house, in my long T-shirt and nothing underneath, the bloody black-leather jacket slung over my shoulder. The pavement was hot on the soles of my feet. It was a clear and beautiful day.

I entered the house and walked quickly upstairs. My dad was sleeping off oral surgery he'd had that morning. The second I got in my room I dialed Jane's number. "Get over here. I did it." I said.

"Oh my God, you really did it?" I had never before heard her awed.

I stepped into the shower and turned it on full blast. I looked down. The water swirling into the drain was red, then pink. The shower stall was splotched. I walked back into my bedroom with a towel on. My Gund Teddy bears were perched in their usual places; James Dean was staring off, sad and cool. That preppy kid Josh was coming in a couple of hours to take me to register for college. I made myself be calm.

Little dabs of blood were everywhere. On my white Formica chair. My phone. My carpet. My desk. I called Jane again. Her father answered and said she'd left. I took deep breaths and hoped like hell *my* father wouldn't wake up before she got there and helped me get rid of the blood. For playing with guns, I thought I would definitely be punished by my parents.

It never occurred to me to worry about the police.

♦ ♦ ♦

13

What Joey Said

◆

Tom! Steve! That was a round we heard! She's been shot!"

At a quarter to twelve—just as a nervous Peter and a blood-soaked Amy were hurriedly U-turning on Adam Road West and driving back to Merrick—Al Cooke, a Hempstead policeman and Biltmore Shores Beach Club member, ran to the street-side fence separating the club from the Buttafuoco property and shouted those words to co-members Steve Salowski, a Nassau Community College mathematics instructor, and Tom Kelly, a retired fireman. Mary Jo and Joe Buttafuoco were friends of the three men, who had been doing some work at the club's marina.

The three bolted to the Buttafuoco house, where Mary Jo's body was sprawled on her small front porch, her wounded right cheek to the ground. "Mary Jo fell down! Looks like she hit her head! I called it in!" Buttafuoco neighbor Joe Slattery, a retired policeman, yelled to the three from his front lawn. In his call to 911, Slattery had reported a possible seizure. He hadn't heard the shot.

But Cooke, a sandy-haired man with a streetwise air, had heard it. Like Slattery and Kelly and many of the beach club's other members, he used Biltmore Shores to *escape* the mayhem and violence his professional life was spent combating. The club was their triumph: proof that the hardscrabble streets they trod on the beat, and had spent their childhoods enmeshed in, had a border, a stop-point with a figurative "No Trespassing" sign on it. A shot fired past that imaginary sign and into this idyllic world they'd built had a jarringly ironic quality, as if a lifetime of bootstrap-pulling had been obliterated.

Kneeling beside his friend, encircled in a pool of her own blood, Cooke now saw two live rounds: one on top of Mary Jo's head, another in her hair.*

He shouted to Salowski, "Get into the house across the street. Use their phone, tell nine-one-one this is a *shooting* victim!"

He checked Mary Jo's wrist—there was a pulse—determined she was breathing, and adjusted her head so the fluids would drain from her mouth. There was no need for CPR, Cooke decided, since she hadn't gone into cardiac arrest.

"Mary Jo, can you hear me?" he whispered in her ear. No response. Cooke wondered, Was this a suicide attempt?

The ambulance pulled up, sirens dwindling to a loud bleat. "What you guys got?" the medic riding shotgun called out.

"Shooting!" Cooke flashed his badge.

Salowski's call hadn't been relayed to the team. "Holy shit!" the medic muttered loudly. Then he and his partner hurtled the gurney and transfusion drip through the doors at the back of the van.

Five minutes later, a phone in the large square homicide squadroom in the Nassau County Police Department rang. Lifting the receiver to his ear, Detective Sergeant Dan Severin heard: "Woman. White. Apparently a housewife. Shot and killed on the front lawn of her house in Biltmore Shores."

The features of Severin's expressive, pugnacious face—with

---

*Later these live rounds would spark an unresolved duel of interpretation between Joe Buttafuoco's attorney, Marvyn Kornberg, and Amy's attorney, Eric Naiburg. Were they (as Kornberg argued) rounds erroneously expelled by a shooter who tried to refire but had not known that the Titan .25, after the first shot, automatically loads a bullet in the chamber? Or were they (as Naiburg maintained) the result of a cheap gun exploding under stress of contact?

its round eyes and ski-jump nose—contorted into puzzlement. This kind of thing didn't even happen in Mob hits. He called out for Detective Martin Alger to be beeped in court and told to meet him at the crime scene, which he now scribbled down. He rushed out of the squadroom, down the flight of stairs, and into his car. Even with the siren on, it would take half an hour to get from the county seat, mid-island Mineola, to Massapequa on the Great South Bay, eight towns away. As Severin's car plowed through traffic, scant miles away, Amy Fisher was washing the blood off herself in the shower.

Adam Road West was in chaos. Neighbors were standing in shocked clusters behind the rope-cordoned area; *Newsday* and local TV reporters were already combing the scene. Severin tore out of his car just as Alger was rushing from his. They were briefed by a Massapequa policeman. The news was a surprise. Contrary to the initial report, the victim was still alive—she'd just been helicoptered to Nassau County Medical Center. But she was not expected to live.

Severin also learned that the victim's husband, Joseph Buttafuoco, was at his place of business when the shooting had occurred. He had been called by Joseph Slattery's wife, Josephine, and had rushed home, arriving at the house just as his wife was being taken off in the chopper. Using his car phone, Sergeant Severin dispatched Detective Richie Lane to the hospital to speak to the victim's husband. He sent additional men to question Cooke, Salowski, and Kelly, and to do a preliminary interview on a crucial next-door neighbor who might have seen a car. Was it a drive-by shooting? What did this woman do to deserve it? Was the victim or her husband involved in something illegal? These questions raced through Dan Severin's mind.

As the crime scene unit men took pictures and samples of the five pints of blood splattered on the steps, and they investigated the footprints found in the garden (these quickly proved to be those of the helicopter medics and firemen who'd arrived on the scene right after the original ambulance). Severin and Alger entered the Buttafuoco home. They walked around the white living room with its flowered couch and recliner, its wood-plank floor—slowly, with their hands in their pockets, so they wouldn't be tempted to touch anything and accidentally disturb fingerprints.

"It was impeccable," Alger remembers.

Severin was even more impressed. "This was the cleanest house I had ever seen in my life."

Confronted with the framed pictures of young children on the walls and in the living room breakfront, Severin walkie-talkied back to Homicide to have local police find out where the children went to school and arrange for them to be picked up by relatives.

Walking through the dining room, the television room, the children's bedrooms, the detectives saw no evidence of a robbery. There was also no money in the house. If these people were into funny business, it couldn't be proven here.

In the sloping-eaved master bedroom, Severin and Alger caught their preoccupied faces in the mirrored headboard. The mysterious shooting of a middle-class white housewife would invite a circus. Severin needed a hard-charging pro; that was why he'd beeped Alger out of court.

"Media up to here." Severin tapped his own chin with the back of his hand.

Alger replied in his tough, low voice: "I won't let the media run my investigation."

Severin knew this would be true. Marty was one serious, no-frills detective. The amiable Severin, on the other hand, enjoyed an occasional schmooze—and joust—with reporters. "You take care of the investigation, I'll take care of the media," he proposed. With that exchange, Severin officially assigned the case to Alger.

Alger walked to the bedroom balcony and let his eyes roam over sun-dappled ripples of Great South Bay. It was the last glimpse of tranquility he would have for six months.

Thin-faced, long-nosed, with a protruding shock of silver-blond hair and a broom-bristle moustache, Martin Alger could just as easily be taken for a professor as for a detective. But his speech was pure working-class Long Island, his key questions often prefaced with a quizzical look and a "Not for nothin' but . . ." He had an earnest, stringent style. Other detectives in Nassau Homicide—Gary Abbondandelo, for example—were warm and avuncular. They could charm a story out of a suspect. Alger was a straight man, but a brilliantly deceptive kind of straight man. Underneath his just-the-facts-ma'am style lay an actor's ability to record precisely every nuance of his interogee's gestures, words, and body language—and to record them inwardly, with scathing accuracy. In a field that depended on bullshit-detecting, Alger was one of the best.

Still, in criminal investigation, what matters is not whether a detective senses that a possible suspect is lying or acting guilty, but whether a charge against that possible suspect can be proved. Then, even with those charges on which the police have proof-positive, the district attorney must decide whether they are indeed worth prosecuting. When such charges are minor or secondary to the main crime, the D.A.'s decision may involve doing a costs/benefits analysis: pitting sentencing yield against manpower outlay and sometimes factoring in the main defendant's credibility and public sympathy for the victim. With these professional realities looming unseen in the future, Detective Martin Alger stepped into the case.

One man would eventually benefit from all of those realities. Martin Alger had not met him yet.

Alger ordered up a background check on the entire Buttafuoco family. Then he walked next door to see Nancy Schreck, the crucial next-door neighbor who had reportedly seen a suspicious vehicle parked across the street. The car she had seen was a maroon sports model. (This later proved correct.) The man sitting behind the wheel had been turning his head so much—and so suspiciously—that Schreck had even moved closer to her living room window to get a better look. But she had walked back to the interior of her house before the shots were fired. In fact, she hadn't even heard the shots.

Alger spent hours trying to jog Schreck's memory, but that was as far as he got. Maroon sports car. Male driver. Shooter? After a third of a day, still a complete question mark.

At 3 P.M. a call came from Richie Lane, who had just finished questioning Joe Buttafuoco. The husband, Lane reported, was extremely upset about what had taken place—yet also, Lane noted, he somewhat composed. He was so surrounded by family members and his attention was so focused on his wife's treatment that the questioning was of limited usefulness. "Marty," Lane said, "we don't feel it's a good time to interview him because his attention is in another direction. He's signing medical forms."

What Lane neglected to mention to Alger was that Joe Buttafuoco *had* mentioned that one person might have had it in for him. A gym owner named Paul. Joe had said that Paul had a girlfriend. He left her unnamed. The girlfriend had loaned Paul money and Joey had told her that Paul was a bum and a deadbeat and that she should get the money back.

Thus, just three hours after his wife was shot, Joe Buttafuoco —despite his presumed shock and anguish, his distraction with doctors and nurses and relatives—did these things: one, he voluntarily introduced the unnamed character of Amy to the detectives, but in a distorted way (as Makely's girlfriend only, not his own); and, two, he presented, in the guise of spontaneous happenstance, a scenario that he had tried to get Amy to effect the week before.

At 9 P.M., Alger himself took a trip to Nassau Community Medical Center to talk to the husband.

Joe—wearing a T-shirt, black jeans, and sneakers—was standing near the lobby of the surgical intensive-care unit when Alger stepped off the elevator. Circling Joe were about a half dozen members of the Buttafuoco and Connery families, waiting for word about the results of Mary Jo's surgery, which had started six hours before. As Alger was introduced to Joe by Richie Lane, most of the members respectfully dispersed. But one man hung close to Joe as Alger approached. He was practically on Joe's shoulder. This was Bobby Buttafuoco, whose constant, intense, almost bodyguardlike presence in relation to his brother would remain, Alger recalls, "throughout almost all of our talks."

Alger recalls, "I immediately sensed Joey was sizing me up: looking at me, trying to figure out where I was coming from." At the same time, he began ingratiating himself with the detective. "Joey was saying, 'I've heard about you, Marty'—right away, it was 'Marty'—'I've heard you're very good; I'm glad you're on the case,' almost like he's patting me on the back." Alger thought this was unusual.

But if Joey was softening Alger, Alger was also softening Joe. He wanted to get as many answers out of him as he could without arousing the man's suspicion that he, like any spouse, was being looked at, too.

Alger eased into the questioning. Then, more bluntly, he asked, "What could have caused this, Joe? You're the only one who can give me answers."

"Honestly, Marty, I don't know! I don't understand how this could have happened!" Joe replied in the theatrical voice that Alger would come to know very well. He was shaking his head, gesticulating broadly. "We're quiet people. We don't bother anybody. I go to business, she minds the kids."

During the conversation, Bobby Buttafuoco was leaning in, aggressively asking Alger questions: "Why are you asking that? What's going on?"

It seemed to Alger that Bobby was more combative than his brother. Bobby also seemed to be more puzzled than Joey was by the day's events.

Ransacking his memory for people who might have done this to his wife, Joey came up with two longshot suspects: one, a man around the corner was a peeping Tom—a "dickie-waver" was how Joe put it; two, a number of months ago Joe had gotten into a fistfight with a fellow at a 7-11 who had made a disparaging remark about Mary Jo. A man who'd witnessed the assault now lived on the Buttafuocos' block. Alger discounted both leads, but he believed Joe presented them earnestly. He had re-created the incident at the 7-11 in great detail.

Buttafuoco also told him about two other events: a day in the recent past when he was driving down Adam Road West and found a lit Molotov cocktail. He stopped his car, stamped out the lit fuse, and reported it to the police. Also, last Thanksgiving, a shot had been fired through his living room window. Joe said he thought both were random acts of criminal mischief. (Both incidents would later be bandied about by the press in connection with the rumors that Joey was a pimp. Alger denies the connection. So, for that matter, do those in the borough escort business who claim they knew Joey as Joey Coco-Pops.)

During a break in the questioning, Lane approached Alger with the story he'd forgotten to mention: the one about Paul-the-gym-owner. The story excited Alger. It provided one major character—"Paul"—and one minor one—Paul's unnamed girlfriend. A tiny window emerged in this closed box of a case.

Alger walked back up to the two Buttafuoco brothers. "I want to ask you something—you mentioned this guy, Paul?"

"Oh, yeah! I forgot about that!" Joey said. "I have a friend. Well, actually, I know her father. She's seeing a guy who's the owner of a gym." Joe repeated the story he had told Richie Lane. Paul's gym was having financial problems. Joey now added a fact—he had known that Paul had been involved in drugs. Joey's female friend had loaned her boyfriend Paul money, and Joey had told her that this had been a bad thing to do.

"When did all this happen?" Alger wanted to know.

"About two weeks ago," Joey answered, apparently condensing his February badmouthing of Paul to Amy with his specific instructions last Wednesday night ("Get the money back from Paul") into a fictional time in the recent past. "I don't know, Marty. Maybe Paul found out what I said to her about him."

"Do you think he would have taken it badly?"

"I don't know. I just thought I should mention it."

Alger agreed. He pressed him for details.

Buttafuoco described Paul Makely, and told Alger the name and location of the gym. He had come as a customer; Paul had helped him with weight training. Their relationship had edged into a kind of friendship. He liked the guy; the guy liked him.

Alger wanted to know more about the girl. "Who's the female?" he asked.

"Oh, this girl Amy. She's Paul's girlfriend." That seemed to be as much as Joe Buttafuoco wanted to say.

Alger got in a few more questions. Then the questioning was interrupted by word that Mary Jo had just been wheeled out of surgery. Through the double swinging doors of the operating theater strode Pradip Sahdev, M.D., who had performed the eight-hour operation. He looked grave and tired in his surgical greens, hair cap, and dangling mask. The family turned tense.

Dr. Sahdev explained the operation in detail. Mary Jo had been shot in the temple, above her right ear. Her carotid artery had to be tied off—a rare, sometimes dangerous procedure—in order to save her. The bullet could not be removed because it was too close to her spine. Only time would tell if the surgery was successful, he said. Two out of every three people who have this operation survive.

The family did not take the doctor's words as good news. They grew confused, alarmed, and emotional. They phalanxed Joe. Joe seemed very upset. Alger knew it was time for him to go.

As he walked to his car at midnight, the detective assembled his few puzzle pieces around the hole at the case's center. The computer check had turned up no illegal activity in the family. The crime stats for the neighborhood were extremely low. A male wheelman had seemed nervous sitting in a maroon car across from the house when the gun went off. The Paul Makely lead was tantalizing. So was the fact that Joe had not offered any details on Makely's girlfriend Amy. He had wanted to steer the talk *away* from her.

Joe Buttafuoco hasn't told me everything he has to tell me, Marty Alger concluded as he drove back to headquarters. In the brightly lit squadroom, Alger initiated a computer trace on Paul Makely. Then he drove home.

While he was driving, the phone in the squadroom rang.

Wednesday, May 20 "Marty," the detective on the other line relayed to Alger, as soon as the detective reached his home at 2 A.M., "the victim's husband just called from the hospital. She's conscious."

Alger hung up and dialed the hospital. Mary Jo Buttafuoco was on a respirator, he was told. She still could not speak. Alger assigned a guard to her room. Her husband, however, would be allowed in the room. That was standard policy.

Alger went to sleep.

An excited voice woke Alger, by phone, in the morning. "Marty, you're not gonna believe this! She's conscious! She's gonna live! She's gonna be okay! She's writin' stuff!" Joe Buttafuoco had taken the role that Alger would see him in for the next two days: the enthusiastic co-detective. "She's writin' the shooter's name on the paper! It's Ann Marie or Jean Marie!"

Alger dressed and raced to the hospital.

Joey and Bobby met Alger at the elevator. Joey handed the detective a folded page of lined yellow legal paper. Perpendicular to the lines on the paper, scattered horizontally across the page, in very neat and very small, slightly rounded lowercase print, Mary Jo had written answers to questions Joe apparently had asked her during the night. Alger gazed at the paper and deduced the questions from the answers. To the apparent first question, "Who shot you?" she had written: "19-year-old-girl." To the second, "What was her name?": "ann marie." To the third, "Where did she live?": "dolphin court." The last entry by Mary Jo was a cryptic half-sentence: "she told me that you . . ."

she told me that you

Alger chose to assume that the sentence was incomplete because the victim was too weak and tired to continue writing. Still, a glance at that paper reveals that the handwriting at the end of the sentence was not at all shaky. Indeed, it was as firm and clear as every prior word Mary Jo had written on the page. *she told me that you:* the truncated sentence was a cliffhanger. It stopped at the precipice of the shooter's declaration that the victim's husband had somehow been involved. No one had been in the guarded ICU room except Joe and Mary Jo Buttafuoco: a strong husband and a severely vulnerable wife. If fatigue made her stop writing in mid-sentence, that fatigue was curiously unexpressed by her penmanship. Maybe it wasn't fatigue. Maybe it was her own survival-necessary rejection of the words in the rest of that sentence—and her husband's appeasing voice, imploring face.

In accounts Buttafuoco later gave to the press about his wife's written replies to his detectivelike questions, he left those five words—*she told me that you*—out.

Alger needed to interview Mary Jo, even if she could not talk. He asked Joe to make the introductions. The ever-present Bobby Buttafuoco followed them into her room. So did Richie Lane, who carried pen and notepad. He would serve as the stenographer.

"Mary Jo, I have to ask you some questions," Alger told the woman. Her body was sheeted; tubes ran from her throat and mouth to a respirator and saliva suction, her face barely visible in the turban of bandaging. "Would you squeeze my hand once for yes, twice for no?"

The victim squeezed weakly—too weakly.

"Then can you nod your head yes and shake it no?"

This proved easier.

"Do you know who did this?"

A shake of the head.

"Was it a female?"

A nod.

More questioning made it clear to Alger that Mary Jo had not seen the gun or the shooting; that the assailant was a nineteen-year-old girl with long brown hair who said she lived on Dolphin Court.

Marty Alger's last question was so blunt it shocked Richie Lane. "Did she say anything bad about Joey?"

Mary Jo nodded yes.

"Joe *immediately* backed up from the bed," Alger remembers. "He had apparently felt safe with the information she had been providing—Ann Marie; Dolphin Court. Now he was brought back in."

"I don't know who it can be, Marty! I really don't!" Joe kept reassuring the detective as the four men moved out of the room and into the hallway. Bobby Buttafuoco was shooting his brother broadly puzzled "Hey-what's-going-on-here?" looks.

Was Joey's theatrical befuddlement on the level? Was Bobby's puzzlement the real thing? Alger didn't know. He left the brothers alone and attended to other parts of the investigation.

When he got a call from headquarters at 3 P.M.—"the victim's been removed from the respirator and is talking"— and raced back to the hospital, Alger figured he might find out now.

With Alger on Mary Jo's left side asking questions, Richie Lane behind Alger taking notes, with Joey on her right side, and Bobby Buttafuoco standing at the foot of the bed, Mary Jo spoke in a raspy voice. She had been painting lawn furniture, she said, when the young girl appeared. They had spoken for ten to fifteen minutes. She had said she lived in Bar Harbor—but she had pointed in the wrong direction. Then she said she lived on Dolphin Court.

"Was anyone else with her?" Alger asked.

"Yes."

"Who was that?"

"She told me it was her boyfriend."

"Where was he?"

"Across the street."

"Did you see the car?"

"Yes. It was a maroon Cougar." (It would turn out that she was close; a Thunderbird and Cougar have the same chassis.)

Listening to these words about the shooter's "boyfriend" in a specific car, Joey was leaning close to his wife, holding her hand.

Then Mary Jo said, "She gave me one of Joe's shirts."

Alger remembers: "Joe immediately let go of Mary Jo's hand. This was the same kind of response as had occurred when I'd asked her, earlier, if the girl had said anything bad about Joe." Only this time Joey beat everyone to the answer. "He backed up from the bed, turned toward Bobby. 'I know who it is!' he said."

The reversal from "I don't know who it can be, Marty. I really don't!" to "I know who it is!" was arresting. Alger was not going to let any detail escape him. And Joey seemed not to want to let any detail of Alger's vigilance escape *him*. For the next thirty seconds, according to Alger, husband and detective scrutinized each other intensely.

"From where my head was, close down to Mary Jo's face, I was watching him to see his reaction," Alger recalls. "*He* wanted very much to go tell Bobby what this new revelation meant, but he was clearly more interested in what *I* was doing, in what my next question to his wife would be. And in her response."

The two men were like competing suitors. Alger questioned Mary Jo softly, keeping his face inches from hers. Joey knelt on his wife's other side, his face positioned even closer to his wife's than the detective's.

"He was holding her hand. He was paying *real* close attention." Alger asked Mary Jo if she had taken the shirt. Mary Jo said no. The shooter must have taken it with her when she left.

The four men left the room and walked down the hall. Alger wanted Joey to himself. Joey, however, wanted his brother near him. When Joey stopped to wait for Bobby, Richie Lane, picking up Alger's cue, held Bobby back. Alger walked Joey to a row of gray laundry bins piled high with soiled sheets.

Safely private in this uninviting nook, he looked the victim's husband in the eye and asked, "Joey, you know who it is?"

"Yeah, I know who it is." He whispered significantly, "You know that girl I told you about last night?"

Alger played cool. "Who's that?"

Young Amy

Amy Elizabeth Fisher, at about eighteen months, holds a toy pet and looks out hopefully at the world, giving no hint of the turmoil that will soon envelop her.

The collection of Roseann Fisher

The Triangle

Tanned and rested after her Caribbean vacation with her parents, Amy, in January 1992, cuddles her dog, Muffin, and looks every inch the picture of a pretty high-school senior well in control of her life. In fact, she is a desperately confused prostitute who recently slit her wrists over one married man and who will, in one month, plunge into a second romance with another older, unavailable lover.

The collection of Roseann Fisher

Joe Buttafuoco

Mary Jo Connery

Joey and Mary Jo as Massapequa High School sweethearts in 1974 (above) could hardly predict the events that would lead them, in the fall of 1992, to confront each other with looks that might be loyalty and love—but also might be her hope that he is telling the truth and his insistence that she believe him.

Dick Kraus/Newsday

Featured Players

Peter Guagenti (above), the son of immigrants, hoped to become a doctor. But on Bensonhurst's high-attitude Eighty-sixth Street, he was enigmatic "Petey G." He sold Amy the gun and drove her to the Buttafuoco house that fateful May morning. Paul Makely (below) was a gym owner with a live-in girlfriend, a child, and a spott[...] past. He became Amy's lover, Joey's rival—and, because of what Joey said right after the shooting, the police's first suspect.

J. Conrad Williams/Newsday

Flanked by lawyers Eric Naiburg and Christine Edwards-Neumann, Amy and Roseann manage an upbeat moment. Eight months earlier, they had talked about daughter following in mother's footsteps by enrolling at the Fashion Institute of Technology. Now they are the defendant and the mother-of-defendant in one of the country's most infamous felonies.

Bill Davis/Newsday

Smooth, sharp Eric Naiburg had a 75/25 win-loss record as a criminal attorney, a way with the press, and a persona of hipness. Still, it took him weeks to convince his jailed young client that Joey Buttafuoco was not going to come to her rescue.

ose greets her daughter at the end of her
xty-six-day jail stay. Elliot Fisher (below)
akes a more tempered appearance. He
ys nothing to the press during his
aughter's ordeal; in December 1992, he
nd Rose file for divorce and he moves to
Florida.

Points of Interest

Photo © by Joann Foster

Photo © by Joann Foster

With Amy's notoriety, Paul Makely's Future Physique became the most famous gym on Long Island. It was here that Amy came, with her friend Jane, the evening of the shooting. It was here, in September, that Paul lured Amy into the "Hard Copy" tape that resulted in the D.A.'s decision not to prosecute Joey.

John F. Kennedy High School, in Bellmore, is one of Long Island's most academically excellent high schools. Despite her considerable intelligence, Amy often cut classes during her senior year.

FREEPORT Motor Inn & Boatel

Seasonal Boat Dockage

AAA APPROVED

Photo © by Joann Foster

was in the *Freeport Motor Inn & Boatel* that, *Amy says, she
d Joey made love, he French-braided her hair, danced with
r, and tested her on her developing knowledge of '70s hit
ngs. The manager and clerk vouch for Joey's appearances—
do the FBI handwriting experts, who verified Joey's
ndwriting on receipts. Joey denies he has ever set foot on
e premises.*

FREEPORT MOTOR INN & BOATEL
445 S. MAIN STREET
FREEPORT, NY 11520

Nº 8725

NAME *Vin Buttafuoco*
STREET *1025 Merrick Rd*
CITY *Baldwin*
REPRESENTING STATE *NY* ZIP CODE *11510*
Car
License
Make
of Car   State
NOTICE TO GUESTS: This property is privately owned and management reserves right
to refuse service to anyone, and will not be responsible for accidents or injury to guests
or for loss of money, jewelry or valuable of any kind.   No. in
                                                                          Party
Date *2/2/91*   Rate

F130

Total *42.02*
Tax (If any) *3.36*
Amount Paid *45.36*

AMERICAN HOTEL REGISTER CO. NORTHBROOK IL 60062-7798
800 323-5686   RAE 246

ROOM *236*
NAME *BUTZAFUOG 10-3*

© John Mantel/SIPA PRESS

The Buttafuoco house, at 1 Adam Road West, after the blizzard of March 1993. The events that took place on the small wood front porch on May 19, 1992, are probably now familiar to more Americans than Paul Revere's ride.

Amy's house on Berkley Lane in Merrick, also storm-tossed in winter. Amy's bedroom is just as she left it; her voice is still on the telephone answering-machine message. Rose Fisher and Muffin live here alone now.

The Two Faces of 1992

From graduating senior (above) to arraigned suspect, all in a matter of weeks. Amy says, "It doesn't take long for a girl to destroy her own life." She hopes that this book will keep other young girls from doing so.

Amy Fisher

Newsday

Amy Fischer 17yrs

© Steve Allen/GAMMA LIAISON

"You know the friend I told you about—Makely? Marty, I gotta tell you, it's *his girlfriend*. It's Mr. Fisher's daughter! Let me tell you, I gotta tell you the whole story."

"Let's start with square one," Alger said. "Who is this girl?"

"Her name is Amy Fisher."

"Where does she live?"

"She lives on Berkley Lane in Merrick."

"How old is she?"

"Seventeen, eighteen, Marty. Something like that."

"What does she do?"

"She goes to Merrick High School."

"There is no Merrick High School. There are two high schools in Merrick, but no Merrick High."

"Well, she goes to one of them."

"What else do you know about her?"

"Her father was a very good customer. Mr. Fisher."

The conversation was making no sense. "Joe, but . . . can you tell me why this girl would have shot your wife?"

"I don't know, Marty! I don't understand!" Joe slapped his forehead. "I'm so shocked."

By this time Bobby had joined them.

"Let me ask you another question, Joe." Alger went on. "Did you give her a shirt?"

"That's how I *knew* who it was, Marty!" Joey answered emphatically. "I only gave *one* of those shirts out—to her father. For her!"

"Those shirts were very expensive," Bobby chimed in, as if scolding his brother for giving even one of them away.

Alger thought Bobby may have been overacting. He *knew* that Joey was.* In addition to overacting, Joey's demeanor suddenly altered. "He started to change, right in front of me," Alger recalls. "His mouth was dry and his lips were sticking together. He was visibly more nervous. Very nervous. He wanted to speak

---

*When interviewed in early December 1992, Martin Alger called Joey's claim that he gave only one shirt away "total bullshit." Alger believes that if Naiburg had been able to subpoena Joe's shirt orders for a trial, it would have been revealed that Joey had ordered a quantity of shirts and had given many away—"at least twenty to females under twenty years old," Alger believes.

to his brother. Bobby picked this up immediately and became more defensive.

"Not for nothin', Joe," Alger asked again, "but what's a seventeen-year-old girl from Merrick doing shooting your wife?"

Joe eagerly resuscitated the story he had told to Alger the night before, and to Richie Lane before that: the story he had tried, last Wednesday night, to get Amy to turn into fact. "Remember Makely? Remember I told you about how she loaned him money and I told her he was no good and she should get it back from him?"

Alger was confused. In that scenario it was *Makely,* not the girl, who had a reason to be mad at Joey. Indeed, Joey was doing her a favor by cluing her in on her boyfriend's poor repayment record and apparent past involvement with drugs. Why would she turn around and pay him back by shooting his wife? The new information Joey had just added—that Amy was the daughter of his good customer—made the act, at least with the motive Joey presented, even more nonsensical.

Still, Alger did not dwell on these inconsistencies. There was too much he knew he didn't know for a nonsensical-sounding story to be a button-pusher—yet. He wanted the shooter, and only Joe Buttafuoco could deliver her. Thus, Alger was willing to look past Joey's original wariness, his evasions, his ingratiation, his brother's combative hovering, his earlier theatrical bafflement about the shooter's identity, his self-interested concentration on Alger in Mary Jo's room, his nervousness, his dry mouth, and his overacted explanation of how only one shirt had been given out.

"How do I find Amy Fisher?" he asked.

Joey pulled out his wallet and gave Alger her phone number and her beeper number. He offered to call Amy for Alger. Alger decided not to act on this offer yet, but he kept it in mind.

Next, Joey told Alger he had a picture of Amy. It was at Complete Auto Body. He had obtained it, he said, because one of his mechanics had admired Amy, and Amy had obliged the fellow with a photo of herself. When Alger said he wanted the picture immediately and would send detectives for it, Joey quickly huddled with his brother. They didn't want the detectives to go *into* the body shop; they would have an employee carry the picture out to detectives who waited at the curb.

Phone calls were made to arrange this transfer of the photograph.

Alger was trying to put things together. In two hours, Joey Buttafuoco had gone from an earnest innocent ("I don't know who it can be, Marty!") to a man who was almost tripping over himself to lead Alger to the shooter. Still, the shooter's motive, as proffered by this extremely cooperative source, made no sense. It was time to circle back to that.

"Joey," Alger asked again, *"why* would Amy Fisher shoot your wife?"

"Maybe because of what I was telling her about her boyfriend, she now wanted to take it out on me. Maybe it was something more. Maybe because of the things that I said."

Alger seized the opening. "What *did* you say? Joey, tell me what you said."

Joe reiterated his claim that Makely was a bad credit risk and had been involved in drugs.

Alger wanted to lock him into a time frame. "When did you tell her this?"

"Had to be . . . last Wednesday night."

"But why would those things you said about Makely give *Amy* reason to shoot her?"

Now Joey augmented his role as messenger of bad news. "I even called another guy to get more information on Makely, and I called her back with it."

Alger effected a quizzical look. "But Joe," he said, "I thought you said you only called her once."

"Well, no," Joe said. "I called her back again."

"When was that?"

"Had to have been a day, two days, after that."

Two days would put that phone call at Friday, May 15: the day Amy got the beeper calls from Joey—at 8:30 A.M. and 11 A.M.

"What did you say in that second phone call?"

"I gave her information about Makely and the drugs."

"Is this as much as you know about Amy Fisher?"

"Yes."

"Is this as much as you know about her motivation to shoot your wife—this money thing with Makely?"

"Yes. It *has* to be that, Marty. It *has* to be that."

Alger wasn't satisfied. He took Joey out to the helicopter pad

185

behind the medical center, where they'd be entirely alone—uninterrupted by Bobby, by nurses. There, Alger questioned Joey "intensely" for forty-five minutes, and Joey Buttafuoco "made certain other admissions." Did Joey admit that he had had an affair with Amy? Alger refused to comment.

At 8 P.M. Alger drove back to the hospital with the picture of Amy Fisher that had been elaborately retrieved from Complete Auto Body. It was nestled in a photo pack the police had assembled of a half-dozen informal photographs of young long-haired brunettes. Getting off the elevator on the ICU floor, Alger was relieved that Joey and his entourage had gone home. He would have Mary Jo to himself.

The detective entered the victim's room. In complete privacy, with the curtain drawn around her bed, he laid out the pictures. Mary Jo unhesitatingly pointed to the one of Amy. She glanced at Alger with a look of surprise. How had he gotten the picture? her eyes seemed to inquire. But she did not ask the question aloud. Instead it was Alger who spoke. "Is that the girl who was on your steps that morning?"

"That's her. Who is she? Why did she shoot me?"

"Now is not the time to answer those questions," Alger said. "Your condition doesn't permit it and I don't have all the answers for you yet, Mary Jo. But I'm working on them."

Alger left the hospital with a sense of urgency and excitement. He had a positive ID of his shooter. A computer check, initiated by one of the other detectives while Alger was at the hospital, had also turned up provocative information about Paul Makely. In the late 1980s, Makely was arrested in Suffolk County, on the basis of a wiretap, for conspiracy to sell marijuana. Makely apparently pled to a misdemeanor and was granted probation. More recently he had been stopped at the airport attempting to board a plane to Phoenix, a known drop spot for marijuana traffic from Mexico, with $38,000 in cash. Makely is currently suing to get his confiscated money back.

If Joe Buttafuoco's relentless words about Makely were meant to turn the gym owner into a serious suspect, then he had succeeded. Alger now believed that Paul Makely was the wheelman. He was eager to get a photo of Makely for identification to Buttafuoco neighbor Nancy Schreck. He would do so as soon as he detailed two cars to sit at the corner of Hewlett and Berkley and secured a warrant for the arrest of Amy Fisher.

As Alger headed back to the squadroom, he thought about Joey's odd stress on the importance of the anti-Makely tip he said he'd given Amy on Wednesday night. ("That's when I gave her the information about Makely!") Joey had also used that same line ("I gave her information about Makely and the drugs") to explain his subsequent conversation with Amy "a day, two days, after that."

The victim's husband certainly seemed to be hard-selling that particular exchange. To deflect what *other* one?, was the obvious question. But Alger had been a detective too long not to know that some exchanges were buried and irretrievable: limited to four ears and four walls. When interviewed in early December, Alger said, "Do I think that Amy probably told Joey, that Wednesday night, 'I'm getting a gun?' Absolutely. There is no doubt in my mind that she did. But that doesn't mean that a reasonable man would have accepted a statement like that without saying, 'What, are you *crazy?*' . . . I can't read Joey's mind to know if *he* thought she really meant it. No one can. And we don't know what Joey's response to her was."

Throughout the two and a half months ahead, Alger would have an uphill battle in building a conspiracy case against Buttafuoco for three reasons: (1) hearsay—as in a friend saying, "Amy told me Joey said he wanted his wife dead"—is inadmissible as criminal evidence. Thus, what Maria Murabito, Lori DeSaro, and Mary Lynn Vise would eventually have to offer was meaningless; (2) "pillow talk" has no investigative value, even if it includes a man's alleged expression of a desire for his wife's demise. "It's assumed," Alger says, "that a man will resort to untruthful remarks just to get a girl in bed"; and (3) prior knowledge of a planned homicide involves the counter-incriminatory element of the hearer's subjective assessment of the speaker's state of mind. The hearer can say he believed that the speaker was joking when she said, "I'm going to kill your wife"—and the hearer will be believed.

In other words, if a man tells an impressionable, naïve young lover he wants his wife dead, and if he listens to and encourages her plans to implement his wishes, and if there are no witnesses to any of these talks, then she can be fully prosecuted—and he can fully elude prosecution. Only a person who actually heard Joey talk conspiratorially to Amy about the shooting could clinch the case that Alger was trying to make. Alger would never be able to find such a witness. Such a witness did not exist.

Much later in the investigation—by way of the brand-new technological process of "dumping a beeper"—Alger was to find records of both of the beeper calls Joey made to Amy, which coincided with the allegedly Makely-oriented conversations Joey had just admitted, in the hospital corridor, that he'd had with Amy. If the case had gone to trial, those beeper calls would have been severely problematic for Joey, Alger believes.

"If Joey had been put on a witness stand by Eric Naiburg and asked what was so urgent on Friday morning, May 15, that he beeped Amy Fisher at eight-thirty-six, waking her up, and then beeped again at eleven A.M., getting her out of her high-school class; and if Joey had answered, 'I wanted to give her information about Makely and the drugs,' he would have had a lot of trouble having that believed by a jury."*

But back on the evening of May 20, Alger's attention was focused on one thing: finding and arresting Amy. He welcomed the prospect of questioning her. "Marty, she'll tell you what happened in a minute!" Joey had enthused, earlier, at the hospital. "She's a kid! She'll give it right up!"

◆ ◆ ◆

---

*Months later, Joey changed his story—to the media. The "information about Makely" disappeared. Rather, the purpose of his beeping of Amy on Friday, May 15, was, Joey explained to WNBC-TV's Chuck Scarborough in January 1993, to respond professionally to Amy's request to have "ground effects" put on her car. Prior to making the "ground effects" remark to Scarborough, Joey suggested that another Complete worker had beeped Amy, then conceded it was "probably" he who had called.

14

The Arrest

◆

Joey loves me. He'll protect me. He wanted me to do this. He'll never tell the police it was me. Those were the truths I kept calming myself down with those two awful panicky days.

"Is she dead?" Jane asked as she walked into my room on Tuesday at about 1 P.M. I was sitting on my bed with a white T-shirt on, sort of frozen and spaced out. She hugged me. "Is she *dead?*" she asked again.

"She wasn't when I drove away," I managed to say. I just kept saying, "I shot her. I *shot* her."

"*Where?*" Jane got down to business.

I pointed to behind my ear. "I hit here and the gun went off here."

"Not too many people live through that. Listen, just *pray* that she dies."

"I'm so scared." What would my mom and dad say?

Jane kept reassuring me that she was dead, that she *had* to be dead. She was bustling around while I sat there dazed. She picked up my bloody black-leather jacket. "Why didn't you wear old clothes?" she asked. "Why'd you wear this?"

I shrugged. "I didn't think." I *never* think.

"Well, we're not throwing *this* away," Jane said. "I'm taking it to the cleaner's." (That's just what Jane did. Right about the time my arrest was making headlines, a commercial dry cleaner must have been handing Jane her just-cleaned black-leather jacket back on a hanger, in a plastic bag. I have no idea what Jane told the guy about how the blood got on the jacket. I just know that Lori saw Jane walking around *in* that jacket, in the nippy days of last fall.)

I looked around the room, with the dabs of blood. The bathroom was even worse. There was blood on the side of the shower and light pink footprints on the tile floor. I was sure my dad would wake up any minute. "How am I going to clean this up?"

Jane wet and soaped some towels and toilet paper and rubbed the blood off my furniture. She cleaned the bathroom, too. Then she sat me down on the bed and said in a soothing voice, "Just close your eyes and lie down and pretend it's a bad dream."

I tried but it didn't work.

So Jane took a different tack. "Cheer up. Try not to think about it. Let's go to Taco Bell."

"Let me call Paul first." I just go running to these men. I never think they'll take advantage of me. I need them too much to think that, I guess.

I called Paul and made up with him for the argument we'd had on Thursday. I needed all the friends I had. He could still take me to my senior prom. We talked for five minutes. Then his friend Jeff came over and Pauly started crying. Poor Pauly, I thought. Paul hung up.

I called my mom and told her I was feeling better from the cramps from my period I had earlier. We talked five minutes about college registration.

My dad, now up from his nap, called out from the bottom of the stairs, "Amy, come and make me a tuna sandwich." With Jane following me, I went downstairs where he stood, a Pall Mall dangling out of his mouth. He had some nerve to ask me to wait on him while Jane was over.

"I've gotta go," I said, and Jane and I walked out.

We got into Jane's Firebird and drove to Taco Bell. I felt like a sleepwalker. I sipped my Coke, watching the dark liquid move up the straw like the mercury in a thermometer. Jane ate like a normal person. She pointed to my taco. "You'll need your strength." I felt too nauseated to eat.

Jane drove me home at about 1:45 P.M. We sat on the lawn. An '82 red-and-white Dodge crawled down the street like the driver was looking for numbers. I made out Josh's face through the front window. I didn't want Jane to leave me. She was like a big sister*—as well as my link to the criminal world.

As Josh slowed to the curb, Jane whispered, "Just act like everything's normal and call me later." She got in her Firebird.

"I like your friend's car," Josh said as we took off.

Nassau Community College was mobbed with seniors from a whole bunch of high schools standing around with their registration forms—the guys goofing around and making rapper gestures, the girls clutching their notebooks and tossing their hair. I saw some kids I knew and talked to them as if nothing had happened. But I kept thinking, I just shot someone. I *shot* someone. Everyone was "up," thinking about summer vacation and graduation more than about being a college student in the fall. The Kennedy seniors who were really psyched for college weren't here. Those were the A students who were going away to really good schools**—some of my girlfriends from before July '91 were going to Ithaca College and American University—and the B students who were going to pretty good local four-year ones, like Fordham and St. John's. Nassau Community was for those of us who hardly studied but who didn't want to go straight from high school to working for minimum wage at fast-food restaurants and mall clothing stores—like Maria and Jane had done. (Lori went to junior college for a semester.)

I registered for a business marketing major. I signed up for five classes and gym. Josh and I left at 4:30. I got home at 5:10 and called Jane. "Get over," she said. "I'm watching the news."

When I got to Jane's house fifteen minutes later, she pulled me through her living room—with its leather couches, deer antlers on the wall, and her father's arm-wrestler trophies scattered around—and into the kitchen.

---

*Three weeks later, in exchange for immunity, Jane testified against Amy before the grand jury. Because Jane's testimony is secret, it is not known whether she therein confirmed or denied the portions of Amy's story that involve her.

**Kennedy High's first-placed graduating 1992 senior went on to Harvard. Ten others went on to Cornell, six to the University of Pennsylvania.

"It was *on*. The lady's in critical, unstable condition. She's going to die. 'No suspect yet,' but they're looking for one."

"Going to die."

Oh, God, I thought, I just killed somebody. After registering for college I had somehow almost convinced myself that it hadn't happened. That nothing happened.

"What should I do?" I asked.

"Look," Jane said. "You wanted this. Joey wanted this. You can't look back now." When I didn't speak, she got firmer. "It'll be an unsolved homicide, like you guys said. It'll be our secret. *Joey's* not going to say anything. He's in this as deep as you."

I wanted to call Joey, but I had promised him I wouldn't. It didn't occur to me he was at the hospital. "I just need to hug somebody," I said. "I need to call Paul."

Jane shook me by the shoulders. "No!"

"I'm not going to *tell* him. I just need to *see* him."

I pleaded. Jane grudgingly gave in.

I drove us to the gym.

Paul gave me a hug and kiss.

I asked if we could take a walk down the block.

"Sure," he said. He threw a jacket over his tank top.

"You're not going to believe this," I said, "but I just shot someone."

He started laughing. He laughed and laughed.

"No," I said. "I *did*. I shot Joey's wife."

"What?!" Paul flew around with this shocked, angry look. "You were *still* with Joey? You were *cheating* on me?" He started yelling—about the cheating, *not* the shooting. He went on about my infidelity for a while.

Paul asked me a million questions and I lied to him about everything—even about Joey putting me up to it.

"Does Joey know you did this?" he asked.

I said, "No."

We walked back into the gym. Jane was waiting, furious. Paul could tell. He wanted to get me away from her so we could still talk.

"Amy, come upstairs," he said, as the pulleys of the weight machines made wheezing sounds and the barbells clanked.

Jane grabbed me by the wrists and said, "I want to go."

"No," I said. "I want to talk to Paul." We went upstairs.

Five minutes later Jane came up, sat down, crossed her arms, and listened to me talking to Paul. Every time I started to say something she didn't like, she'd roll her eyes up and demand, *"What* are you doing?" She finally pulled me down the stairs and pushed me out the door.

I was shaking, so she drove. "Paul said I should go to a lawyer," I said.

"No!" she said. "Unsolved homicide, remember? You go to a lawyer, you'll go to jail for the rest of your life!"*

After Jane left I went up to my room and called Paul back. I drove back to his gym and we sat and talked.** Customers came in and said, "Did you hear about Mrs. Buttafuoco? Isn't that terrible? Who could it have been?" I went in the bathroom and threw up. I went home and went to sleep.

I was too panicked to go to school the next day, Wednesday. I slept half the day and called in sick. I drove to The Quintessential Look and Jane excused herself from her customer, pulled me into the employees' area, and pushed *Newsday* in my face. It listed Mary Jo's condition as "still critical."

"I don't know how she lived this long. She'll die," Jane said.

Jane bought me a sandwich from the deli next door. I took two bites. I got in my car to drive home. I told her I wanted to call Joey.

She said, "No! I'm going to come over tonight and take you for a drive instead." On the radio that song "Jump!" by the thirteen-year-old "pimps" was being played for like the hundredth time that day.

---

*Immediately after her apprehension by police the following week, Jane hired an attorney who stanched the extensive questioning Detective Alger sought to put her through. This cut-off of a valuable witness crippled the police investigation, particularly in regard to the identification and apprehension of Peter Guagenti. Located at her new job in November 1992 and asked to talk about those six days in May for this book, Jane refused, saying, "I was dragged into this from day one. I don't know anything about it. I'm sorry, I have nothing to say."

**At this point—10 P.M. Tuesday evening—Marty Alger had just acquired the identity of Makely and his girlfriend, "this girl Amy," from Joey. It would be another few hours, however, before surveillance of Future Physique was set up.

That night Jane picked me up. A friend of hers, a girl she grew up with, was with her. We all took a walk on the beach. The friend's mother worked at Nassau County Medical Center. She said she would call to check on Mary Jo's condition.

Back home, on Wednesday night, I sat hunched up in my bed, watching TV. My legs were jacked up to my chest under a big T-shirt stretched around my knees like a tent. Mary Jo Buttafuoco's shooting was still "a mystery," the news announcer said. I reminded myself, Joey will never tell them my name. Joey loves me too much to do that.

♦ ♦ ♦

The Police

Thursday, May 21 By Thursday, Marty Alger had Amy Fisher's house under surveillance; her parents, at Stitch 'n Sew, under surveillance; and their two cars—Elliot's Cadillac, Rose's station wagon—under surveillance. But where was Amy? And where was her black LeBaron? Alger had the kid's file; her parents' reporting of her as a runaway to the Nassau County D.A.'s office, and their description of her as "totally uncontrollable," did not inspire great confidence that the girl was going to sit tight while her captors massed or go quietly into the good night.

Any number of things could have happened, Alger figured. She could have told her parents—and they could have put her on a plane. She could have run away herself. Or she could be in her house. The Fishers' garage door's windows were covered, a surveillance team member's walk down the street had revealed. There was no way to know if the LeBaron was inside, or if Amy Fisher was home.

By late afternoon, Alger had acquired a photo of Makely. He eagerly brought it, in a photo pack, to Nancy Schreck to identify. When the neighbor who had seen the man in the maroon car stared intently at the six photos and finally sighed and concluded, "No, it wasn't any of these," Alger was thrown halfway back to square one. No wheelman. And where was his teenaged girl shooter? In Merrick—or halfway around the globe?

Alger made the spontaneous decision to walk the 200 feet to the Buttafuoco home. He would take Joey up on the offer he'd tendered the day before: to call Amy. In the ensuing months, Amy's lawyer and the press repeatedly asked a suspicion-laced question: Why did the police never offer a tape recording of the call Joey made to Amy to get her to leave her house? (It was almost inconceivable that the police would not have recorded, or at least listened in on, such a call, which might reveal as much about the caller's culpability as it would about the suspect's.) The answer to this question is this: There was no tape of the phone call because the call was not made from a monitored phone at police headquarters, as was widely assumed; it was made, due to a spur-of-the-moment—even slightly desperate—decision by Alger, from the Buttafuocos' home.

Alger rang Joey's bell at about 5:45 P.M. Joey answered the door, shirtless. He seemed surprised to see Alger. He'd just come home to take a shower and feed the kids, he explained. Then he was going back to the hospital. He went on about how tired he was. The kids were playing in another room. "I told him, 'I want you to page Amy,'" Alger recalls. "He was somewhat taken aback by my request."

"What do you want me to say to her?" Joey asked.

"I want you to find out where she is," the detective answered.

Joey reeled around. "You mean you haven't *found* her yet?"

"No, we haven't *'found'* her yet," Alger said, with an annoyed touch of sarcasm.

Why don't all these jokers who think police work is so easy—*especially* defense attorneys—take a crack at solving the cases for us? he thought.

"I just want you to find out, in your conversation with her, where she is," Alger said.

He sat Joey down and they went over a little script. Joey picked up the living room phone, dialed Amy's beeper, punched 007. Joey assured Alger that Amy would respond to his page fast.

Still, Alger was startled at *how* fast. No sooner had Joey stood up and started pacing—"He was certainly nervous about the upcoming call," Alger recalls—than the phone rang.

Joey picked it up. Alger listened closely as Joey said, "Hi, babe, how ya doin'?" Then he sat down on the couch. He determined for Alger that Amy was in her house, then started whispering, "Did you hear what happened, babe? . . . Yeah, she's still pretty bad but she's doin' better."* This part of the conversation hadn't been scripted by Alger.

Now Alger scribbled *Say, I want to meet you* on a pad.

"I want to see you, babe. I want to see you," Joey growled into the mouthpiece, "but I've got to go back to the hospital." There was a pause. "Okay. Eight."

Joey hung up the phone. He was visibly shaken. "I can't believe it, Marty," he said, shaking his head. "No reaction. No emotion. She's like *ice.*" Joey stood up. "I have to put on a shirt. I'm cold."

Before getting the shirt, Joey told Alger what Alger needed to hear: Amy was leaving the house for an appointment. Alger hopped on the phone to the squadroom and detailed the plainclothesmen on Hewlett and Berkley, James Kelly and Tony Mascoli, to make the arrest.

♦ ♦ ♦

Amy

I had spent that morning, Thursday, at The Quintessential Look with Jane. (So much for the Nassau PD's great surveillance of me!) Jane's friend whose mother worked at the medical center called and tried to find out Mary Jo's condition. We couldn't get the information. By late afternoon I was very upset.

At 6 o'clock, just as I was about to go out the door, Joey beeped. I thought it was weird. Then I figured maybe he thinks the phones are tapped and he wants to cover everything up, have a "normal" conversation to show anyone who was secretly listening that both of us were innocent.

I called him right back.

He's like, "Hi, how ya doin'? Oh, did you hear? My wife got shot." I couldn't believe how he sounded! As casual as if he was giving me a lesson in local current events!**

---

*Amy did not infer from this that Mary Jo was conscious.

**Amy's assessment of Joey's tone of voice on the telephone predates the interview in which Alger recounted Joey's assessment of Amy's.

I played along. "Oh, yeah, I heard something about that last night."

Both of us were trying to act casual—to play the shooting as something neither of us had anything to do with.

He said, "You want to get together later?"

I was surprised. He told me he wasn't going to call me for a couple of months! I asked, "Just to talk? Nothing more?"

He answered, "No, no, no—just to talk."

He was taming down everything I wanted to say. Every time I started to say something he cut me off. He was making it so that I couldn't even slip if I wanted to.

The last thing he said was, "I love you."

I said, "Yeah, okay, Joey." We hung up. I thought, Odd, if he thinks his phones are tapped, that he would say "I love you." It sounded so final, the way he said it.

I flew out the door—and the police ran me down with sirens blaring. They cornered off my car, got me out, and brought me to headquarters.*

I want everyone to know:

I didn't want to go with them. I didn't want to talk to them. I kicked and screamed the whole way.

I was ready for them. I was going to weasel my way out of it.

Like everything else in my life, there was no way in hell I was going to take this arrest without fighting back.

♦ ♦ ♦

The Police

Detective Sergeant Dan Severin was the only one in the squadroom when patrolmen Kelly and Mascoli ushered in the

---

*Amy's attorney, Eric Naiburg, contends that Amy's arrest was made without sufficient probable cause, and that the police improperly used Buttafuoco to find out if Amy was voluntarily leaving the house—and to effect such departure, if necessary. Only with her out of the house on her own were they able to stop her to ask if she would "consent" to go— conspicuously lawyerless and parentless—to the station for questioning, at which time the Miranda-rights-reading would be virtually a moot point, anyway.

suspect. She had purple-hued hair and wore shorts, a white T-shirt, and sneakers. She was taken into the interrogation room. "'I know what this is all about. I was fucking Joey Buttafuoco,'" Severin recalls her having said after he introduced himself.

Severin told her to make herself comfortable—that Detective Alger was coming in to question her in a moment.

The suspect sat down, leaned back in her chair, put her feet on the desk.

Severin frowned.

"You better treat me like a lady," she warned.

"You'll be treated as you act," the sergeant admonished.

Severin pegged her as a kid who'd developed a very big muscle of a defense against male authority figures.

"This is a very calm kid," Severin asided to Alger, as he entered the squadroom, fresh from the Buttafuoco home, at 7:20.

"Hey, don't you even smile?" Amy Fisher asked Marty Alger, her feet still on the desk.

According to Alger and Severin, Amy was read her Miranda rights twice—once by each of them. Twice, they say, she waived them. (Eric Naiburg thinks both of the policemen's assertions are unlikely.) Alger's notes indicate that Amy said she understood what her rights were and was willing to answer questions without an attorney. "'Ask me what you want,'" he says she said. Repeating what she had said in the car, she told Alger, "You know, I just spoke to Joey. He called me. He must have told you about us. I couldn't believe he called me. His wife is in the hospital. Why did he call me? It upset me. He wants to meet me later. He's going to beep me at eight P.M." Still, she had no idea the extent to which Joey was behind her visit to headquarters. This was still a game to her, not an arrest.

For an hour and a half, Amy told Detective Alger a calm and elaborate story of how she had heard about the shooting of Mrs. Buttafuoco at Paul Makely's gym Tuesday night. She backtracked and detailed her entire Tuesday—school, the sick pass home because of her cramps, the visit from Jane, the fight with her father over the tuna-fish sandwich, the lunch at Taco Bell, Josh, registering at Nassau—leaving out the shooting, glossing over the little window of time, 11:30 to 12:15, that it had taken.

Alger was amazed at her cool. "She was a very, very tough interview. Cocky. Confident. Calm as could be. She was *not* going to give it up. She was *not* like a seventeen-year-old."

Alger was getting impatient. Round one of the interrogation —wherein the suspect palms the bullshit alibi—had gone on a little too long.

"It was time to go into round two. It was time to bang her between the eyes." Alger leaned in on his tough little charge. "You know, Amy, your biggest mistake was that you walked away and your victim survived. You left someone who could identify you. She *did* identify you. So we're not going to sit around and debate this anymore. *You* did it, and *we* know it. You can't tell me that you weren't there on the porch because Mary Jo's living and breathing and *she* said it was you. Here's why she said it was you." He whipped out the picture Joey had given the police. "She saw this and pointed at it. *Joey* gave this to us."

According to Alger, Amy's whole face changed. Her glib confidence broke in a second.

"She was shocked. I mean, *she* was *shocked.* She knew right away that Joey had betrayed her, that Joey had given her up."*

Now Alger tightened the screws.

"You're not leaving here tonight," he said. "You are going to be arrested, and you're going to be charged with a crime. And you're going to go to jail."

Amy's tone changed in accordance. She stopped being glib and confident. Now she was tightening up.

"Whatever we were going to get out of her, we had to pull."

All Amy would admit to was that she had been on the porch with Mary Jo that day. She did not admit to pulling the trigger.

"Who were you with?" Alger asked.

"I can't tell you," Amy answered. "I promised not to tell. He'll get in trouble." Joey's betrayal of her may have been beginning to fan out in her consciousness. Now it was *Peter* whom she aimed to protect.

By 9:30, Alger was inwardly cursing Joey's breezy "Marty, she'll give it right up!" This kid was as tough as nails. To break

---

*Does Amy's shock indicate that a pact *had* been made between Amy and Joey? "That's all interpretation," is all Alger will say.

Amy's tightness, he sent the serology team in to take hair samples from her head and a sneaker print.

After the serology team left, Alger got this story out of Amy: Last January, Joey, her lover, had given her a "ladies' gun"—a .25. (This, of course, was untrue.) Last Wednesday, he arranged for her to meet a fellow, "Anthony," in Brooklyn, who would get her bullets—"because Joey told me the gun was useless without bullets." The description of "Anthony" was exactly the same as the description of Peter Guagenti (whose brother's name is Anthony), from his hair to his car.

The crucial confession was still being withheld. Alger and Severin could both tell that Alger's hard-charging style was something this girl had spent her whole life pushing against— and surviving. Alger was a disciplinarian. She would continue to butt heads with him if they sat there all night and all morning—as it increasingly looked as if they would.

Alger brought in Gary Abbondandelo.

A pleasant-faced man with an easy-going air, Abbondandelo calls himself the "father confessor" type. He exudes empathy and sets suspects at ease. His weapon is not the threatening club, but the honeyed bait. At 10:45 P.M. he walked into the small interrogation room to talk to Amy, whom he could see was very upset. "I've got a daughter about your age," Abbondandelo said. "She even looks a little like you. I feel sorry for you. I want to make you feel better." Abbondandelo remembers that Amy didn't say much, but she listened to him as he softened her up.

By the time Alger reentered the room, forty-five minutes later, she gave herself up. "Her whole attitude changed," Alger marvels. "At nine P.M. she was a kid who'd gotten away with twelve stickups. By midnight she was a scared juvenile. 'I've never been involved in anything like this before. I've never even been to the principal's office.' But the real emotional break came during the oral confession."

Amy's confession briefly detailed her affair with Joey, included the false declaration that Joey had given her the gun and had introduced her to "Anthony," and mentioned Jane coming to her house after the shooting. Contrary to the widely held assumption that her lawyer came up with her description of the shooting as accidentally resulting from a blow to Mary Jo's head, Amy gives that account herself. While she implicated Joey—falsely—by saying he bought her the gun and led her to the bullet supplier, she continued to protect him by concocting a motive that implicated *only* herself. After recounting Joey's bad-mouthing of Paul Makely during the week, she said, according to the statement the police wrote, "I was thinking about how Joey was trying to mess things up between me and Paulie [sic]. I hadn't spoken to Paulie since Thursday and I was very upset. I thought about how I could get back at him and decided to go tell Joey's wife that he was having an affair. I wanted to put a lot of tension in his marriage."

Two things are notable in this sadly guileless mélange of reality and invention: one, both Amy and Joey had used Joey's recent persistent remarks about Paul in their proffered shooting motives—except that Amy had used them to protect Joey, and Joey had used them to protect himself; and, two, the most truthful thing in Amy's "motive" was how upset she had been at Paul Makely. But her upset had sprung from a fact she refused to mention to the police: her fear that Paul's son had been abused.

Eric Naiburg says, "Amy's statements to the police are a combination of truth and fiction. In them you can see how she protects everyone but herself."

During her confession, which she finally signed at 2:30 A.M., Amy paused to ask Alger, plaintively, worriedly, "Do you have to tell my parents about this?"

Phew! What a complex kid, Alger thought.

Alger's questioning of Amy went on all through the morning. She was allowed a short nap at 5 A.M. She continued to claim that Joey had given her the gun. Never once did she come close to implicating Peter Guagenti by name, or Jane by deed.

As for Joey, "She went from giving him up to protecting him and back," Alger recalls. "By six-thirty-five A.M. she'd had so many different statements, I didn't know whether she was covering for him or not. There was only one way to find out."

At 9 A..M. Alger dispatched detectives Richie Lane and Don Daley to bring Joey in.

Friday, May 22 According to Alger, Joey probably missed leaving the hospital in handcuffs by a very small accident of fate: Bobby Buttafuoco, his self-assigned bodyguard, wasn't at the hospital that morning when Lane and Daley came to bring Joey to Nassau Homicide for questioning.

Instead, Lane and Daley were able to walk right up to the unguarded Joey and ask that he accompany them to headquarters.

"What's going on?" Joey asked when the pair approached. "Are you arresting me?"

"No," Lane said. "We got her. She's under arrest. Marty wants to talk to you."

"What does he want to talk to me about?" This is the point at which, had there been any balking or resistance, the handcuffs would have been whipped out. Had Bobby Buttafuoco been there and had that balking occurred, then Joey's lawyers' months of skillful, effective distancing of him from any original suspicion of culpability would never have come to pass.

Instead, Joey went willingly, but worriedly, to headquarters. He walked into the squadroom and pumped hands all around.

In the adjacent interrogation room a few yards away, Amy asked Alger, "Can I talk to him?"

"No," Alger said. "He probably doesn't want to talk to you."

After Joey had finished greeting the detectives, he was led into another interrogation room—he and Amy were catty-corner to each other, about fifteen yards apart—where his concern, according to Alger, was single-minded.

"He thought I was going to collar him for statutory rape. He kept asking me questions about it, like, 'Can you explain the law, with a sixteen-year-old?' "

But Alger was far more concerned with Amy's assertion that Joey had given her the gun. This Joey vehemently denied. Alger, who had closely watched Joe Buttafuoco's various layers of guile and bravado for three days, was very impressed with his truthfulness.

Alger now went to check in on Amy. She knew that Joey was being held mere yards away. "Can I talk to him?" she asked Alger.

"He doesn't want to talk to you," Alger replied. "He wants to wring your neck."

Joey Buttafuoco was released from questioning. Before he

went back to the hospital, he heartily expressed his gratitude for Amy's arrest.

When Alger called the Fishers and told Elliot Fisher where his daughter was, Elliot dropped the phone and called out, "Rose!"

The Fishers immediately called the lawyer, Christine Edwards-Neumann, who was handling their lawsuit against Kennedy High, prompted by Amy's fight with Madeline Cioffi. Through their nightmare of a summer, Chris Edwards-Neumann soon became the family's Rock of Gibraltar and Rose Fisher's best friend. She immediately stepped in, by phone, to stop the police videotaping of Amy. But for an attorney to be contacted after a client as young, voluble, and self-destructive as Amy Fisher has talked to police for *fifteen* hours straight is to lock the barn door after the horse has already galloped not off the farm, but clear to another state. Chris Neumann remembered a sharp, impressive, handsome criminal lawyer who had done local television commentating on several notorious local cases. She would shortly put a call in to the man—Eric Naiburg—whose job it would soon become to, as much as possible, ride the horse back toward the barn.

As to who had that role in the opposite camp, the answer would soon become clear to the case's chief. Before he met the press that afternoon, Detective Sergeant Severin sought out Joe Buttafuoco. "You know, all this is going to come out," the senior officer warned the victim's husband. "I don't know any way that we're going to be able to hide that you were having an affair with this young girl."*

"Don't worry about it," Severin says Joey reassured him. "You do what you have to do. I'll cover my end of it, with my wife."

* * *

---

*In early December 1992 Severin said: "It was obvious to us right away, based on what both of them told us, that Joey was involved with Amy when she was a juvenile. He never recanted it to me or to Alger. The hard factual information we have on Joey is that he had sex with Amy before she was seventeen. We never had hard proof that he was involved in a conspiracy or that he introduced her to the escort service.

AMY FISHER

At 3 P.M. Amy Fisher was led in handcuffs to her arraignment at Nassau County Courthouse. She was booked on the charge of attempted murder. "Your Honor," Assistant District Attorney Fred Klein said, "we have a very strong case. We can prove she purchased the gun, was driven to the location, rang the door-bell, and with a twenty-five-caliber semi-automatic handgun shot the victim and left her on the doorstep to die. . . . She then disposed of the gun and clothing that was bloody . . . and attempted an alibi."

Amy was held without bail and led to jail.

Jane was apprehended by two detectives at The Quintessen-tial Look the next afternoon. No sooner was she in the squad car than the beauty-shop owner called her mother at home—"and fireworks started," Marty Alger remembers. "The mother is tough and high-strung, just like Jane. She showed up at the stationhouse—she knows a homicide detective—and had an attorney call right away to cut us off from questioning her daughter."

As for Peter Guagenti, he hid his maroon Thunderbird in his locked Bensonhurst garage. He kept a low profile for nearly a month, going to work by day, hanging out as "Petey G." in Caesar's Bay by night, perhaps never fully appreciating how much Amy had protected him.

Right after Amy's arraignment, Dan Severin faced a crowd of reporters and cameramen that would only continue to mush-room over the summer and fall. He announced the arrest of the Kennedy High School senior and answered the thundering questions. One reporter inevitably asked: Did the relationship between the victim's husband and the perpetrator involve sex.

Severin said, "Yes."

"Then this is like *Fatal Attraction*," the reporter said.

Severin again said, "Yes." (Later *Newsday* reporter Susan Forrest properly corrected him, noting that since no one had died, it was a "*near*-fatal attraction.")

The tabloids had picked up the tag line and gone wild.

The next day Marty Alger went to meet Joey and Bobby Buttafuoco to get more information. The brothers were ex-tremely displeased that the news of the affair had been let out.

* * *

My Story

On Monday, May 25, Maria Murabito and Lori DeSaro spent the day together. Worried and shell-shocked by what was whirling around them, the two innocent members of The Lady Mobsters had tried to see Amy in jail but were not allowed in. Whenever they called Jane's house now, Jane's mother screamed and hung up.

A friend of Maria's was in Nassau County Medical Center after an accident involving a chainsaw. After lunch at Taco Bell, the two girls went to visit him. As they left the boy's bedside, Maria asided to Lori, in her knowing, peppy voice, "He better watch it. He's dating two girls at one time." Look what happens in these triangles, the two girls marveled. Look what happened to Amy, to Mary Jo. And yet, come to think of it, Maria wondered to Lori, the *females* always ended up getting hurt, while the two-timing *guy* stayed untouched.

Both girls felt grateful that they had nice boyfriends.

While they were waiting for the elevator, Lori was taken aback by a sight down the hall. She whispered to Maria, "Isn't that Joey over there?" Lori had never seen Amy's boyfriend in person, although she had, these last three days, seen him on TV. Maria was the only one of the group who had hung out in Joey's shop with Amy—had even endured that stupid blind date that day that Joey was all over Amy at Paddy McGee's.

Maria turned her head in the direction Lori had cocked her chin. Yes, it was Joey. Maria met his eyes.

Maria has sworn in an affidavit that this is what happened next: "I looked over at him and when he saw me his face turned ash white and his jaw dropped open."

♦ ♦ ♦

PART

◆

4

15

"Lolita"

◆

I want you to understand something: I'm not saying I should have gotten away with it. I did something terribly, terribly wrong and I'm where I should be: in prison. But my logic is this: If they weren't going to investigate Joey, then why did they give me the maximum sentence? I think the fair thing would have been this—either prosecute both Joey and me to the maximum, or don't prosecute either of us.

I mean, *I* was the dingbat who came up with the plan—he wouldn't have. But you saw how he knew about it and encouraged it. That's "participation"—that's "conspiracy," isn't it?

To me, Joey just got away with it. To me, Joey is much worse than me.

Here is what life in Albion prison is like. Here are the things an official here would say to a visitor. (They've said these things to my official visitors—people who have come here to work on this book.) Forty percent of the women here have AIDS. Many are here because they have killed their children or babies or participated in drug-related crimes.

I have gotten used to it here, but to the outsider, Albion can be a pretty scary place. Women who are considered difficult are taken in here chained by their ankles and wrists. There are cells, bare except for toilets that are visible to the guards and drains in the middle of the floors. There is plastic instead of glass on the windows. That's where they take prisoners who are considered harmful to themselves or others. They hose them off in those rooms and hold them there.

The picture of me on this book cover, with its soft pink background and nicely glamorous look, was taken very near one of those cells.

I've made one friend here. I've learned there are good people everywhere. There were good people at Nassau County Jail, too.

I have gained twenty-five pounds in two months.

The women in my prison do factory work. We make the badges that state officers wear and the grilles on the gates of state parks and the aluminum rubbish barrels for state and city parks. (License plates are made in men's prisons.) So the next time you pitch your leftover lunch into a park trashcan, take a look at that trashcan and think of me.

The work I do is in the kitchen—eight hours a day. After work, I take business-management courses three hours each night. It's not the same as at Nassau Community College, I guess, and after getting up at 5:15 and working all day, it's sometimes hard to stay alert, but I am grateful for the opportunity to learn. When I get out of here, I want to continue to study fashion management—hopefully at the Fashion Institute of Technology, where I went that day and saw Liza Minnelli's Halston gowns, just before I slit my wrists over my breakup with Joey.

We get half an hour to eat breakfast, half an hour to eat lunch, half an hour to eat dinner. I brush my teeth after every meal. For some reason, keeping my teeth clean has become an enjoyable little project for me.

Prison is a very regulated place—not just with time, but with clothes. The uniforms we wear every day are dark green. (The red scoop-necked sweater I'm wearing on the book cover was just for the photo shoot.) When I get out of here, I am *never* going to wear dark green again. The bras supplied to prisoners are simple white cotton and very unattractive. I brought my own bras. If I close my eyes and shut out the noise, it's like I'm twelve years old again and wearing my first training bra.

My Story

Albion prisoners are allowed to wear only certain colors, and you're not allowed to wear things that are two-colors-in-one. Somebody brought me a red-wool cap (it's freezing cold in this very northern part of New York State), but it had tiny flecks of blue in the pompom, so it was confiscated. Towels have to conform strictly to size regulations. Anything half an inch bigger than allowed is confiscated. (They really do measure them.) I guess they think that even slightly larger towels can be used to try to escape or to do harm to ourselves or to fellow inmates.

Telephone calls can be made only collect, and only to the people who are approved to be on an inmate's phone list. That way the prison can keep track of who you're calling—as well as what you're saying. Calls are monitored. And guards listen. There is not much privacy here.

I get hundreds of supportive letters a week from people all over America who understand that I shouldn't have been punished for this all by myself. Thank you all.

There's a chapel, and it gives me comfort to go to it. A lot of the prisoners go there. We're real people—just like everyone else. We're worth redeeming. See, I think of myself as a prisoner now, a member of a population of troubled women. The other day, when I was thinking of the turnpikes and streets around my house and how a person would get from Bensonhurst to Berkley Lane, I found I almost forgot them. I've been away a long time. Still, I'm so homesick I just ache. I wish more than anything I could be on the beach near my house, holding my little dog in my lap. I've forgotten what freedom is like. I'm just eighteen.

I've been in solitary because of the threats to me, so my room is very small and there's a mattress on the floor. In solitary, you're not allowed to use the phone, so my communication with my family and with Eric has been through letters. Hopefully, by the time you read this, my solitary will be over.

I just wanted to say all this now to bring you face to face with the reality of me today. I am a grim, chastened person, a prisoner living for the foreseeable future in a place you would not want to be in, you would not want your daughter or your sister to be in. I am paying my debt to society. Yet sometimes when I look back on the feast the media has had with me, I wonder, Did the "novelty" of my age and gender and the fact that my family was prosperous and my father bought me cars—did all those things lead to my getting the kind of animal-in-a-zoo attention I did?

Do people think I deserve to be here because I was a "privileged" and a sexually active girl?

♦ ♦ ♦

Amy's arrest brought headlines—first local and tabloid, eventually national—daily more provocative and titillating. It was a "serious" news period—a presidential election was coming and both parties were about to mount their conventions; the unraveling of the daily-more-incredible tale of the suburban teenaged girl was just what summer spot-news readers needed to take them away from the nagging economic woes that all three candidates obligatorily insisted needed facing.

The headlines kept the story tracked along the selling lines of lasciviousness and shock value:

FATAL ATTRACTION

A TEEN OBSESSED

OBSESSION: TEEN JUST HAD TO HAVE HER MAN

LONG ISLAND LOLITA

The fiercely competitive tabloid-TV market—featuring shows like "A Current Affair," "Hard Copy," "Geraldo," and "Inside Edition"—saw gold in the story, and were willing to pay for it.

Very quickly, there were takers. One week after Amy confessed, an escort client she had seen several times—a short, heavy salesman from Levittown—sold secret videotapes he had made of her to "A Current Affair." Peter DeRosa was not one of Amy's three regulars, but after he booked her through ABBA the first time, he claims she told him to call her directly in the future. His three dates with Amy, in the spring, cost him, he claimed, $185 (this was the ABBA rate), $100, and $150, respectively.

Confined to her cell in Nassau County Jail—still unarraigned, still held without bail—Amy was to discover that she had *not* been alone in the room with the smarmy man from Levittown who had asked her if she would participate in S&M sex with a party of men. What had happened was, arguably, worse than submitting *to* those other men: Amy's customer had set up a video camera in his bedroom closet and had secretly videotaped their encounter, their sex, their talk. He had done it as a joke for his friends.

But now that DeRosa, along with all of New York, had discovered how notorious the young prostitute had suddenly become, the lascivious chuckles and the arousal he had shared with his friends escalated into a highly profitable arrangement. Through a representative, Peter DeRosa negotiated to sell his grainy tape to "A Current Affair" for $8,000. Since it had cost him only $435 to acquire the three hours of her services, chunky Mr. DeRosa had, in effect, netted $7,565, by procuring sex with Amy.

Mr. DeRosa's entrepreneurial act would cost Amy far more. The day the secret filmmaker cut his deal, Amy had been indicted by the grand jury—key evidence was Mary Jo Buttafuoco's positive identification of her shooter, relayed to the jurors from her hospital bed via closed-circuit television. With her arraignment and bail determination coming up the day after the show's airing, the timing could not have been more unfortunate. Throughout the next several months, the release of secret videotapes that men had made of Amy Fisher, *a day before* key legal hearings, would be a leitmotif of the case.

"A Current Affair" producer Steve Dunleavy, a cutthroat veteran of tabloid gossip journalism, went all out to advance-bill his coup of a show. Dunleavy chose to underscore the sensationalism of the suburban high-school girl's secret life by having some of his show's staff drive to Kennedy High with a camcorder. They parked down the street from the school and asked students on their way home if they would like to view the videotape. Five students watched as the tape played on the camcorder, perched atop the car. When these students confirmed that the girl they saw was, indeed, Amy Fisher, "A Current Affair" had a wrap.

Amy's classmates saw the grainy tape of a leotarded Amy and her portly customer talking and settling their fee, Amy protesting DeRosa's invitation to appear at a stag party, and—fuzzily—Amy and DeRosa making love.*

That, of course, wasn't all. The day before the show aired, "A Current Affair" invited tabloid reporters to view the tape, thoughtfully providing a full transcript of the dialogue.

The reporters fed the show's publicity release right into their stories, giving the show headline fanfare. HIGH SCHOOL STUDENT BY DAY, CALL GIRL BY NIGHT was the *New York Post*'s offering. That night at 7:30, much of New York watched the tape. The most-quoted line was Amy boasting, to DeRosa's first mention of the bachelor party, "I'm wild. I don't care. I like sex."

That sad little boast would frame her image with the public, certainly with the Buttafuoco attorneys—and, most important, with the D.A.

Less remembered was the fact that right after she let loose those words, Amy, for all intents and purposes, took them back. The conversation reveals both her guilelessness and the limits she put even on the sexual limbs she'd climbed out upon. It also reveals her customer as an entrapper, egging her on to agree to group sex, while his closeted cameras were rolling.

When DeRosa asks her if she would come by herself or with a friend, a startled Amy says, "Oh, no. Nobody knows I do this." After he talks about the S&M sex, she rejoins, "I wouldn't sit and let a whole bunch of guys slap me around. I would *never* do that. If you paid me two thousand dollars, I would not do that. I *can't* do that."

DeRosa then restates, "I'm just saying for my friend."

"Oh, *no way*. Uh-uh. Forget about it."

---

*Economist Sylvia Ann Hewlett, a noted critic of America's institutional disregard of youth and children, has pointed out in her book *When the Bough Breaks* that our nonregulated and strictly profit-driven TV industry has given us the phenomenon of a glut of 4-to-6-P.M. programs heavily keyed to true-sex-and-violence confessions. Through these, kids left alone at home after school learn about behavior. "A Current Affair"'s bringing the car and camcorder to Kennedy High, it might be said, pushed that "learning" to the student-participatory level, at the expense of one student's privacy.

The customer is persistent. "That's why I said . . . you and your friend would do it."

Amy is firm. "My friends don't know I do this."

Interviewed on the show, DeRosa admitted that Amy "was not your average hooker. She didn't wear makeup. She was quiet. She seemed kind of shy. At the same time, she was easy to talk to—definitely not the type of girl you would expect to be a call girl."

This was forgotten as well. What was remembered was Amy's boast about being "wild" and "lov[ing] sex."

Assistant District Attorney Fred Klein, a rising star in the Nassau County D.A.'s office, was ready to seize upon Amy's instantly notorious prostitution when he walked into Judge Marvin Goodman's courtroom for her arraignment the next day, June 2. To land a $2 million bail was his goal. Such a bail—for a seventeen-year-old girl—would be a feather in any prosecutor's cap.

A pleasant-looking dark-haired man with a sometimes incredulous air and a high-pitched voice, Klein, forty-one, had the eager, unslick demeanor of an earnestly helpful son-in-law. But inside he was steely and tough. A George Washington University Law School graduate, Klein had been with the Nassau D.A.'s office since 1979. He had two preadolescent children at home, yet on the job he had recently acquired a specialty of staunchly prosecuting youth.

Klein had just come off a victory: guilty pleas for twelve youths—and a murder conviction for a thirteenth—involved in a stabbing that occurred during a rap concert at Nassau Coliseum.

He had another hot youth case under way, as well—coincidentally involving a defendant who, like Amy Fisher, was a young, attractive white middle-class South Shore native with one Catholic and one Jewish parent, who had dealt a victim serious physical injury that did not result in death. Five months from now, Klein would prove successful in getting that defendant, a twenty-one-year-old man named Shannon Siegel, convicted of one count of assault in the first degree (against the principal victim, student Jermaine Ewell), and two counts of assault in the second degree. Siegel would be sentenced to seven to fourteen years in November 1992, shortly before Amy would be sentenced to five to fifteen.

But both of those sentences lay unforeseeable in the future on this hot early June day in Judge Goodman's court. Fred Klein stood solemn and ready to pounce as he prepared to talk, his fingertips drumming the wood table.

The court clerk recited the litany of charges against the girl who had "never thought about the police" when she stood dripping blood in her bedroom, hoping Jane would arrive before her father came upstairs to punish her: "Amy Fisher, on May 29, 1992, the grand jury of the County of Nassau, State of New York . . . indicted you for the crimes of attempted murder in the second degree; criminal use of a firearm in the first degree; an armed felony; assault, first degree, two counts, one count of which is an armed felony; criminal possession of a weapon in the second degree, an armed felony; and criminal possession of a weapon in the third degree, an armed felony." The clerk asked, "How do you plead to the indictment, guilty or not guilty?"

Amy said softly, "Not guilty."

Klein went on the attack. He had been lucky in drawing a judge of Goodman's pro-prosecution leanings. Two years before, Goodman had presided over a murder trial that would eerily foreshadow Amy's case as a sorry example of South Shore life in extremis. In that case, Kelly Tinyes, thirteen, was killed by her neighbor, Robert Golub, twenty-two, an unemployed bodybuilder and one of two brothers who had often baby-sat for her. The torture-death took place in Golub's home gym in the family basement. Golub was convicted.

What gave that case its oddity was that the Tinyes and Golub families continued post-trial life in Hatfields *versus* McCoys–style warfare: screaming at one another on the street, sideswiping one another's automobiles. Much later, after Amy was imprisoned and young Katie Beers was the Long Island scandal *du jour,* columnist Pete Hamill called Long Island America's "new Tobacco Road." The Tinyes-Golub behavior—as well as three wife-murders by Nassau men (two of whom committed suicide soon after) in the single month of January 1989— perhaps preheated that unfortunate image.

Judge Goodman had given Golub the maximum sentence:

twenty-five years to life. Still, with a thirteen-year-old victim and a brutal torture-murder, what judge would have been lenient?

Amy's newly hired criminal attorney, Eric Naiburg—who'd been recommended to the Fishers by their civil lawyer, Christine Edwards-Neumann—stood before Judge Goodman. Naiburg hoped that the judge would see big differences between the Golub case and this one. For starters, this case was *not* a homicide.

Fred Klein, on the other hand, may have been hoping that the judge's lack of mercy toward the one youthful defendant, Golub, would extend to the young girl now before him. The Fisher case was a career-making piece of rare luck for any D.A., and Klein was sufficiently political to rise to the occasion. He was well liked in the D.A.'s office and by the police. "You'll be hearing from Freddy. He's a comer, he's ambitious," Nassau detectives said admiringly about the man. Here was Klein's moment to come out swinging.

He did so—heaping scorn on the possibility that the shooting was in any way unintentional. "The defendant went to Mrs. Buttafuoco's home with a loaded semi-automatic, twenty-five caliber handgun. What kind of accident is this? The defendant's conduct after the shooting is completely inconsistent with an accident. She did not call for help. Students, friends, even her own family, who saw the defendant within minutes and hours and days of the shooting have confirmed that they saw nothing unusual in the defendant's conduct during this period of time . . . hardly an indication of a woman who accidentally shot a stranger in the head."

Klein now zeroed in on Amy's prostitution, emphasizing the fact that she had "cheated" the escort service out of its share of profits by turning service referrals into private customers. The irony of a prosecutor in the *one* greater New York county that battled escort services defending the *one* service owner who had successfully flouted the D.A.'s office for years and had cagily resurfaced after a recent major bust was a rich one. But it went unnoticed.

Klein brought up the Fishers' missing-persons report of the previous year, highlighting Elliot Fisher's fateful remark that his daughter was "totally uncontrollable." These two words,

uttered in exasperation by probably half the parents of teenagers in America at one time or another, were Klein's selling
point to Judge Goodman. "Totally uncontrollable." The words
stuck.

With a sexually active, self-destructive seventeen-year-old
girl, Klein could have it two ways: He could pitch Amy both as a
wily adult—"this *woman*"—and he could appropriate the
hyperbolic terms of frustrated parental domination ("totally
uncontrollable"), out of context, to demonize her.

And if there were any doubts that demonization was the
direction Klein was heading in, they were laid to rest with these
sentences: "One might describe this defendant as a seventeen-
year-old girl who lives home with her parents and goes to high
school. That would be about as accurate, Your Honor, as
describing John Gotti as a businessman from New York City."

"You really know John Gotti, Jr.?" Amy had said on Joey's
boat, after he'd allegedly bragged of his gun use, his past
cocaine addiction, just before he'd shown her his chop-shop
operation, handcuffed her during lovemaking, suggested employment as a stripper, and handed her an open Yellow Pages,
pointing to "ABBA Escorts." *"You really know him??"*)

Klein pushed on, handily shifting his imagery from Amy the
Mafia don to Amy the spoiled child: "It would mean nothing to
this defendant for her to flee, and her parents would lose
everything. . . . Your Honor, this defendant is uncontrollable,
manipulative, violent, and extremely dangerous. I respectfully
ask you to deny bail at this time. If you *must* set bail—and I
strongly recommend against it—I suggest that it be in the
amount of at least two million dollars."

Judge Goodman set bail at the requested two million, then
struck his gavel. Gasps rose from the Fishers and Amy was led
back to jail.

Eric Naiburg was furious. The cool, trim, chiseled-faced
forty-nine-year-old attorney had formally asked for a bail of
$50,000. In fact, he was prepared to hear it set at $250,000,
tops. The astronomical $2 million was beyond his most pessi-
mistic guess. It would be unmeetable by the Fishers.

If Fred Klein was the favorite-son-in-law type, Eric Naiburg had a more suave, cooler, less artless demeanor. He gave off a whiff of street smarts, courtesy of his native Brooklyn, but he was also very smooth, very polished. He had a clipped, deliberate way of speaking. As lawyers went, he was movie-star handsome—and Long Island's local Channel 12 had made use of this by making him their commentator for high-profile local trials, including that of Robert Golub. (If Fred Klein was pleased by the selection of the pro-prosecution judge, Naiburg uncomfortably remembered how his televised remarks had been harshly critical of Goodman.)

Naiburg was hip. He called his wife "babe." On weekends, he and his family repaired in their Ford Raider (he also had a Mercedes and a Saab) to their house in Woodstock, New York, long the retreat of choice of the counterculture. His weekend gear—cowboy boots, jeans, suede jackets—was classic "maturing '60s person."

When Christine Edwards-Neumann, the Fishers' civil lawyer, had deduced that this smooth, style-conscious attorney whom she'd seen doing Channel 12 commentary would be perfect for Amy, she hit the bull's-eye. Amy was to grow exceedingly attached to Naiburg. Over the next months, he would become her best friend, savior, mentor, a platonic and positive corrective for every other alternate father she had, disastrously, chosen.

Naiburg's appropriateness for Amy was not, however, superficial. He was a man who had a serious respect for women. He was the father of two daughters, both law students. He referred to them proudly as "geniuses." He and his wife, a professor of communications, had been high school sweethearts and married when he had finished—and she was still in—college. He was an avid supporter of women's rights, a voter who often pulled the lever solely on the basis of a candidate's pro-choice commitment. Naiburg was keenly aware that Fred Klein's boss, Nassau County District Attorney Denis Dillon, was vehemently anti-choice, refusing to arrest marchers who lined up to barricade abortion clinics. "My God," Naiburg says, "Dillon was right up there, standing *with* the marchers!" (It would later be discovered that Denis Dillon and Mary Jo Buttafuoco's mother, Mrs. Patricia Connery, belonged to different branches of the same pro-life organization.)

Naiburg had met the Fishers the day after Amy's arrest when Chris Neumann had tracked him down in Woodstock. Rose and Elliot drove upstate, bearing their grief, disbelief, and the front-page headlines. Naiburg's take on the family was instinctive and correct. And, of course, he knew instantly that the case would be high-profile and glamorous. Naiburg recalls: "It had media, it was an interesting fact situation—it was not your run-of-the-mill homicide."

Naiburg had a 75/25 win–loss record. He was known as cerebral, occasionally haughty; very aggressive in cross-examination; creative in front of juries.

His most admired victory was the 1985 acquittal, on a murder charge, of James Triano, accused of participating in a Satanic cult murder. "It was a case I wasn't supposed to win," Naiburg admits. In his defense of nurse Richard Angelo, the porcine "Angel of Death" brought to trial on four homicides and a multitude of assault charges, Naiburg's defense operation was a success but the patient died—the jury took an impressively long eight and a half days to reach a decision, but that decision resulted in two convictions.

When Naiburg met Amy in Nassau County Jail, he saw "a scared little kid who was mistrustful and didn't understand the complexity of the situation. She didn't have a true comprehension of why she was in jail, of what had happened, about why everyone was making a big deal about her. And she was *convinced* that Joey was going to ride to the rescue and take care of everything.

"I remember telling her, early on, 'Joey is *not* your friend. He supplied your name to the police. He gave them your photograph. He said bad things about you. He got you out of your house and *he turned you in.*' She resisted understanding this. She thought Joey was doing all this for some purpose. It was weeks before she started to comprehend that Joey was not on her side. She was like Hedda Nussbaum with Joel Steinberg*— absolutely."

* * *

---

*In late October 1989, New York City was stunned by the beating death of six-year-old Lisa Steinberg, the child (illegally adopted, it turned out) of

Naiburg had presented this picture of Amy—as the gullible victim of a Svengali—to Judge Goodman. It was an image he was to hammer home to the media throughout the summer. It was a successful spin.

Speaking before Klein had gone on the attack, Naiburg had begun his appeal for reasonable bail by stressing Amy's roots in Long Island and the fact that she knew nothing else *but* Long Island. Given her lack of money and the great attention the case had been given, how could she successfully flee?

Then he appealed on the basis of her parents' decency and devotion, and the fact that they were willing to put their home and life savings up as bail. Rose and Elliot Fisher, Naiburg said, "will assure this court by word and deed that Amy will return when this court mandates it . . . They are willing to put everything they have, everything they own, on the line. . . . *That's* how confident we are that Amy will return to the jurisdiction of this court and abide by the processes of this court."

Then there was the fact that high-school graduation was imminent and Kennedy principal Fred Cohen was arranging for Amy to be tutored at home in order to take her final exams.* Finally, Naiburg asked the judge to show some understanding of the fact that his client "was in a crisis situation and has suffered trauma because of the abuse that she has suffered at the hands of another person involved in this case. . . . Judge, I have to get help for her. . . . I have to have her home for that. She needs . . . a psychologist or psychiatrist who will help her understand the difficulties she is going through, help her assist me in the defense."

The latter point was critical. Naiburg and his investigator, Richie Haeg, knew that their debriefing of Amy and their work with her on her defense would be severely crippled if it had to be conducted in the jail's crowded visitors' room, where intruding eyes and ears were everywhere.

Joel Steinberg, a Greenwich Village attorney, and Hedda Nussbaum, a children's-book editor. The city was equally shocked that Lisa's "mother," Hedda, had for years been battered from head to toe by her mate, Joel—and had apparently acquired, in the process, a bizarre belief in Joel's godliness.

*Amy took her final exams in Nassau County Jail.

Still, Judge Goodman had dismissed all Naiburg's arguments and set the bail at the record-breaking $2 million. Naiburg left the arraignment intent on getting the outrageous bail reduced.

The next day, things got worse. Stephen Sleeman followed Peter DeRosa's example and sold his extensively fabricated tale to "A Current Affair." A day later Chris Drellos came forward. Now *three* men whom Amy had trusted had profited from impugning her. All had said they'd had sex with her.* Much worse, Sleeman's and Drellos's highly publicized stories established the intent motive that Fred Klein was eager to have by claiming that Amy had been looking for a gun for months.

HIT PARADE was one punnish headline. Its subhead was: "2nd Man Links Amy Fisher to Sex-for-Murder Plot." The same attorney, Bruce Parnell, who had just ushered Sleeman to fame and fortune on "A Current Affair" was now treating reporters to a heady dual story. The trouble is, the profit motive for the peddling of the tales somehow got lost under the sizzling allegations—and the fact that Parnell had assumed representation of Drellos quickly and only briefly (Drellos's parents cut this alliance off and hired their own lawyer) was also not known until later. Here is what Parnell, before he was dismissed by Drellos's family, asserted:

"He [Drellos] had a sexual relationship with Amy beginning last May through August. In early August, he had a car he wanted pinstriped and Amy brought him to [Complete]," and there disappeared with Joey for about forty-five minutes. "Afterward my client started asking her what the hell was going on between her and Buttafuoco. She told him she had a relationship with Buttafuoco and that he was madly in love with her. . . . About a week later, Amy approached my client and

---

*When Peter Guagenti was arrested (with information supplied to the police by Amy through Naiburg) on June 11, *his* lawyer, John Esposito, followed suit and declared that an "expectation of sex" from Amy was part of his motive for supplying the gun. Amy says, "Peter was *not* attracted to me, and he was very close to his girlfriend, Rory." Esposito also called Guagenti "a victim and unwitting pawn" of Amy, and, at Guagenti's February 4, 1993, sentencing (to six months in prison), he reiterated the expected-sex allegation.

asked him to kill Mrs. Buttafuoco. This went on day in and day out and she repeatedly asked if he could get her a gun.''

Parnell continued: Drellos "decided to pass her off to Steve [Sleeman] because Steve had a rifle.* He figured he could kill two birds with one stone—get rid of Amy" and obtain sexual favors for Sleeman.

The lies about the sex hurt and frustrated Amy the most. From her cell, Amy watched in hurt and disbelief as Drellos— the charming, hapless mooch she had given hundreds of dollars to, apartment-shopped for, and to whom her family had fed countless dinners—wove his headline-grabbing tale. She was revolted that Sleeman—the infatuated loser who rushed to her house with her requested burgers, the pest whose persistent calls she had changed her number to escape—lied to all of New York by saying she'd had sex with him in exchange for the promise of a gun.

Chris's lawyer Bruce Parnell's cavalier words—Chris had "decided to pass her off to Steve"—reeked of the presumption of female servility. So had Peter DeRosa's persistent imploring of Amy "and a friend" to perform for a party of men.

No one blew the whistle on these cheap shots. To the contrary, these sex-with-Amy tales were wind to the sails of Fred Klein, who, at Amy's June 6 hearing for bail reduction, went out of his way to highlight her prostitution, torturing logic in order to push easy buttons. Amy would be a "horrendous, horrendous" bail risk, Klein said, because, if released from jail on the lowered bail, "she could slide into that sleazy world [of prostitution] and she'll be able to support herself very well, and no one would ever find her." (Regarding that last claim, what Klein failed to consider was the virtual certainty that, if Amy *did* jump bail and go back to prostitution, there would be *dozens* of Peter DeRosas waiting to turn her in for tens of thousands of tabloid-TV dollars.) Klein added, here with more logic than grammar, that "her engagement in prostitution for months is the equivalent of a person involved in crime." Naiburg's attempts to get the bail reduced fell on deaf ears. The notion that teenaged prostitution can as easily bespeak a girl's

---

*Amy says, "I never saw Stephen Sleeman with a rifle. I don't know if he has a rifle or not."

enormous emotional problems and self-brutalization as the
wiliness and resourcefulness Klein alluded to, was unad-
dressed. Bail remained at $2 million.

Before and after every visit Amy received—most were from
her mother and from Eric Naiburg—she was frisked and strip-
and cavity-searched. This would go on for almost sixty more
days.

One columnist defended Amy from a feminist perspective,
accused the D.A.'s office of sexism, and eschewed the sleaze-
shows' throwing money at the sex-with-Amy bandwagon-
jumpers. This was the *New York Post*'s Amy Pagnozzi. But
women columnists from the so-called better papers—Anna
Quindlen of the *New York Times* and Ellen Goodman of the
Boston Globe—were mum. This was perhaps surprising since,
months before, insensitive reporting on Patricia Bowman (Willie
Smith's accuser) in *The New York Times* had made sexism in the
media a large, embarrassing issue. Thereafter, coverage of
exploited women—strong and virtuous ones, anyway: Anita
Hill, Desiree Washington, and the Tailhook victims—had been
squeaky clean. Yet that same higher press, which had exerted
such noble vigilance on its "own" stories, was now looking off in
distaste as a tabloid gang-bang was being conducted on one
palpably troubled teenager.

Silent, too, were the feminist eminences who had empathized
with or in one way or another supported such controversial
judged women as Jean Harris, Hedda Nussbaum, Bess Myerson,
Mary Beth Whitehead, Tawana Brawley, and Betty Broderick.
Perhaps Amy Fisher put off many otherwise-expected support-
ers. For one thing, her victim was a woman—and a person who
had done absolutely nothing to provoke her. City snobbism
about Long Island mall culture may have also made the story
seem inherently base and unresonant. (Mayhem that might
seem more random or banal if committed elsewhere—say, the
gang rape and bludgeoning of a young professional woman by
ne'er-do-wells, or the strangulation of a prep-school girl by a
private-school boy—becomes anointed with social significance
when they occur in Manhattan.)

More, the women's movement had spent twenty years distancing itself from the so-called sexual revolution. The fight now

was *against* forced and pressured sex with men—whether at the office, the convention, the hotel room, or the beach. The abiding presumption was that the *man* was doing the forcing, the pressuring, the enjoining. A girl—so young!—who sought sex, bragged about sex, wasn't monogamous, a girl who seemed to go out of her way to get herself exploited: She was snipping a thread in a polemic fabric that was being carefully and effectively knit.

Whatever the reason, groups and writers on women's issues seemed not to know what to *do* with Amy Fisher. It was a preelection summer and the pro-choice fight was dominant. Let this one stay a sleazy tabloid story representing nothing beyond itself, seemed the unspoken consensus.

Amy stayed in jail, losing weight from nervousness, fear, and an inability to stomach the jail food. Eric Naiburg fought for bail reduction and alienated the police by feeding leads first to the press. (The leak of the affidavit of Anthony Saciolo—the prison inmate and ex–gas station employee who asserted that Joey had sold him cocaine and had offered him a girl through the escort agency—had led to Saciolo's fear of harassment in prison and his concerted retraction. This press-currying act of Naiburg's particularly angered Nassau Homicide.)

Meanwhile a slumbering giant awakened: the innocence and virtue of Joey Buttafuoco.

◆ ◆ ◆

16

Perfect Husband

◆

One night, around June 15, at about 10:30 P.M. (I lost track of days and hours in jail), I sat down in my jail cell and wrote my parents a letter about how lonely and scared I was.

I reported to them the sounds I was listening to: the dripping faucets, clanging metal doors, and the screams of other inmates. I told them how I got most depressed at this hour—when my link to them, the telephone, was cut off. I told them how I hated to hang up from my evening phone conversation with them. "I feel," I said, "like a piece of me is being taken away."

I expressed what I guess you'd call my dependence on them by telling them that I always counted on them to make my pain go away—and, even though I logically understood that they couldn't make *this* pain go away, something in me still thought that somehow they could do that. I told them how I missed them, how "I dream about what it will be like if I ever come home."

It takes an experience like jail to see how lucky you are, and as I was writing the letter I looked around and saw women so much worse off than me—women who had no one. I had my parents, who, I finally realized, had given me so much. I told them how grateful I was that they were my best friends. I told them I wanted to come home and be with them and have everything be all right again.

226

I told them I was going to try "to pretend I am elsewhere" as I tried to fall asleep. "I decorated the letter with lots of happy faces and sad faces and hearts. I signed my name with lots of X's and O's and, right after my name, I wrote: "(confused)."

By now it was sinking in that many people I had counted on were not helping me. Peter had just been arrested, but he completely denied he knew what I wanted to do with the gun. Jane was walking around, uninvestigated: scot-free.* Stephen Sleeman had a movie deal!** There were some good people: Maria, Lori, and Rob were giving me support and love when I called them from jail. Eric was my hero and lifeline. And I was getting very attached to Paul—very attached.

As for Joey: Joey was the perfect husband. Never had sex with me—ever. Here's what happened, in case maybe you forgot.

♦ ♦ ♦

For two weeks, Eric Naiburg had been presenting Amy as a "pliable young girl," "repeatedly raped by a married older man." He called Joey a "Teflon bum and a classic pimp" and he'd waved the specter of an indictment of Joey on charges of rape in the third degree—vernacularly, statutory rape.

For those same two weeks, the media took at face value the presumption that Amy and Joey had been lovers. "A Long Island teen who admits shooting *her married lover's wife* . . . ," read one news story lead. "A year ago Joseph Buttafuoco *began a romance with* a quiet but determined teenager," began another; ". . . Buttafuoco, *who admitted to* an affair with the high-school senior. . . ." a third announced.

---

*Eric Naiburg says Jane would have been "critical" in terms of establishing Joey's part in the conspiracy. As for Guagenti, "We gave the police Guagenti," Naiburg says. "They wouldn't have gotten him on their own." Even though Guagenti, very quickly served by a lawyer, maintained limited involvement, Naiburg claims his arrest served Amy's defense because it led police to the gun (not found until August), which, being "a Saturday Night special that [Naiburg maintains] exploded on firing, was good for us: corroborating Amy's story."
**In short order, the writer and producers of the NBC-TV movie omitted Sleeman as a source.

[Emphases were added.] Not an *"alleged* affair or lover" in the lot.

Early on the morning of Friday, June 5, all of that changed.

The case had become the daily stuff not just of pre-prime-time tabloid TV and the city's daily newspapers—the New York *Daily News, Post,* and Long Island's *Newsday* (which provided the best coverage), and intermittently *The New York Times*—but of the region's radio call-in shows as well. One of the most controversial of these shows was that of Howard Stern, on WXRK-FM, airing from 6 to 10 A.M.

Howard Stern is a six-foot-five, thirty-nine-year-old, long-dark-haired South Shore native whose stock-in-trade is something called shock rock. Add Andrew Dice Clay to Lenny Bruce, give him the look of a massive heavy-metal roadie just prodded out of a long nap on the couch of his parents' pine-paneled basement, and there you have him. Pendulous breasts, mastur-bation, bovine lesbians, men who play pianos with their penises —those who take their morning coffee and doughnuts with Stern count on such patter as condiment. Howard Stern is an equal-opportunity offender; he has made not only anti-black and anti-Jewish cracks (he is Jewish), but also a sick joke about his own wife's miscarriage. The raunch is cut by Stern's female sidekick, Robin Quivers, a stylish, black, former air force nurse and radio reporter. If Stern can be said to be Regis Philbin, then she is his Kathie Lee Gifford.

Stern is heavy on inventive party games—his third in a series of $29 videos is titled *Butt Bongo Fiesta,* as in the percussive use of bare female derrieres. (The previous two were *Howard Stern's Negligée and Underpants Party* and *Howard Stern's U.S. Open Sores.)* His firing from his previous station, K-Rock (which Amy started tuning to after she met Joey), was, Stern believes, occasioned by RCA Chairman Thornton Bradshaw's chance hearing of his "Bestiality Dial-a-Date" in the corporate limou-sine. But then, blueblood executives like Bradshaw don't "get" Stern's message. Rather, he provides a kick-bag for lower-middle-class turnpike males who felt ripped off by the yuppie thieves of the 1980s and who, to add insult to injury, now have to eat a lot of Martian-seeming mandates on political correct-ness. Stern has 1.2 million listeners in New York alone. He is their designated hitter as they open their eyes every morning to a world they didn't make.

Stern's show inspires outraged complaints to the FCC. His New York syndicator, Infinity Broadcasting, has been fined for facilitating obscenity on the airwaves. Still, the show's immense popularity renders Stern's transgressions a manageable business risk and positions him, however improbably, as a Christlike martyr to the prudish and multicultural thought police. *Crucified by the FCC* is Stern's latest video.

On the morning of June 5—three days after Amy's $2 million bail was set, four days after the DeRosa tapes aired, right before the Sleeman and Drellos stories came out—Joey Buttafuoco picked up the same phone he had used, at Marty Alger's behest, to lure Amy Fisher into captivity, and called Howard Stern.

Joey was an avid Stern fan. Stern "spoke" to Joey—just as John Belushi had, just as Steely Dan had. On this particular morning, a caller to Stern's show had claimed he had worked in the backyard of the Buttafuoco home and that Amy had been in the pool. Since there *was* no pool in his backyard, Joey felt compelled to set the record straight. Maybe, too, he wanted to curry support from the audience most ready to scorn and leer at his hapless jailed lover, most ready to take his word against Amy's. Or so he might have supposed.

Shortly after he dialed Stern's call-in number, Joey Buttafuoco was put on the air.

Thousands of listeners turned their volume knobs to the right and blinked. According to Maria Eftimiades's book, *Lethal Lolita,** this is what they heard:

"I had a feeling you'd be a listener," Stern said.

"I'm definitely a listener," Joey allowed.

"How is your wife feeling?"

"Mary Jo is feeling a little better, man. She really can't do much for herself. I'm doing everything, bathing her, doing her hair. Whatever she did, man, I'm doing. Like I couldn't afford to pay her to do what she does, I'm telling you, man."

Perhaps Joey was chastened to learn the depth of the real

---

*St. Martin's Paperback, October 1992.

daily contribution of the woman he'd long complained, to Amy, of "sitting around all day doing nothing while I'm out there busting my butt."

Howard Stern perhaps heard the subtext; he decided to rub it in. "Let me tell you something," he said. "I feel guilty about my wife when I don't do stuff? You've got to be the guiltiest husband in the world."

Joey took advantage of the opening. "No, I'm not guilty."

"You've got to be riddled with guilt."

"Nooo."

Now Robin perkily asked, "Why not?"

". . . Because I have never in my life with her minimized what she has done," Joey responded, contradicting his months of resentful remarks to Amy.

"But we're talking about what *you've* done," Robin clarified.

Stern turned gleeful. "Wait till she realizes you were cheating on her. She's going to kill you."

Here came the opportunity Joey was waiting for. Remarking that Stern's was a good question, Joey announced, "Howard. I wasn't cheatin' on my wife. . . . I was faithful to my wife."

Across Radioland, listeners' eyes collectively widened. Was the guy kidding, or what?

"Really?" Stern shot back. This coup was unbelievable.

Joey said firmly, "Yes."

"So this stuff in the press is a lie? . . ." asked Robin Quivers. "Are you into that 'deny at all costs'?"

"I can't believe you guys are trying to bury me this morning," Joey said.

After a little more patter, Stern asked for a restatement. "So you're claiming that the papers are lying when they call you Amy's lover?"

"Absolutely yes."

Howard Stern was left to say, "Wow."

"You're getting a first, Howard," Joey reminded his host.

Robin Quivers was appropriately thankful. "Well, then I'm sorry for everything I've said about you."

Joey laughingly thanked Robin.

"I guess that yearbook stuff was true," Robin said. Under Joey's senior picture in the Massapequa High yearbook, no activities were listed; it simply stated, "I love Mary Jo." (What about his friend's girl, the girl he said he *really* loved? Amy would wonder when she heard about the yearbook.)

"Absolutely. Absolutely. She's my high-school sweetheart. I've been dying to be with a thirty-seven-year-old girl all my life. . . . What the hell am I going to go back to a sixteen- or seventeen-year-old throwback?"

That odd—and thereafter much-quoted—explanation for his claimed marital fidelity was praised by Robin Quivers. "This is a good defense," she said. "I like this."

Stern was a tad more cynical. "Listen," he advised, "whether this is true or not, I would stick with this. I would be in complete denial."

"It's just how I feel, Howard," Joey said earnestly. "It's where I'm at in my life right today."

Stern and Quivers tried to get Joey to admit that his idealism may have been slightly off the factual mark. But he was steadfast.

"I have a very beautiful wife," Joey said.

Stern: "You're saying you are clean as a whistle."

"Yes."

"In all of this."

"Absolutely."

After a few more minutes, Stern asked, "And you are now claiming that Amy Fisher is totally hallucinating that she had a relationship with you?"

"Yes."

Both Buttafuocos were being represented by Michael Rindenow, a portly and gentlemanly family friend, a man who had been the attorney for Complete Auto Body for twelve years. But with this bizarre outreach of Joey's, Rindenow decided that Mary Jo's husband was a little too irrepressible to remain his client. If Joey was going to nurse any more urges to pop up in undignified forums while his slowly recovering wife lay abed, he would need an attorney with a tough style and a strong muzzle.

Joey needed a criminal, not a civil, lawyer anyway. There was the issue of the possible statutory-rape charge. There was the introduction of Lorraine Wurzburg and her ABBA escorts into the picture and the floating allegations of Joey-the-prostitute-canvasser, Joey-the-drug-dealer, Joey Coco-Pops. These had to be stopped.

That afternoon, Rindenow called his friend, Marvyn Kornberg—a hard-hitting Queens-based police-brutality specialist. "'Marvyn,'" Kornberg recalls Rindenow saying, "'I'd like to consult with you with respect to a possible criminal case.'"

Marvyn Kornberg listened. A few minutes later he called Joe Buttafuoco, who was eager to hire him.

Kornberg remembers his opening words to his new client: "The next time you decide to speak to Howard Stern, you can get another lawyer. My clients *do not* make any public statements unless they're cleared with me."

Kornberg, fifty-eight, was a tough, loud, gravelly voiced courtroom bulldog. He had successfully defended a fair share of major drug dealers and "just as many charged with murder." In 1992, he got charges dropped against three police officers and a not-guilty verdict in the trial of a fourth after all four were charged with the beating and strangulation murder of a man named Federico Pereira in Queens; and, crossing to the other side of the police/suspect divide, he successfully represented alleged marijuana salesman Mark Davidson, who was tortured by police using a highly controversial interrogational aid. This well-known "stun gun case" (named after the aid) resulted in indictments for all of the officers involved.

Moving back to the other side of the line, Kornberg then represented firefighters who were charged with homicide when they hit a driver while on their way, in their fire truck, to a Chinese restaurant meal. All the firemen were acquitted.

Kornberg wanted Buttafuoco as a client. At that point the D.A.'s office was being pressured to prosecute Joey for statutory rape. Kornberg is, in his own words, "a major cross-examiner. I latch on and I *don't* let go." He wanted—to use a favorite term of his—to get a crack at Amy Fisher. He figured he could take her apart. In the meantime, the gruff, bellicose Kornberg would have a great time trying to best suave, cool Eric Naiburg at the media game. In the coming months—including well after

Joey's exoneration and Amy's imprisonment—Kornberg's appearances with his client on "Donahue" and other shows would, many believe, do *him* more good than his client.*

Kornberg emphatically denied the escort-service rumors and the drug-dealing stories. Since Alger and his men at Nassau Homicide found the escort-service rumors baseless and the drug-dealing stories irrelevant to the case at hand, both of these issues were quickly buried. Kornberg vowed to sue Eric Naiburg for calling his client a "pimp." He made Naiburg his whipping-boy, accusing the lawyer of pulling a Joey-made-me-do-it defense out of thin air and spinning publicity gold from it. As time went on, he would also heap grand sarcastic scorn on Amy.

He released a statement, admitting that his client had had a substance-abuse problem (the word *cocaine* was not mentioned, though it did receive candid play in the CBS-TV movie, for which the Buttafuocos had acted as consultants), and had spent twenty-eight days at a detox clinic. "He has been free of that problem for three years and eight months," Kornberg said in early June, "and he is not ashamed of the fact that he is one of the people that beat that problem."

Detective Marty Alger was convinced that Lorraine Wurzburg had absolutely *no* relationship with Joey Buttafuoco. Though his office was getting a number of "vengeance calls" from self-identified prostitutes, he didn't waste time pursuing these;

---

*Sources close to the case believe that Kornberg was frankly currying publicity on those programs; that Joey's boasting (with Kornberg at his side) that the D.A. didn't get him—"when in reality the D.A. was *inches* away from getting him," one source says, "amounted to Joey's making a fool of the D.A.'s office. He tried to stick it in their ear! So they *reopened* the investigation of him"—on the statutory-rape charges—in late February 1993. The instigating cause was the resurfacing of former Complete employee George Nessler (who had made an anonymous call to the "Howard Stern Show" after Joey's interview thereon), who claimed that Joey bragged that he'd given Amy her first orgasm. Nessler, it should be noted, has an arson conviction and is a former drug addict, both facts that Marvyn Kornberg notes with glee. Still, if Joey is finally indicted for statutory rape, Kornberg will get the chance to show off his talents as a "major cross-examiner" to unparalleled media attention.

past the possible ABBA link, which Alger had nixed, Joey's relationship to hookers was not relevant to the case.

Alger *was* hungry to stick Joey with conspiracy, however. For this he needed a witness. So eager did he seem that during one of his questionings of Amy, Amy briefly contended that Jane had been present when she and Joey were planning the shooting—"because she didn't want to disappoint me," Alger says wryly.

Alger and Severin were "positive" of the statutory rape. They had *thirteen* motel receipts, and the FBI handwriting experts had positively confirmed Joey as the signator on the majority of these.

Still, the Joey who now emerged with Marvyn Kornberg in tow was his wife's nurse-redeemer. "I am absolutely her caretaker," he told a reporter. The "power of prayer" had brought her back to health. "Everything's an effort. She can't eat solid food. I'm feeding her mashed potatoes. Everything I fix for her I fix in a blender. I feed her. I bathe her. I do her hair."

More, the Connery and Buttafuoco families became an army, touting Joey as the perfect husband.

Shortly after Joey's words to Howard Stern had turned a perceived certainty—that he'd been Amy's lover—into a suddenly open question, Mary Jo's mother, Pat Connery, made a phone call to another, decidedly middle-of-the-road morning radio show, John Gambling's "Rambling with Gambling."

All of New York had come to have great sympathy for the valiant shooting victim who had made the remarkable recovery and who, in fragile health and with an uncertain medical future, was trying to come to terms with her life. Mrs. Connery took a few moments to describe her daughter's condition. "Mary Jo is in a tremendous amount of pain," she said. "She still has double vision. She still has tremendous amount of problems with her ear, can't hear. . . . she's in pain twenty-four hours a day."

But Mrs. Connery's call had a greater purpose: to support Joey.

". . . I told you before, John, and I will say it again," she said to the sympathetic host, "I will lay down my life for my son-in-law. And they'll have to go through me to get to him."

The notion of *another* woman (the victim's mother, no less) taking a hit for the pecadillos of Joey Buttafuoco may have seemed a bit jarring. In this family, support for an innocent and valiant suffering wife translated into protestations of her *husband's* valor and purity.

John Gambling asked Mrs. Connery, "You don't buy any of this."

She continued: "None of it. Absolutely none of it. I have known him since he was sixteen years old, and he is my son. I don't consider him my son-in-law. He is my son. He's one of my kids."

Mrs. Connery reiterated that she didn't believe the reports that Joey *had* admitted his affair with Amy to the police ". . . one iota. Not one bit." And Mary Jo? "Exactly the same. They're devoted to each other. That's all I can tell you."

The next day, Caspar Buttafuoco's voice joined the family chorus in support of Joey's innocence. With an earthier take on the same words his in-law had used, the body-shop owner said, "If I thought my son was guilty even one iota, I'd gladly send the sunuvabitch to hell and let him burn for eternity. I love my son and it's really rough to have to sit here and listen to all these lies about him. It makes my blood boil. . . . I wish I could tell you what the *real* story here is. That girl makes poison ivy look good. I'll tell you this: I will go to hell and back for this boy, because he is one hundred percent right."

Both Joey's mother-in-law and father had just stated that they were willing to lay down their lives for him, for his goodness and honesty. In an earlier decade, that brand of family loyalty would have seemed deeply admirable. In the truth-obsessed early 1990s—when wives were not supposed to, as Hillary Rodham Clinton had so memorably put it, "stand by their men, like Tammy Wynette," when families were expected to confess their myriad dysfunctions, seek help and "grow," not hunker down into know-nothingism—it seemed inappropriate.

But it was not the elder family members' servant-to-the-pharaohs' attitude toward Joey that most piqued the public's incredulity; it was Mary Jo's. Starting with the Buttafuocos' press conference following Amy's sentencing in December and running through their television appearances ("CBS Good

Morning," "Donahue"), during the publicity for "their" TV movie (for which Joey co-profited in the $300,000 rights fee), Mary Jo's public attitude was one of unswerving belief in her husband's post–"Howard Stern Show" story. One reporter at the press conference voiced a question that many people had been asking silently: "Mrs. Buttafuoco, why is it so inconceivable to believe that your husband and Amy Fisher could have had an affair?"

"I know what I live with," she responded instantly, not missing a beat. "You've asked me this before. I know what my life was like. I think you people can *see* I'm *not* a stupid woman. I feel like I'm an intelligent woman who knows what's going on in my own life. I'm thirty-seven years old. I just *know*. I know what I live with." It was an answer that could not be shaken. Here and elsewhere, Mary Jo's elaborated answer was that her charming big bear of a husband had been so nice to pathetic Amy Fisher, had paid her attention that no one else ever had—so Amy had fantasized the affair to match her dreams. The CBS-TV movie *Casualties of Love* was faithful to this, the Buttafuoco version, chapter and verse.

The police had tried to tell the truth to Mary Jo, on October 22, 1992. Both Detective Sergeant Dan Severin and Detective Marty Alger had enormous admiration for the victim, whose shooter they had apprehended and sent to justice. And so when District Attorney Denis Dillon decided—after the airing of Amy's setup tape with and by Makely—that Amy was non-credible, that Joey would not be indicted for statutory rape, Alger in particular felt he owed Mary Jo the whole truth: the eleven motel receipts and the verification of Joey's handwriting by the FBI. Then she could decide what to do with her future.

Alger wanted Fred Klein and himself to be able to present the evidence they had against Joey to Mary Jo alone. But it had been the Buttafuoco family's practice, all summer long, to flank Mrs. Buttafuoco with lawyers and/or family members whenever the police talked to her. It was almost as if they were subordinating her interests to Joey's. In this, Alger did not think she had been well served.

For this particular meeting, Alger did *not* want the lawyers,

Rindenow and Kornberg, present. This was certainly too personal for that. So Alger called Mary Jo's mother, with whom he had a good relationship, on Wednesday, October 21, the day before the no-indictment announcement was to be made. "Mrs. Connery," he recalls saying, "I'd like to sit down with you and Mary Jo tomorrow. There are several things we'd like to discuss." Perhaps guessing what was coming, Mrs. Connery replied that there was nothing that Alger had to say that would ever change her mind about anything. "She was very defensive about meeting with me," Alger remembers.

In fact, she refused to meet.

"When the Connerys backed out of the meeting, I had to go another route, and the only route left was through the attorney," Alger says. Fred Klein made the appointment, and the following morning, October 22, at 10 A.M.—just as an announcement was going out that the D.A.'s office would not indict Joey—Alger and Klein went to Michael Rindenow's East Meadow office to meet with Mary Jo and her attorney.

According to Alger, when Mary Jo was told that her husband was not going to be indicted, "She was wracked with emotion. There was immediate relief, tears came . . . and she said, 'Thank God.'"

Alger continues: "At this point Fred Klein said, 'If you wish to ask any questions about what we found, we'll be more than happy to speak to you about it.' Rindenow stopped the conversation. Fred Klein and I were ushered into another room so Rindenow could speak to Mary Jo alone. Basically what he wanted to do at that point was shield her from the truth. That's been the scenario that's been written by this attorney during this whole thing: shield her against the facts. His line has always been: 'Because of her health, because of her injuries, because of her recovery, this may not be the right time . . .'"

After Rindenow had private words with his client, he left her to go back to Klein and Alger. What were they going to tell Mary Jo? the attorney wanted to know.

Klein and Alger replied, "The truth about what we found out."

Then Rindenow asked, "Can you be more specific?"

"Well, Michael," Alger replied, "if the woman asks a question, and there's an answer we can give her about whether or not her husband had an affair with this kid, we're going to answer that question."

"Okay, fine," Rindenow said, and the foursome reconvened.

Mary Jo had "fewer questions than you'd think she'd have," Alger says. Mostly, they were about the motel receipts. She listened intently as Alger and Klein went through receipt after receipt.

"At that point, she began to take a defensive posture," Alger recalls. "Her questions turned into statements. She began to counter what we were saying. 'Well, don't you know that *Naiburg* said that . . .' 'Well, my husband can *prove* where he really was that night.' 'We were with people.' 'I keep a calendar.' 'Marty, you know . . .' this, 'Marty you know . . .' that."

Alger liked this brave woman, into whose bandage-wreathed eyes he had solemnly gazed that late May evening, when she had first regained consciousness. Her overingratiating husband was gone that night; the husband's defensive, hovering brother was gone, too. "Why was I shot?" she had whispered. Her eyes begged for the truth. Alger told her he would find out. Well, he had that answer for her now. But her eyes had changed.

"Mary Jo, you must understand, there's more to this," Alger said. "Your husband signed more than one motel slip. We have as many as a dozen. They haven't been forged. His handwriting's been confirmed by a special document examiner with the FBI. We have receipts of the people who were in the room before him and receipts of the people who were in the room after him. They weren't forged. You have to understand."

But Mary Jo had already made up her mind about what the truth was. Everything Alger was trying to tell her stopped at a shield of tough certainty—forged from the same steel that had helped her to beat the medical odds and recover so extraordinarily.

"She was past denial and into *total resolution,*" is how Dan Severin would come to see it. "She is through with the anger and blame. She has turned the tables on her victimhood. A psychologist told me that one of her defense mechanisms was to say, figuratively, to Amy, 'You're not getting me. You may have shot me and it may have been because you want my husband but, uh-uh; I didn't die. And *I've* still got him. And *you're* in jail.'"

At one point in the meeting, Mary Jo had even challenged Klein and Alger. If they or anyone said they had a dozen motel receipts, "then a dozen times, *I'll* just say that *I* was in that motel room with him," Mary Jo is reported to have said.

♦ ♦ ♦

17

Overdosing and Overcoming

♦

I love Cher. She's my idol. I started off loving her because she looked so much like my Aunt Mary Lynn. One of the last things I did in my state of interim freedom—during the part of that stretch of time between June 28 (when I was freed from Nassau County Jail on the $2 million bail) and November 5 (when I voluntarily went back to jail) that I wasn't in the psychiatric hospital—was go to a Cher concert in Manhattan. Eric, my lawyer, took me. We tried to send a note to her backstage, but either it didn't get to her or the people around her thought it would be too controversial for her to acknowledge that I was in the audience and to invite me for a backstage visit.

I wish Cher would give a concert to the inmates of Albion. We do bad or stupid things because we're dependent on men and then we get in trouble, and that's when men start *really* swooping down to take advantage. In our desperation we don't see through them; we think it's love. We think it's concern. And—boom!—there we are: in prison.

I stand here in the Albion kitchen thinking, *Cher* was a young, wild girl when she hooked up with *her* older man, Sonny. How did she get out from under his spell and realize her own power? Maybe one day I'll get to meet her and she'll tell me.

My Story

If I ever meet Cher and we start kidding around, I'm going to ask her to do me this really big favor. Actually, it's more of a fantasy than a favor. She—the fittest of the fit, the gym-workout queen—sashays into Future Physique in her hottest leotard. While everybody's watching amazed, she walks up to Paul Makely and gives him one of her all-time cool "you're-a-wimp-and-a-creep" glares. And then she says, "That was from Amy."

I think Paul and that videotape are why Joey wasn't prosecuted, and Paul is why I almost didn't live to tell this story. I thought Paul really cared about me. I thought he was my friend. Obviously, I have very poor judgment when it comes to men. *That's* going to change by the time I leave Albion. I swear, if it takes every cell in my brain working triple overtime, *this* story isn't going to repeat itself.

◆ ◆ ◆

After the appeals court refused to lower Amy's bail, Eric Naiburg put out this somewhat novel call: Any Hollywood production company or studio that secured Amy's $2 million bail could have the full rights to her story. Almost every major studio and production company contacted him, but none was able to secure the money. It was certainly easy enough for any number of successful Hollywood producers to come up with the *bond* of $100,000 or $200,000 (the non-returnable 5 percent or 10 percent of the $2 million) needed to initiate the bail process; but Hollywood had to put its money where its mouth was. Such a producer would either have to collateralize his $2 million Bel Air home; standing ready to forfeit it entirely if Amy skipped town; or he or she would have to find a bail bondsman willing to personally insure that $2 million. For a fee of $1,000 or $2,000, that was a tall order to ask of such a bondsman—and producer after producer could not find a willing gambler in the bail-insurance industry.

One New York agent came upon a promising lead. Ron Yatter, a twenty-five-year veteran of the William Morris Agency who was now president of the Producers' Agency, was representing KLM Productions—consisting of two men, Alfred Kelman and Phillip Levitan, who together and separately had produced a dozen notable television movies, including George C. Scott's *A Christmas Carol* and the biography of Raoul Wallenberg. Through a mutual friend, Yatter spoke to Ron Olszowy, a New Jersey–based national bondsman, and conveyed his sense of Amy, culled from conversations with Naiburg and with Rose Fisher, as a girl who needed her family and would be, despite Fred Klein's exhortations, a safe bail risk.

Olszowy worked very closely with the nation's largest bail insurer, International Fidelity Insurance Company of Newark. He set up a meeting for Yatter, Naiburg, Rose Fisher, and the principals of KLM with the company's owner and chairman, a dapper, white-haired eighty-year-old man named Philip Konvitz. Konvitz had been in the bail business for fifty years. He made decisions by weathered and confident instinct. At the unusual hour-long meeting, he was moved and impressed by Rose Fisher, and was struck that she and her husband were willing to stake all they had—their home, stock portfolio, business assets, and life savings: $900,000 total—on their utter conviction that Amy would not flee.

Rose brought to the meeting a letter that Amy had written from jail. (This letter is referred to at the beginning of the previous chapter of this book.) She handed the letter to Konvitz, who read it slowly. The sartorially conscious octogenarian—he favors white suits in summer, with colorful handkerchiefs fluffed in their pockets, and wears brown-and-white wingtips that he bought in 1946—is a man whose views about human nature are as secure and unambiguous as his taste in bootery.

In Amy's plaintive, ingratiating words to her parents, Konvitz saw a frightened girl begging to return to the lost certainty of childhood. Young girls who yearn for such safe harbor do not flee and leave their parents destitute, he believed.

Konvitz set the letter down and, alone among major national bail insurers, said, "I'll do it."

"I didn't think anyone was ever going to get me out!"

Amy said as she was led out of jail on Tuesday, July 28, 1992. She had been incarcerated for sixty-six days. She had lost almost twenty pounds. She looked wan but happy. Her hair was fixed in cornrows, courtesy of a big-sister inmate.

The tabloids played up the contrast of a thrilled Amy— FREED!; AMY FREE!—and a furious Mary Jo. Absent in the stories was any mention of KLM's role in securing the bond. (The *Post* alluded to AMY'S MYSTERY $2M.)

When Fred Klein found out the next morning about the production company's participation, the hearing in Judge Goodman's courtroom turned into considerably more than what it was supposed to be: the simple issuance of a restraining order for Amy to stay away from the Buttafuocos.*

Klein angrily accused Amy's lawyers of deception. "It is very odd to me," he said, "that all this financial information was jammed down our throats yesterday afternoon, but no mention at all was made about a production company being involved. . . . I asked that woman," he said, referring to Christine Edwards-Neumann, "yesterday where the hundred thousand dollars came from. She knew that part of the premium of sixty thousand dollars was put up by a production company, but she never told me that, and she never told a court that."

The scolding over the deception was merely Klein's warm-up. He had a larger issue in mind: bail remand.

"I think it is against the public policy of this state to allow defendants to sell their rights to how they committed a crime

---

*A restraining order barring Amy from going near Mary Jo would have been appropriate and sufficient. To word the order such that eighty-pound, seventeen-year-old Amy Fisher was the aggressor against Joey, Bobby, and Caspar Buttafuoco, large adult males daily hunkered down in their power-tool- and metal-filled body shop, was telling. There were some who thought that Mary Jo (who told reporters she would *"never, never, never"* believe her husband had an affair with Amy) was being protected from the truth. Says Marty Alger, who could not speak to her without lawyers or family present, "I think Mary Jo was badly served by the people surrounding her."

and then profit by that by getting a bail bond,"* he announced sternly.

"Is he going to send me back to jail?" Amy asked, panicked.

Naiburg hugged her but he looked grim. He was prepared to fight. "She is presumed innocent, Your Honor," Naiburg stated loudly. "That is the foundation, the premise, the basis of our entire judicial system. Let me have my client back so I can prepare her defense. . . . She is here, Judge. Please don't deprive her of liberty." Goodman agreed not to do so.

Amy settled back into her gray-and-white bedroom with the Floridian curtains and sheets, but life now on Berkley Lane was not the life she'd left. The phone calls to Maria and Lori were stilted now; a chasm of crime, jail time, and unimaginable notoriety gaped between Amy and her former buddies. Jane severed contact. The media posted photographers in front of the house day and night to catch glimpses of the "Long Island Lolita."

Emotionally fragile and woefully impressionable to men under the best of circumstances, Amy had Eric Naiburg as her male anchor. He was close at hand but not on call twenty-four hours a day. (Chris Neumann, however, was. She virtually moved in with the Fisher family, helping her client and best friend Rose Fisher through a painful experience that Rose has said "*Webster* has no word for.")

Most frightening, Amy had not yet gotten over Joey. Richie Haeg, Naiburg's private investigator, noticed this as much as Naiburg had. "When we'd see her in jail, I would say to her,

---

*New York State Supreme Court eventually confirmed that KLM's payment of monies in connection with bail proceedings was proper, and that Mary Jo Buttafuoco did not have a right to such monies in connection with her civil suit against Amy Fisher. Rather, the court decided, Amy was exercising her constitutional rights to raise her bail in any legal manner. KLM posted $80,000 of the nonrefundable $100,000 bond to Konvitz: $60,000 when bail was made, another $20,000 (by way of reimbursement to the Fishers) when their NBC-TV movie aired in December 1992. The Fisher family thus lost only $20,000 on the bail insurance, having staked the entirety of their assets on Amy's return to court for what was then expected to be her trial date.

'Amy, *he gave you up.* You're going to do all the time and he's going to go free. He's *not* a knight in shining armor coming in here to get you. Now: Do you still love him?' And she'd say, 'Yes.' That attitude didn't evaporate with the bail bond."

Haeg is a man whose easygoing charm belies the fact that he was a marine sergeant who served with distinction in Vietnam, a New York City rackets investigator, and Suffolk County detective who chaired the Detective Association's Political Review Board. Like Naiburg, who has two daughters close to Amy's age, and KLM agent Ron Yatter, who has one, Haeg's experience with his own two teenaged girls led him to understand Amy. "The vulnerability of a girl that age who wants love is enormous. You meet her and realize why we *do* have statutory-rape laws."

Eric Naiburg went over a limited list of friends considered safe company for his confused and fragile young client. Paul Makely was on that list. The thirty-year-old gym owner had a likable manner and a convincing self-depiction as the man who cared about Amy as a whole person. "Tell me the truth; I need to know the truth; I won't leave you," he had gently urged her in April, when he had heard of her prostitution. Stories like this were impressive—even to Haeg and to Naiburg. Besides, the bottom line was: He was much better than Joey.

By now Joey had become a parody of hulking, foot-in-mouth braggadocio. With his call to Howard Stern and his frequent appearances—in boots, shades, and tight T-shirts—in swaggering postures in front of his house and his body shop, his persona begged for the poetic justice of an opposite: a macho but sensitive New Man. Makely filled the bill of Amy's "nice" boyfriend, the reluctantly seduced (*if* seduced) older brother prodding Amy to her better self. Many who dealt with the unfolding story—investigators, journalists, lawyers—found this image to be a handy missing fragment; they snapped Paul Makely, in the hero role, into the Amy Fisher puzzle board.

As such, Makely was getting away with a great deal of the doubt. He was still officially denying that he had ever been Amy's lover. He had not told the police that, as Amy claims, she had told him, twenty hours *before* she was arrested, that she had shot Mary Jo. His past alleged involvement in two drug cases was handily unknown to reporters. He had so far eluded the messy fate of Peter DeRosa, Peter Guagenti, Stephen

Sleeman, and Chris Drellos; there were no pictures in the tabloids and on the TV screen touting Makely as one of "Amy's men." Even his biggest secret—that he had a hair weave—was safely hidden.

But Makely wasn't silent. He was profiting from Amy's travails. Future Physique was getting free publicity. Its membership rolls were burgeoning. Many of the new members were reporters, hoping to catch a glimpse of the gym's most celebrated young female member. Makely took advantage of this surge in business by refusing to give the reporters cancellations or refunds when their iron-pumping stakeouts proved fruitless.

Makely was reportedly paid as a consultant for *People* writer Maria Eftimiades's paperback book on the case, *Lethal Lolita*. (That book reports as fact that the first time Paul learned of the shooting was *after* Amy was arrested and she called him from jail to report, "Paul, I really screwed up.") Even the screenwriter for the KLM-produced NBC-TV movie was sufficiently impressed with Makely's persona, and needy enough of a script "throughline," so that the story that eventually aired presented Makely in a very flattering light. (Makely was, however, condemned by Amy at the end of the movie.) Makely received $21,000 for the depiction.

Amy was now falling in love with Paul and relying on him greatly. She had sent him letters and tapes from jail and had called him from jail. True to his persona, he presented himself to her as an anchor, a confidant.

Although Eric Naiburg was preparing to go to trial, the possibility of a plea bargain hovered. It was not an unattractive option. Amy knew she had done wrong and was not looking to elude punishment through an acquittal from a jury. With Elliot Fisher suffering a recurrence of his heart ailment, he and Rose were not eager for the ordeal of a trial, which would, among other things, put their parenting on the witness stand and open up their daughter's childhood to gleeful and intense press scrutiny. Another factor reared its head: Sleeman's and Drellos's statements and the consequent possibility, strongly implied by the D.A.'s office, of a conspiracy charge added to that of attempted murder.

If proved, the conspiracy could add at least eight and a third years of prison time to that same minimum sentence accruing from an attempted-murder guilty verdict. The *maximum* time on such consecutive sentences would be *fifty* years. Thus, under this worst-case scenario, if Amy's in-prison behavior were poor and parole boards unsympathetic, she could live behind bars until she was nearly seventy years old. With a girl who had proved so vulnerable to self-destruction in the *best* of all environments, was self-destructive behavior in the worst of all environments—prison—so unimaginable? Pleading guilty to first-degree assault would bring Amy's minimum time served down to five years, her maximum to fifteen years. However skillful Naiburg was at trial work, however sympathetic Amy might appear as a defendant, however skewerable Joey was as an instigator-accomplice, the plea option bobbed like a life raft in risky waters.

If a plea bargain for Amy was attractive to Naiburg, to an even greater degree, immunity from prosecution for Joey was a desperate goal of the Buttafuocos and their attorneys. Michael Rindenow made no secret of the fact that his client would accept a lesser charge against Amy in a plea, in exchange for the guarantee that Joey would not be investigated.

In mid-September, two different kinds of behind-the-scenes negotiations were going on: one by Richie Haeg with Paul Makely; the second prompted by a call to Eric Naiburg by Michael Rindenow. No one expected that they would be colliding.

If any one investigator believed Joey Buttafuoco was guilty of conspiracy, it was Richie Haeg. Haeg knew that Joey and Paul Makely had been friendly in the fall and winter (Amy would not otherwise have met Makely); Haeg suspected they might even have had past drug-related business dealings. Makely was being charming and helpful with Haeg, as he was with everyone.

Haeg wasn't going to let lie the curious hand-over of Amy to Makely by Joey last February. Why did Joey do that? He had a feeling that Joey would be back in Paul's gym, possibly saying something such as "Send Amy a message." According to Haeg, Paul Makely agreed to let Richie Haeg wire Future Physique with microphones in hopes of catching Joey Buttafuoco during an incriminating moment.

The gym was wired. Nothing happened. The wiring was dismantled. But Paul Makely had just been given a good idea about how to entrap someone—and, quite possibly, to make a lot of money in the process.

Shortly after Haeg unwired Makely's gym—late in the week ending September 20—Eric Naiburg was on the phone with Michael Rindenow. Naiburg was seeking to subpoena three different records from Complete Auto Body: its employment records (to see if any employee had ever seen Amy and Joey together*; its shirt orders (to judge whether or not Joey had been lying when he claimed that the reason he knew Amy was the shooter was because "we only gave one of those shirts away—to Mr. Fisher's daughter"); and its phone records, to document the frequent calls from Joey to Amy, especially during the week preceding the shooting.

Rindenow was now asking Naiburg if he would accept a sworn statement about the employment records, instead of the records themselves. Both attorneys, however, seemed to feel that something else was in the air between them. "There was a pregnant pause in the conversation," Naiburg recalls, "I sensed Mike wanted to talk more."

The subject of the plea bargain was broached. Rindenow had gotten word of the numbers Naiburg was talking with the D.A.'s office. "Five to fifteen?" Rindenow asked.

"That's right," Naiburg said.

"We have a common interest," Rindenow allowed, according to Naiburg.

"Yeah, I know we have a common interest," Naiburg responded. Naiburg recalls today: "That common interest was expressed, in sum and substance, as: I'm looking for less time for my client, Amy—and he's looking for Joseph Buttafuoco not to be prosecuted."

Naiburg remembers the conversation proceeding thusly:

RINDENOW: "What are you looking for?"

NAIBURG: "Two to six."

---

*George Nessler, who five months later claimed he heard Joey brag about having sex with Amy, was the then-unknown employee Naiburg sought.

RINDENOW: "That's much too low."

NAIBURG: "Well, look—there's a lot of room between two to six and five to fifteen."

RINDENOW: "That I agree with."

Three to nine years would have been the logical middle-ground.

NAIBURG: "Let's meet."

RINDENOW: "Do you mind if Kornberg comes along?"

NAIBURG: "I'd rather not."

RINDENOW: "Look, I'm not familiar with criminal law, and Kornberg is, and he's representing Joey."

NAIBURG: "All right, if he wants to meet, let me know."

Ten minutes after hanging up, Naiburg got a call-back from Rindenow saying he'd just spoken to Kornberg and that Kornberg was "very excited." The three attorneys set a meeting at a Nassau County restaurant for Monday night at 6:30.

Over the weekend, Naiburg had extensive negotiations with Fred Klein. The lawyer weighed his options. One was that he could meet with Kornberg and Rindenow on Monday night and hammer out a quid pro quo, consenting to immunity for Joey in exchange for a prison term of less than five to fifteen years, then go straight to Judge Goodman and say, "Look, this is what we, the defendant and the complainant, agree to." But such a move would risk Klein's anger; Klein *wanted* to prosecute Joey. Or he could go with Rindenow and Kornberg and that same agreement—but to Klein instead of to Goodman. Naiburg believes, however, that Klein would not have gone along with granting Buttafuoco immunity, so his attempt to get Amy less than five to fifteen in the plea would have failed.

In the end, Naiburg canceled his meeting with Rindenow and Kornberg and went with Klein's deal: five to fifteen for Amy and immunity for her in exchange for her testimony against Joey. This was the best deal for Amy in the long run, he decided. Among other things, the psychological benefit would be significant. She would get to set the record straight, see Joey share in the blame, and watch justice being administered evenhandedly. "Fred Klein is someone you can trust," Naiburg told his client.

So there were two men Amy was told she could trust:

Assistant District Attorney Fred Klein, and her boyfriend Paul Makely.

The announcement of Amy's plea, on Monday, September 21, led to fury in the Buttafuoco camp. The thing they most wanted, the thing they would have traded less prison time for Amy for—immunity for Joey—was out the window.

" 'The bullet couldn't kill me but the judicial system may,' " an angry Rindenow quoted his client as saying, with a curious turn of logic.* Rindenow threatened that if the plea was allowed to stand, "my client will not approve and will write to Judge Goodman to ask him to deny it."**

Kornberg added his ire: "To sell out for five to fifteen years without the consent of the victim is outrageous. [Mary Jo is] repulsed by the district attorney's handling of the case."

On Wednesday, September 24, 1992, Amy stood before Judge Goodman and described her crime thusly: "I went up to [Mrs. Buttafuoco's] doorstep with a loaded gun in my pocket. I proceeded to talk to Mrs. Buttafuoco for approximately ten to fifteen minutes. She turned around to walk away and I hit her on the back of the head. I went to hit her again and the gun went off. I guess, obviously, I shot her. She fell on top of me on the ground. I tried to get her off me. I hit her—I think twice more. Then I left. I ran away."

Fred Klein remarked, "We got one fish. Now we are going to look for more fish."

All of this outraged Mary Jo. "She tried to kill me and now she's taking my husband and she's trying to destroy us. It's frightening that one person can do so much damage. This girl is an attempted murderer, a liar, a prostitute, and the D.A. is

---

*After Amy finally made her $2 million bail, Mary Jo was quoted as saying she would never feel safe as long as Amy was free; yet she was now eager to accept an *earlier* prison release date for Amy (as long as it meant that the truth about her husband would not get onto the judicial table), the denial of which (as part of that deal) she now angrily said was part of the judicial process that would "kill" her.

**According to New York State law, the victim's wishes must be taken into account during the negotiation of a plea bargain or the administration of a sentence.

accepting her statement that she and Joe were together. Something's wrong here, real wrong. I am behind [Joey] one hundred percent. . . . Everything [Amy] is saying is a lie."

The headlines over the next two days framed the situation as it *appeared* to be:

AMY CUTS DEAL; JOEY'S LAWYER FEARS RAPE CHARGE

AMY PLEADS; JOEY SWEATS: MARY JO FURIOUS AT DEAL. LABELS AMY'S STORY A LIE

AMY FISHER PLEADS GUILTY TO ASSAULT: HUSBAND OF THE VICTIM IS SUBJECT OF INQUIRY

AMY'S BIG DEAL: BUTTAFUOCO IN PROBE'S SPOTLIGHT

JOEY'S LAWYER PREDICTS RAPE RAP

But things would turn out differently.

Just before the plea bargain, Paul Makely apparently looked around his gym, freshly shorn of the microphones Richie Haeg had placed there. Maybe he got an idea. At any rate, he was soon on the phone with Rafael Abramovitz, a producer for "Hard Copy." The show, a direct competitor to "A Current Affair," had featured anti-Amy coverage all summer long. It is not known whether Makely or Abramovitz initiated the call, but a figure of somewhere between $10,000 and $50,000 seemed to have been part of the conversation. Paul Makely's certification as Amy's lawyer-approved boyfriend was a strong selling point.

Here is how Amy remembers what happened the night before she appeared in court for her plea bargain.

♦ ♦ ♦

I had always thought of Paul as an improvement over Joey because he didn't manipulate my mind, didn't play games with me. He laid things on the line. He was a straight shooter.

One of the things Paul could always do (which Joey couldn't do) was make me laugh. As it came time to go to court for my plea bargain, I was getting very nervous and very scared. Paul called me the night before I was supposed to be in court to accept my fate.

"Come over, we'll have a good time," he said. He offered to take my mind off tomorrow.

I wasn't in the mood for a "good time." But he sounded convincing.

"I don't want to talk about your case. Come on, we'll just have a good time. I'll take you out. I'll make you happy."

Then he said—and these were his exact words: "I have a surprise for you."

"What is it?" I asked. I wasn't sure I was in the mood for a surprise any more than for a good time.

"We're going to talk about five things that we're going to do together before you go to jail," he said.

Five things? He was putting so much into this attempt to make me feel better, I felt touched. So I said, "Okay, I'll come over." I figured, why not? (That's the *last* time I'm ever going to figure "why not?")

People who know me will tell you: I go out of my way to please people, men especially. I feel I'm responsible for making things good for them. I told the police Joey gave me the gun (when, of course, he didn't) because that seemed to be what the police wanted to hear from me. I withheld Peter Guagenti's name so long because I promised him I would protect him. Marty Alger has been quoted in this book, saying how I said Jane listened in on an incriminating conversation between me and Joey because I didn't want him [Alger] to feel so frustrated in trying to find a conspiracy witness. And later in this chapter Eric's law partner, Matthew Rosenblum, will tell you what I said to *him* two days after the plea bargain, when I came to in the hospital. To make a long story short, I don't like to disappoint men.

So there I was on the phone with Paul. He wanted me to be happy and have a good time. I was nervous—tomorrow was D day. But I didn't want to let him down.

I went to the gym and we sat in the lounge and I was kidding, I was joking around. He played this game of asking me the things I most wanted before I went to prison, but I didn't see through it; I just answered. A lot of the things I said were absolutely ridiculous because *that was the mood Paul was setting*—that was part of our agreement about the evening: a carefree good time. Anyway, the things I said weren't so terrible.

I *did* say that I felt remorse for what I did to Mary Jo. And when Paul kidded around about us eloping to Vermont, I *did* say, "No. Then my parents will lose everything." When I said I wanted a Ferrari for all my pain and suffering, that was supposed to be ironic. I was going to prison. You can't bring a Ferrari to prison! It's like making a joke about the *Titanic*. Gallows humor, I think they call it.

My attitude with Paul that night had nothing to do with my feelings about the crime I had committed and everything to do with wanting to be cute and funny, because Paul had made it very clear that he expected me to be that way.

◆ ◆ ◆

Amy spent the entire day of Friday, September 25, in Eric Naiburg's office being debriefed by Fred Klein and Marty Alger, as part of their vigorous investigation of Joey. "By the end of the day she was exhausted—she was haggard," Naiburg's law partner, Matthew Rosenblum, remembers noticing. "It was a grueling process. It's emotionally exhausting to rat on someone you were madly in love with and controlled by."

News of Paul's betrayal came in by way of the tabloid headlines: LAUGHING LOLITA: AMY BRAGS ON TAPE ABOUT PARTYING, DESERVING FERRARI FOR HER SUFFERING, said the *Post*. *Newsday* was more circumspect: CANDID CAMERA: HIDDEN LENS CAPTURES FISHER TALKING ABOUT SEX, PUBLICITY. The *News* took a middle ground: AMY: FAME IS MY FORTUNE: SEZ PAIN IS WORTH A FERRARI.

All three front-page stories touted the "Hard Copy" show that would air that evening, which would feature the videotape Paul Makely had lured an unknowing Amy into starring in. Goading her into a display of materialism that would sound appropriately startling in sound bites, Paul had asked Amy what she most wanted before she went to prison. All the sad, silly replies she accommodated her older boyfriend with—her flirtatious request that Paul marry her so she could have "conjugal visits" in prison; her flippant line: "If I had to go through all this pain and suffering, I am getting a Ferrari"—were promised in the evening's broadcast.

So eager were the papers to deliver the hot news quickly that the reporters inadvertently turned their stories not merely into wholesale "Hard Copy" press releases, but also into virtual

AMY FISHER

broadsides for the Buttafuocos: perfectly timed, since the "Joey probe" they furiously sought to quash was barely off the ground in the D.A.'s office. The news stories: (1) did not question Rafael Abramovitz's assertion that Paul Makely was paid no money for the tape; (2) did not question Paul Makely's denial of knowledge of the tape's existence; (3) went with Makely's denial that he had ever had an affair with Amy; (4) featured grave warnings from a show spokeswoman that a second, "more disturbing" tape of Amy would follow on Monday evening; and (5) were peppered with quotes from Marvyn Kornberg: "It's just Amy Fisher doing what she does best: lying and prostituting herself"; and, "I'd give a quarter to see [Nassau District Attorney Denis] Dillon's face tomorrow morning."

Amy insisted on seeing the show. Rose Fisher wanted her to view it with an attorney present and Naiburg had already left for his weekend house. So Rose got on the phone with Matthew Rosenblum and the two worked out an arrangement by which Amy would not view the show alone and would *not* be allowed, after viewing it, to drive her car home that evening. Both Rose Fisher and Rosenblum predicted that Amy would be thrown into emotional turmoil.

Rosenblum drove Amy to a friend of his and Naiburg's. They turned on the set just as Abramovitz was lambasting Amy in the show's wraparound narrative. Amy sat still in the friend's living room and stared at the screen as her private "fun" evening with Paul was grainily and grotesquely played back to her.

"As soon as the tape started rolling," Rosenblum says, "she fell on the floor, crying, writhing in pain, calling out, 'Not Paul! No! Not Paul!' She just kept saying it, over and over. I thought she was going to vomit. I turned off the set, said, 'Let's get out of here.' I almost had to carry her back to the car. She was crying hysterically as we drove to the office."

There she called her mother. She spoke, Rosenblum recalls, of how disturbed she was not only by Paul's entrapment and betrayal, but by the fact that people were getting the wrong picture of what she was like.

Rosenblum said, "She was terribly upset. She was physically and emotionally bankrupt."

Rosenblum took her car keys and drove her to a quiet restaurant, Orlando's, for dinner. Nestled at a corner table, she drank club soda, picked at her food, and struggled to be cheerful for her male company.

Rosenblum reassured her, as Naiburg had, that Fred Klein was a fair prosecutor. "I told her, 'I had a couple of murder cases with him. He is a man of his word, the best prosecutor on the island, if not in the state. Justice will be done evenhandedly.'"

Rosenblum dragged the dinner out as long as he could and then, at about 9:45, announced, as per his plan with Rose, that it was too late for him to drive Amy back to the office to get her car; he would simply drive her home now and pick her up to retrieve her car in the morning.

Rosenblum drove Amy home, waited until she got inside, then drove to his own home. As he walked in the door his phone rang. A panicked Rose Fisher was on the line with the news that Amy had gone straight into the bathroom and swallowed a quantity of the tranquilizer Xanax. Rosenblum, Rose Fisher, and Chris Edwards-Neumann conference-called. Then each called every doctor he or she knew to find out if Xanax could produce a fatality; all said no. "We wanted to avoid the publicity of Amy entering a hospital," Rosenblum says, "but we wanted to make sure Amy was all right." Rosenblum contacted a resident from Huntington Hospital who made a house call and determined that Amy was safe for the night.

The next morning Amy went back into the bathroom, this time swallowing eighteen tablets of the more toxic Lorazepam, the tranquilizer prescribed for her father for his heart condition.

Rose Fisher called Naiburg; Naiburg called Rosenblum to help him. Both lawyers rushed to the Fisher house and struggled to carry a moaning and nearly comatose Amy out of the house and into Eric's car. "She was like dead weight," remembers Rosenblum. "We were just handing her off to one another, she was so limp and heavy. She kept saying, 'I just want to die . . . Let me die . . .' Eric had tears in his eyes. I was blurry-eyed also."

After driving 100 to 120 miles per hour and communicating with Huntington Hospital emergency admissions by car phone, the lawyers got her admitted. Her stomach was pumped and she was hooked up to an IV.

"As soon as she came to, she told her mother she wanted to

see me," Rosenblum says. "Her words, from her hospital bed, were: 'I just want you to know: It had nothing to do with you.'"

On Monday, September 28, "Hard Copy" played an extremely personal audiotape Amy had made for Paul. In it she alluded to "terrible" things her father had done to her. She used the word *abuse.* "I just don't understand why my mom ever had me," her voice on the tape said to Paul.

The betrayal, the exposure, the misrepresentation, the stress, and the inability to know where to turn had led to the two suicide attempts. Amy was kept in the psychiatric unit of Huntington Hospital, too fragile to testify against Joey. Meanwhile, the "Makely tape" was souring the atmosphere at the Nassau County district attorney's office. Questions were tossed around: Could the star witness against Joey Buttafuoco be considered credible after such a prime-time display? Wasn't there a standing order in the D.A.'s office that rape in the third degree not be a prosecutable offense? Was it worth the office's manpower and reputation to go after stat-rape when the girl was on the highest end of the age range—sixteen—and had only been under age for a month and a half of the ten-month affair? Was such a case winnable? Especially with the adultery charge Klein had tacked on, how would it make the office look— puritanical? overzealous? frivolous? sycophantic in the face of public pressure?—if the case against Joey were lost? Finally, what about Mary Jo Buttafuoco? Hadn't she suffered enough?

Those questions would not have been entertained had the Makely tape not been aired.

In Huntington Hospital, where Amy stayed for a month, she formed a group of friends with three other patients: a thirty-two-year-old male would-be rock producer, a thirty-year-old Wall Street accountant, and a fourteen-year-old girl named Vicki. Vicki, an Italian-American girl from Bellmore, was recovering from severe depression and soon became Amy's morning-to-night best friend. They played pool before and after group and individual psychotherapy sessions; loaded up on junk food—potato chips, Hershey's Kisses, Doritos, Snickers, mini-marshmallows; and hoarded the little packets of hot chocolate they got in the morning.

Amy also poured her heart out to Vicki. "She broke down and

cried when she thought about going to jail," said Vicki. "She told me how much it hurt her, to see what Paul did to her, but that she kind of understood that she shouldn't try attempting suicide again. I told her"—Vicki's high-pitched, Long Island-accented voice is just like Maria's and Lori's—" 'From what I was reading about you, I thought you would be a psychomaniac!' She was one of the nicest, sweetest people I ever met."

On Thursday, October 22, 1992, Nassau County District Attorney Denis Dillon announced that no charges would be brought against Joseph Buttafuoco. "We determined that the Buttafuoco family had suffered enough," Dillon said. "To continue the investigation would only bring greater suffering to Mrs. Buttafuoco." Fred Klein termed Amy's words in the tape "revolting" and assailed her credibility. Joey declared himself "exonerated" and flashed a cocky smile, while his wife looked at him adoringly as the cameras flashed.

Thus, Amy had met her final betrayer—the district attorney's office: She had refused to try to get herself a lighter prison sentence because she refused to assent to Joey's being immunized from prosecution. Now she was being given the maximum sentence—*and* Joey *wasn't* being prosecuted.

On December 1, 1992, Amy went to prison.

◆ ◆ ◆

When I attempted suicide it was because I didn't want to live anymore. I felt I had nobody. I didn't think of it as dying—I just wanted to go to sleep and have all my troubles go away and never have to deal with them again.

Prison is the opposite of that sad dream of death. Prison is hard reality. It keeps you awake. You get up at 5 A.M. for a reason: to face life. The thing about prison is, there's nowhere to run to, to drive to—even in your mind. I look back at the men I loved from this distance, from behind this barbed wire, and I know that part of coming to terms with it all is remembering an experience in all of its complexity. Joey told me I was "angelic." He sucked my toes. We had foreplay, afterplay, during-play. It was a very special relationship, not just some dirty thing. I want to be able to hold on to that tiny bit of the good, as well as to learn from the bad.

As for Paul, right before he betrayed me I sent him a tape from jail and said, "I guess the worst guy I ever met in my entire life"—meaning Joey—"made it possible for me to meet the *best* guy I ever met: you. When you came along I realized that I could date a man. And I could love him. And I could still have fun. Before you came along I never experienced all three of those things put together. I didn't think you loved me back. And now I know that you did."

Well, some love *that* turned out to be. But, still, being realistic is being able to remember the good, even when it turned into the bad.

After all, it was to Paul that (in that tape from Nassau County Jail) I spoke these words: "Now I'm starting to realize that I can't run away from my problems anymore; that I'm going to have to face them and even though it's real hard sometimes, I'm just going to have to." Shortly after I said them, I did try to run away: by dying. That's not going to happen again.

Just the other day I was telling somebody the first thing I am going to do when I leave here is change my name. Amy Fisher will be gone. I'll disappear into a new name and a new life. I already have a first name picked out. (I'll give you a hint: It's the name of a big, exotic country.) I don't have a last one yet.

Other times I think, No. I was born Amy Fisher, and despite everything that's happened, that's who I'll stay. I'll battle to have a better life from the inside out, instead of thinking a name will change everything, instead of just running away.

The second choice would be harder. Much harder.

I'm leaning toward it more every day.

◆ ◆ ◆

Epilogue

♦

Just when the Amy Fisher story seemed to be over for a while, it broke wide open again.

After having reopened its investigation of Joey Buttafuoco for statutory rape on February 11, 1993, the Nassau County district attorney's office announced on March 25—just as this book was about to go to press—that it will present witnesses to a grand jury over a two-week period.

Amy will be the star witness. At press time, she had already been transferred from Albion Correctional Facility to Nassau County Jail. She will soon be telling her story in front of a grand jury investigating Joey. By the time this book is shipped to America's bookstores, other witnesses, too, will be telling the grand jury their stories. Some of these stories will be provocative.

The story is still unfolding.

THE CHRONOLOGY OF
AMY'S STORY

◆

November 1, 1990: Amy first meets Joey Buttafuoco, briefly, when her father brings her car in for repairs to Complete Auto Body. According to Amy, Joey makes an admiring but off-color reference about her to her father. Amy is nine and a half weeks past her sixteenth birthday.

Late May, 1991: Amy brings her car into Complete after she has broken the sideview mirror backing out of her garage. She begins a friendship/flirtation with Joey.

July 2, 1991: Joey drives Amy home from the car-sound-system installer. He asks to see the inside of her house, then makes a physical advance toward her in her bedroom. They become lovers. That evening he takes her to the Freeport Motor Inn & Boatel for the first time.

July 15, 1991: Amy, bothered by a rash, goes to her doctor and learns that she has contracted a sexually transmitted disease. She tells Joey, who, she says, talks her into exonerating him in front of her parents so they won't have to end their love affair. Joey begins to talk persistently, according to Amy, about his desire to see Mary Jo "have an accident."

August 21, 1991: Amy turns seventeen.

Mid-September, 1991: Amy, at Joey's suggestion, becomes a prostitute through ABBA Escorts.

Late September, 1991: Joey tells Amy to break off her relationship with her aunt and confidante, Mary Lynn Vise. Out of fear of losing him, she does so.

November, 1991: Amy tearfully asks Joey to choose between her or Mary Jo. Joey refuses. Amy breaks up with him. Amy slits her wrists. Amy goes to the Buttafuoco house, pretending to sell candy, to get a glimpse of Mary Jo.

January, 1992: After Amy's father has initiated new auto-repair work with Joey, Joey recontacts Amy and wins her back.

Late January, 1992: Joey asks Amy to join Future Physique, the gym he has recently joined, so they can work out together.

February 1, 1992: Amy joins Future Physique.

February 6, 1992: Amy and Paul Makely become lovers.

February, March, April, 1992: Amy carries on affairs simultaneously with both Joey Buttafuoco and Paul Makely; sees three regular clients as a prostitute; becomes close to Jane; starts hanging out in Bensonhurst. Joey continues to refer to Mary Jo being "out of the picture" and "having an accident."

May 13, 1992: Jane tells Amy she wishes she had a gun to shoot the girl with whom her boyfriend is cheating. Amy asks Jane how she can acquire a gun. Plans are made for her to do so. Amy tells Joey about these plans. Joey, according to Amy, gives Amy instructions to carry out the killing of Mary Jo. Joey instructs Amy to get $2,000 back from Paul Makely that she loaned him. Jane and Amy drive to Bensonhurst to make contact with Peter Guagenti to acquire a gun.

May 14, 1992: Amy has a fight with Paul Makely over what she sees as disturbing behavior in his son. Paul tells Amy to get out of his house.

May 15, 1992: Joey beeps Amy twice in the morning—once, waking her up; the second time, getting her out of class. Beeper records later recovered by the police confirm this. Amy says these calls were inquiries about her obtaining the gun from Peter Guagenti. Joey also inquires if Amy got the money back from Makely. Amy reports her fight with him.

May 18, 1992: Amy and Jane steal a pair of license plates to cover Peter's car's plates on the forthcoming day of the shooting.

May 19, 1992: Peter drives Amy to the Buttafuoco house. Amy confronts Mary Jo on her front porch. Mary Jo is shot. Her recovery seems unlikely. Joey raises the possibility, with Detective Richie Lane and then Detective Martin Alger, of Paul Makely as a suspect.

May 20, 1992: Mary Jo regains consciousness. She describes the events that took place on her front porch. When the COMPLETE AUTO BODY T-shirt is mentioned, Joey exclaims that he knows who shot his wife. He gives Detective Alger the name, address, and description of Amy Fisher. He supplies a photograph of Amy, which Mary Jo identifies. He offers to phone Amy to entice her into a police dragnet. Paul Makely is still suspected as the wheelman. Amy's house is staked out by police.

May 21, 1992: After a witness fails to identify Paul Makely as the wheelman and Amy has not been found, Detective Alger goes to the Buttafuoco house to get Joey to call Amy to lure her out of the house. He does so. Amy Fisher is apprehended, arrested—and questioned for fifteen hours without having a lawyer present.

May 22, 1992: Amy Fisher is arraigned. She is charged with the attempted murder of Mary Jo Buttafuoco. She is jailed without bail.

May 23, 1992: Jane is apprehended at The Quintessential Look, the hair salon where she works, and is brought to the Nassau Homicide squadroom. Her mother and an attorney appear. Jane is effectively cut off from questioning by police. Meanwhile, "Teen Fatal Attraction" becomes the tag line in news stories that state that Joey Buttafuoco was Amy's lover. There is no denial from Joey.

May 29, 1992: Grand jury indicts Amy Fisher for attempted murder of Mary Jo Buttafuoco. Jane's testimony helped effect the indictment.

June 1, 1992: Peter DeRosa's tape of Amy as a prostitute is aired on "A Current Affair." Stories begin to surface about Amy's work for ABBA Escorts and as a prostitute on her own.

June 2, 1992: Amy pleads not-guilty before Judge Marvin Goodman. Nassau County Assistant District Attorney Fred Klein calls her "totally uncontrollable" and compares her to John Gotti, Jr. Bail is set at $2 million.

June 3, 1992: Stephen Sleeman comes forward, first to "A Current Affair," and then to the police—with his sex-in-exchange-for-a-gun story.

June 4, 1992: Chris Drellos similarly comes forward.

June 5, 1992: Joey makes a surprise call-in to "The Howard Stern Show" and summarily denies he ever had an affair with Amy. Michael Rindenow quits as his lawyer. Joey hires Marvyn Kornberg after abiding to Kornberg's condition that he is never to speak without Kornberg's permission.

June 6, 1992: At the bail-reduction hearing, Eric Naiburg fails to get Amy's bail reduced from $2 million.

June 7, 1992: Naiburg appeals to Hollywood producers to bail Amy out in exchange for exclusive rights to her story.

June 10, 1992: Apparently responding to rumors and stories about his alleged participation in drug-selling and prostitution, Joey admits he is a former cocaine addict who spent twenty-eight days in a drug rehabilitation center. He denies that he ever sold drugs or was a pimp.

June 11, 1992: Peter Guagenti is arrested during his lunch break in Brooklyn.

June 12, 1992: Peter Guagenti is arraigned. He admits he sold Amy the gun; he follows DeRosa's, Sleeman's, and Drellos's lead in claiming he was led to expect sex from Amy. He denies knowing what Amy was going to do with the gun. His lawyer calls him an "unwitting pawn" of Amy.

June 23, 1992: Naiburg tries—unsuccessfully—to have Amy's bail halved to $1 million. She has been in jail one month and one day.

June 30, 1992: Mary Jo Buttafuoco identifies Amy Fisher in a police lineup.

July 28, 1992: KLM's negotiation, via agent Ron Yatter of the Producers' Agency, with bail bondsman Ron Olszowy, president of Nationwide Bail Bond, and Philip Konvitz, owner of International Fidelity Insurance Company, successfully raises $2 million. Amy is freed on bail.

July 29, 1992: Fred Klein finds out about KLM involvement, protests that he was never told that a production company was involved, and calls the bail arrangement improper. Judge Goodman rules that Amy may remain free on bail.

August 7, 1992: Mary Jo Buttafuoco sues Amy, Amy's parents, and Peter Guagenti for $125 million. The Buttafuocos' attorneys attempt to rescind her bail. Supreme Court Justice Edward Hart protects KLM's $60,000 bail contribution from seizure by the Buttafuocos by saying, ninety seconds into the hearing, "[Amy] is presumed innocent, and that it is her constitutional right to raise her bail."

August 14, 1992: The Titan .25 semi-automatic that Guagenti sold Amy is found in a sewer near Amy's house, where Guagenti disposed of it.

August 21, 1992: Amy turns eighteen.

September 14, 1992: "A Current Affair" producer Steve Dunleavy (who broadcast the DeRosa tape) hints at a new videotape of Amy, purportedly taken by one of her clients, that will prove Joey was not Amy's lover. Paul Makely denies involvement with Amy.

September 15, 1992: Nassau County D.A. Denis Dillon announces that he is considering adding a conspiracy charge against Amy. The charge is thought to be linked to the assertions of Stephen Sleeman.

September 22, 1992: The night before Amy's plea bargain, Paul Makely lures Amy to Future Physique, where hidden "Hard Copy" cameras are recording her responses to his baiting questions.

September 23, 1992: Amy accepts a plea bargain—five to fifteen years—and Fred Klein announces that his office will now go after Joey.

September 25, 1992: The "Makely" tape of Amy is the New York tabloids' front-page story. It is aired on "Hard Copy." Just before its airing, Amy is debriefed for eight hours by Marty Alger and Fred Klein, as part of their investigation of Joey.

September 26, 1992: Eric Naiburg and his law partner, Matthew Rosenblum, rush Amy to Huntington Hospital to have her stomach pumped after she is nearly unconscious following a suicide attempt. Amy says she feels betrayed by Makely, grossly misinterpreted by the tape—and is upset that her statement of remorse for Mary Jo's shooting was cut from the tape, that she "doesn't want to live anymore." Amy begins an extensive stay in the psychiatric unit of Huntington.

September–October 1992: The three networks race to put Amy TV movies into production and on the air. CBS has bought the Buttafuocos' rights for a reported $300,000; NBC will mount the KLM/Michael Jaffe Films production, which encompasses Amy's exclusive story; with Makely, Sleeman, and Maria Eftimiades' rights having been acquired. ABC purchases the journalism of *New York Post* columnist Amy Pagnozzi and will base its story on the public record.

October 1, 1992: St. Martin's Paperbacks publishes *Lethal Lolita* by *People* magazine writer Maria Eftimiades; it's a paperback compiled largely from press accounts. Two hundred thousand copies are in print.

October 22, 1992: Mary Jo Buttafuoco weeps when she is told, in a private session with Fred Klein and Marty Alger, that her husband will not be prosecuted. When Alger tries to tell her about verification of most of her husband's motel receipts, Mary Jo denies their legitimacy. The D.A.'s office announces it will not prosecute Joey. Dillon cites the family's suffering and the pall cast over Amy's credibility by the Makely tapes. Joey says he is exonerated.

October 28, 1992: Amy is released from Huntington Hospital, vowing that she wants to live.

November 3–4, 1992: Amy begins work on this book.

AMY FISHER

November 5, 1992: Amy voluntarily returns to jail.

November 9, 10, and 11, 1992: Amy's "Inside Edition" interviews are telecast.

December 1, 1992: Amy is called a "wild animal" by Judge Goodman and is sentenced to the maximum, five to fifteen years. She is handcuffed and sent back to Nassau County Jail, soon to be transferred to prison. Joey hosts a press conference with Mary Jo after the sentencing; he smiles for photographers, and repeatedly calls Amy a liar. The Buttafuocos fly to Los Angeles to meet the actors who portray them in their TV movie.

December 22, 1992: Amy's interview on NBC's "Dateline" airs.

December 28, 1992: The NBC-TV movie *Amy Fisher: My Story,* starring Noelle Parker and Ed Marinaro, airs, earning a 19.1 rating. Amy is in Albion Correctional Facility.

December 29, 1992: Roseann and Elliot Fisher announce that they have separated and will file for divorce.

January 3, 1993: In a move unprecedented in TV history, two networks —CBS and ABC—present, during the same hours, competing movies about the same story (Amy's), which was featured in the third network's (NBC's) movie the week before. Despite skepticism that people had their fill of the story the previous week, the ABC movie, *The Amy Fisher Story,* earns a 19.5 rating; and the CBS movie, *Casualties of Love: The "Long Island Lolita" Story,* earns a 15.8 rating.

January 4, 1993: The *New York Post*'s front page does advance promo for "Hard Copy"'s second, "steamier" Makely tape of Amy. Eric Naiburg assails the exploitation as "despicable."

January 5, 1993: The Buttafuocos and their attorneys appear on "Donahue." During the show, the highest rated in that program's history, the audience waxes raucously skeptical about Joey's innocence. The Buttafuocos angrily claim they were "ambushed" by Donahue.

January 15, 1993: Joey and Marvyn Kornberg appear on a specially prepared NBC-TV show, "It's Joey's Turn," hosted by Chuck Scarborough. Joey denounces Phil Donahue for stacking his show's audience and reiterates his denials of having had an affair with Amy.

January 16, 1993: Spoofing Sinead O'Connor's ripping-up of a photograph of the pope on a previous show, Madonna ends a song on "Saturday Night Live" by tearing up a photo of Joey Buttafuoco while saying, "Fight the *real* enemy."

January 17, 1993: After receiving an apparently threatening phone call, Joey is allegedly shot at by an unknown gunman. He emerges unscathed.   Kornberg rails against Madonna's exhortation and says that Joey has initiated intense personal security measures.

February 4, 1993: Peter Guagenti is sentenced to six months in jail for his role in getting Amy the gun.

February 10, 1993: After an inmate has "seriously threatened" Amy, says Christine Edwards-Neumann, the young prisoner is put in protective custody at Albion. Instead of having a bed in a group dorm, she is placed in solitary, sleeping on a mat on the floor in a cell. She loses her telephone privileges.

February 11, 1993: Nassau district attorney's office reopens the investigation of Joey for the rape in the third degree (statutory rape) of Amy. Former Complete Auto Body employee George Nessler—who claims Joey bragged of giving Amy her first orgasm—is questioned extensively by Marty Alger at Nassau Homicide.

March 25, 1993: Nassau County District Attorney Denis Dillon announces that his office will present to a grand jury "certain allegations made by Amy Fisher."

AUTHOR'S NOTE

♦

Amy Fisher and I spent four long days together, talking about her life, her love affairs, and the events of the tumultuous last year that led to the shooting of Mary Jo Buttafuoco. According to the terms by which KLM Productions had secured her bail the previous summer, I was the only writer allowed to obtain her story from her.

Our first two days of interviews took place in an elegant two-bedroom suite at the Hotel Westbury in Manhattan on November 3, Election Day, and November 4, 1992. Amy started off in a good mood; she had just been to the Cher concert. Eric Naiburg was in the next room, watching the election returns, for almost half of our talks. He occasionally joined the interview and she often ran in and asked him if she should or could say something to me.

Later that evening he would take her out to a fancy Italian restaurant for dinner. (She proudly modeled for me the tiny black starlet dress and push-up bra she wore.) As Amy and I began our talk, televisions lodged in the suite's mahogany armoires brought word of Clinton's hour-by-hour gains. For a while, anyway, it was easy to pretend these two days in Manhattan were not a prelude to Amy's five years in prison. We called our digs—all chintz and dark plaid and framed pictures of hunting dogs—the Di-and-Fergie Suite, and Eric and I custom-topicalized our Election Eve quips.

(Q: How did Mary Matalin and James Carville's campaign-long affair go undetected? A: They must have conducted it at the Freeport Motor Inn & Boatel.) The grown-ups were treating Amy like a celebrity, and Amy—who, one instantly sees, aims to please—obliged.

Late that evening, things changed. Eric was gone. Amy's mood became wistful and grave. As the taxis rolled up Madison Avenue below our window, Amy slipped a *Hotel California* tape into my tape recorder. "Listen to this song. It's a very sad song," she said, fast forwarding to "Lyin' Eyes." She sat still on the couch and looked off in the middle distance. Her eyes were at once blank and close to tears. I told her that I, too, had had a perfectionistic, short-fused father with a chronic heart condition; that when you came of age in the late sixties, as I did, you understood how a swaggeringly juvenile older man could make an embarrassed-to-be-middle-class girl feel she was in the presence of a glamorous outlaw. "Yeah?" Amy asked, her eyes lighting up. "You know about that?" Our book began in earnest.

Amy couldn't sleep that night, I found out later. The contrast between the coddled glamour she had enjoyed for the last couple of days and the long prison term that lay in store filled her with sadness and panic. She lay in her bed and called her mother and her friends. When I came upon her in the suite's living room at 9 A.M. the next morning—standing barefoot, her hair uncombed, in her long T-shirt over panties, taking a Snickers bar and Coke out of the refrigerator for her breakfast—she was startled.

"Oh, you scared me!" she said, slapping her hand to her chest and slumping.

She looked for all the world like a twelve-year-old on a first baby-sitting job, worried that she would get in trouble for having wandered into her employers' kitchen. (Later she said, "If I had known you have to pay for everything you take out of that little refrigerator, I wouldn't have taken anything out!")

A few hours later, when we went to a three-star restaurant with the publisher of, and agent for, this book, she gazed, intimidated, at the menu, pointed by rote to the first entrée listed—cod—and whispered to me, "I thought you said we were going to go to McDonald's? That's the only place where I know how to order!" The maître d' smiled significantly at her, came over and wished her luck, brought her a special chocolate dessert—and beamingly announced that Al Pacino had just put him in a movie. An hour later, as I gave Amy a hug (I now felt like her mother) and helped her into the car that would be driving her back to Merrick, she looked forlorn. What was this bizarre celebrity the world had fashioned for her, anyway?

The day after our meeting, Amy voluntarily went back to jail. The stress was too much for her; she was a prisoner in her own home—these were the reasons cited. Similar to what she had said to Matthew Rosenblum, who had taken her out to dinner before her suicide attempt, she reassured me, from the jail phone, "It had nothing to do with you!"

My second two meetings with Amy were very different in tone and setting from the first. These took place on an icy-cold day in early January—just after the TV movies about her had aired to astounding ratings, the day NEW AMY SEX TAPES was emblazoned on the front page of the *New York Post*. I was checked for weapons as I entered Albion prison and was ushered into a large, grim common room. Amy, wearing her green uniform and a sweater, was led down a hall by a guard. She did not look happy—either to be there, or, perhaps, to see me. She feared that she had said too much the first time we talked. She didn't know what I was getting from my other interviews. She was wary, tired, and terse.

Her reaction to the three TV movies made about her and the SEX TAPES headline was a simple and defiant one: "There *won't* be any Amy Fisher when I get out of here. I'm changing my name! Amy Fisher won't exist!" This was also her reason for not wanting certain things put in the book that, I had been pleading with her, would make people sympathize with her and understand her. Her logic (to use a favorite Amy word) was: Since there won't be any more Amy Fisher, why would this nonexistent person even require sympathy or understanding?

To break our Cartesian deadlock, I gave her the presents I had brought along: soaps, sachets, a little Teddy bear, a knit cap with a pompom for the cold. She smiled and patted the bear and the pompom. Then the guard came and permanently confiscated them. Her face fell.

We weren't in the Di-and-Fergie Suite, charming each other anymore. There was no refrigerator packed with Snickers bars and smoked almonds, no fawning maître d' in a three-star restaurant— only guards and fellow inmates, one of whom audibly grumbled, "Who she think she is, anyway?" Amy, who was gaining weight and had developed acne, had worked in the prison kitchen five hours already that day, as she would every day for the next almost-five years. And I was not the Manhattan media hostess I may have looked like in that posh, Anglophilic hotel, but instead a pushy, frazzled writer, huddled against the draft in a parka: uncoolly asking her to restate times and dates and details, glancing nervously at my tape recorder to make sure its spools hadn't stopped winding.

Amy was a good soldier. She talked for six hours straight. When, on the second day of the prison visit, the guard came to say we had only fifteen more minutes, Amy asked me, "Do we have the story?"

I told her we did. "It will be a good book. People will finally understand you," I said.

She nodded weakly, as if to say, I've heard *that* one before.

To prove it, however, I handed her the Prologue. She read it quickly and voraciously. "I love it! It's the truth! It's how I feel!" she said.

"See, I told you I wasn't going to exploit you," I said.

Her face was very vulnerable—in fact, embarrassed—as she said, half under her breath, "You'd be the first one who didn't." As the guard led her away, she said, "I'll call you."

But I knew that she wouldn't. Her calls are monitored; anyway, she still felt ambivalent about trusting me. The expression on her young face was that of a much older, resigned person. *You can go home to your family*, it said. *I'm the one who has to stay here.*

Marty Alger called Amy "a very complex kid." Well, she is. She has the guilelessness, the innocence—the lack of protective emotional cover—of a child half her age. Her willingness to trust, her pliability, can take your breath away. At the same time there is a gravity, a bluntness, a somber toughness to her that is far beyond her years and circumstances. We think of suburban teenaged girls as talking with airy words and gestures. They move their heads around, punctuate their talk with "y'know" and "like." Even during our first meeting, before she became a prison inmate, Amy did not talk that way. She looks you in the eye, talks very literally without jargon or fluttery equivocation, and she does not smile.

Still, her priorities are those of a teenager—and the juxtaposition of those concerns with the chilling information she had to deliver was sometimes jolting. For example, a few minutes after she'd talked unselfconsciously about Joey's telling her he didn't want to wait seven years for the insurance money on Mary Jo's death, she asked me to turn the tape recorder off so she could say something particularly sensitive. I pressed the Stop button, prepared for a bombshell. Instead, she started disclosing details of Kennedy High's popularity totem pole.

But Amy is not coy, and my efforts to ingratiate myself to her were met with her sensible literalness. "I write a lot about women," I had told her when we first met at Eric Naiburg's office, several days before the hotel interviews.

"I'm not a woman," she corrected, almost sternly. "I'm a girl. A confused girl who's had a lot of stress."

She is also a girl who has a lot of integrity, sweetness, solemnity and—despite the skills she had to develop as a prostitute—an eschewal of bullshit. She is a girl who is very confused and who, I believe, has been damaged. She needs first-rate psychological help much more than she needed this bizarre, two-faced celebrity we've heaped on her. Serious help alone, and not the prison term that she has never denied deserving, will save her. She is a young woman very much worth saving.

This was a dream assignment for a writer: to take a person everyone knows and yet nobody knows and turn her from a ridiculed icon into a human being. I wish to thank The Producers' Agency's intrepid president, Ron Yatter, and the gracious KLM partners Alfred Kelman and Phil Levitan for the project's existence. I thank my wonderful agent, Ellen Levine, for calling me up the minute she heard about the project and for negotiating tirelessly— from Johannesburg. I thank Ron and I thank Bill Grose, senior vice-president and editorial director of Pocket Books—a true gentleman of great warmth—for selecting me for the project and for putting their faith in me. Thanks to Molly Allen, Jennifer Weidman, Jonathon Brodman, and Joe Gramm, who, along with Bill, made it such a joy to work with Pocket Books. I thank my assistant, talented young journalist Myung Oak Kim for the research, transcribing, scrapbook-assembling, library-storming, cooking, and kid-sitting that allowed me to meet my deadline.

The trust and approval of Eric Naiburg was singularly essential. I would have had no relationship with Amy at all—and no book— without them. I felt Eric's support from the beginning. It was his idea for me to have extended time, in an overnight setting, with

AMY FISHER

Amy. I thank him greatly for comprehending my desire to portray her richly and accurately. I hope this book lives up to the trust he afforded me. Thanks, too, to Matthew Rosenblum, for contributing an important part of the story.

I am enormously grateful for the generous cooperation of Marty Alger and Dan Severin, who gave me the full story of the police investigation, something that no other journalist had been able to obtain. Marty, Dan—you guys are the greatest. Thanks, too, to Gary Abbondandelo.

Invaluable assistance was given by private investigators Richie Johnson, Tom Dixon, and especially my buddy Richie Haeg. Remember our deal, Richie: I'll teach you how to write a book if you teach me how to be a detective.

Gratitude to "Sonny" for going out on a limb and repeatedly helping me where others who had less to lose wouldn't. And thanks to Alexandra Cohen for getting me to him. Kiki, thanks—and good luck staying clean.

The journalists who covered the Fisher case from the beginning provided the groundwork for my catch-up research. I am especially indebted to the outstanding daily reporting of *Newsday*'s Susan Forrest and Shirley Perlman, the latter a professional I have long admired.

To Amy's friends Maria Murabito and Lori DeSaro, I owe gratitude for their trust and candor. Maria particularly helped me start to understand the guido world; Queensborough College sociologist Dr. Donald Tricario, who has studied and published on this subculture, took that understanding further. Dr. Joseph Scelsa of the Calendra Institute, historian Dr. Sal LiGumina of the Long Island Studies Department of Nassau Community College, the information assistants at the Queens Public Library and its Long Island Room, the editors of *Newsday*'s *The Long Island Experience,* the work of Barbara Ehrenreich, Donna Gaines's *Teenage Wasteland,* and demographer Fred Wolfe of the Long Island Planning Board also aided my understanding of Long Island history and sociology.

On the subject of teenaged development and teenagers and violence, thanks to Dr. Ralph Lopez, to Harvard University's Dr. Deborah Prothrow-Stith, to Ron Stevens of the National School Safety Center, and to the studies collected in the work of economist and author Sylvia Ann Hewlett. Dr. Diane Glazer was invaluable in my understanding of middle-class prostitution, and the writings and studies of Dr. Mimi Silbert of the Delancey St. Foundation and Dr. Judith Herman of Harvard helped me learn about the link between sex abuse and prostitution. Lucy Berliner, M.S.W., and Dr. Gail Robinson shared their considerable expertise on the futures of abused girls, as did Judith Klein, C.S.W.

Jim Flateau and Linda Faglia at the Department of Corrections in Albany made my visit to Albion red-tape-free.

Thanks, too, to Mary Beth French, Kelly Leisten, Sam Schmidt, and Jose at 380 Services.

John and Jonathan Kelly—human-development author extraordinaire and fifth-grade sports star, respectively—got, for four months, a pie-eyed figure wearing the same clothes days in a row, perpetually hunched over a computer, instead of a wife and mother. Thanks, guys, for not complaining—or divorcing, Jonathan's consolation was that he got to keep the "Naughty by Nature" tape, got to wax authoritative on makes of cars, and got to ask cool questions like, "So who were you on the phone with, Mom? Another escort service owner?"

The usual crew—Liz, Helen, Carol, Eileen, Mark, Jean—was grandly supportive.

I wanted to interview Rob, but despite many messages left on his answering machine and two actual conversations, this interview never materialized. Peter Guagenti was not contacted since his lawyer's statements were public record, as were those of representatives for Stephen Sleeman and Chris Drellos. I drove out to Jane's place of employment in an effort to arrange an interview. She summarily refused to talk to me.

I *very* much wanted to interview Roseann Fisher. At the onset of this effort, I almost thought I could, or should, not write this book without her blessing and participation. She refused to be interviewed. I salute Roseann—that she has been able to survive the nightmare of the last year with her sanity, dignity, courtesy, and even her good humor intact speaks volumes for her strength of character. I also wished to speak more substantively to Christine Edwards-Neumann, a lawyer of resplendent tenacity, grit, and loyalty. I had many incidental conversations with both of these women, but their decision not to contribute to this project remained unswerving. Their refusal to participate also precluded my speaking to Mary Lynn Vise and to Elliot Fisher.

AMY FISHER

I repeatedly told Rose and Chris that my intention was to write a book that would let people understand Amy in a way that might genuinely help her. I don't pretend that they will love this book; and I know that almost everything written about Amy strikes Rose—in a way that I, as a mother myself, understand—as unwanted. Nevertheless, I hope that they, more than anyone else except Amy herself, can see from these pages that I care about Amy's future and that my heart was in the right place when I sat down to help her tell her story.